PRAEGER LIBRARY OF U.S. GOVERNMENT DEPARTMENTS
AND AGENCIES

The Department of Justice

The
Department of
Justice

Luther A. Huston

FREDERICK A. PRAEGER, *Publishers*
New York · Washington · London

160706

FREDERICK A. PRAEGER, PUBLISHERS
111 Fourth Avenue, New York, N.Y. 10003, U.S.A.
77–79 Charlotte Street, London W.1, England

Published in the United States of America in 1967
by Frederick A. Praeger, Inc., Publishers

Library of Congress Catalog Card Number: 67-20482

Printed in the United States of America

This book is dedicated to those who, in years gone by and in crucial present times, have given full measure of devotion to the cause of making justice a reality, not a byword, in the United States.

Foreword

by WILLIAM P. ROGERS

Attorney General of the United States, 1957–61

Since the founding in 1789 of the Office of Attorney General and its establishment in 1870 as the Department of Justice, the federal government's law enforcement agency has undergone many changes in structure, methods, and policies. A mural on a wall in the Department's headquarters proclaims that "the life of the law has not been logic, but experience." Although I would not want to endorse this terse summary without reservation, it is true that the Justice Department, as it exists today, is the product of 178 years of giving life to the law by experience in administering it.

During those 178 years, great political, social, and economic forces shaped the maturing democracy of a vigorous, progressive, and diversified people. The evolvement of a government of right, not privilege, of equal justice, not tyranny, came about in measurable degree because from the beginning men learned in the law gave guidance to statesmen who made the laws and officials whose responsibility it was to enforce them.

Too little is known of the role of law and of the lawyer in the history of the United States. Too little is known of the origins of our legal system and of the men who gave life to the law and thereby helped to preserve liberty.

An obvious need for a comprehensive story of the Department of Justice is filled by this book. An "information gap" concerning the history of the Department, the lawyers who have headed and staffed it, and the part they have played in

building and administering a distinctly American system of
equal justice under law has been closed.

The lawyer, the layman, the teacher, and the student will
find in this book enlightenment on the application of the
principles of law to the problems of past and present genera-
tions. As a knowledge of aerodynamics is valuable to one
who would know what makes a jet plane fly, so the detailed
accounts presented here of the functions and responsibilities
of the Department's divisions and bureaus provide essential
information to those who would know how the government's
law office performs its duties and how it fits into the federal
system. Knowledge of these things is basic to understanding
the American system of government and how it operates.

When I became Attorney General, one of my first appointments was that of Luther A. Huston as Director of Public
Information. As a highly respected and admired correspon-
dent of *The New York Times,* he had covered the Department during several previous administrations and was familiar with its operations and known to its personnel. Out of his
journalistic and official experience, supplemented by abun-
dant research, he has produced a readable and informative
story of the development and activities of the Justice Department. Students of government will find it very valuable.

Preface

Because democracy means a government of laws made by the people and justly administered by their chosen agents, it is difficult to conceive of a democratic nation without a law enforcement agency, whether called a department of justice or some other name. Yet even among the world's democracies, there are those that have no agency vested with such comprehensive powers to enforce the laws and administer justice as the Department of Justice of the United States. And, certainly, the autocratic and totalitarian governments have no counterpart to protect the rights of men and punish transgressors.

Mankind's concept of justice began to develop ages ago as the human race struggled upward toward higher levels of civilization. Inherent in the groping minds of men, never content with things as they were, there seems always to have been a goal of protection for all and just punishment for those who transgressed the simple laws of primitive society. The upward climb was tortuous. What appeared just at one stage became tyranny in a later age. But the idea of justice was always a beacon on the pathway to a better civilization. No matter how often pilgrims stumbled, the movement was forward. After centuries, the concept is still developing.

In this book, the author has endeavored to tell the story of how the New World, borrowing from the Old World but building anew with the materials of democracy, has created a system for the administration of justice.

The system is not perfect and its architects tinker with it constantly. None will contend that pure justice has always been served, nor that it ever will be. But neither will any perceptive person deny that, as the system has been built stone by rough stone from the quarries of experience, the aim has been to erect a structure that administers justice in the interests of all.

The chapters that follow purport to set forth how the system has developed and to show how it operates in the hands of fallible human beings to protect those rights that free men cherish in a democratic government.

Some of the material herein came from the author's own files of stories written during his assignment as a reporter covering the Department of Justice. Other knowledge and background were acquired during the four years he served as director of the Justice Department's Office of Public Information.

The cooperation of assistant attorneys general, the Federal Bureau of Investigation, the Bureau of Prisons, the Immigration and Naturalization Service, and the Office of Public Information of the Department of Justice is gratefully acknowledged.

LUTHER A. HUSTON

Washington, D.C.
March, 1967

Contents

*The Department of Justice organization chart
appears on page 55.*
A section of photographs follows page 84.

The Department of Justice

I

Learned in the Law:
The Attorney General, 1789–1870

The U.S. Department of Justice is the product of a system of government that evolved in the New World, a manifestation of concepts ingrained in a government wherein the people make the laws and officials administer them under popular mandate. To be sure, the seedlings from which the American governmental system grew were brought from the Old World, but, nurtured in a political soil and climate conducive to new ideas, the trees that took root bore fruit of a different form and substance from the parent stock.

What has resulted is a Department of Justice that incurs its obligations and derives its powers from laws passed by Congress. Its administration of those laws is always under the watchful eye of the judiciary. Because the Attorney General and his principal aides are appointed by, and may be removed by, the President, they are subject at all times to the mandates of the executive. Sometimes, they may be impaled upon a three-horned dilemma. They must approach enforcement of a law mindful of the purpose and intent of Congress when it passed that law. They must interpret and adhere to rules promulgated in decisions of the Supreme Court. And they must not deviate further than the law requires from the policies of the Presidential Administration of which they are a part.

OUT OF RUNNYMEDE

Concepts of justice and the application of law underwent many changes in England long before the colonists left. At Runnymede, Englishmen had received the Magna Carta, the first great charter of liberty from monarchical oppression. But despots, though curbed, had not been shorn of their powers, and tyranny, though abated, still trampled upon the liberties of the king's subjects. Some of these tyrannies followed the colonists to the New World and led to the revolt that established in North America the union of states, replacing the colonial federation.

In a true democracy, the rule of law prevails. Laws, however, are made and administered by men, and the effectiveness of government depends upon how men apply the laws to the need and problems of their times. Justice is the arm of law. The law can be majestic in its power for good or vengeful in its power for evil, depending upon its administration.

In the United States, law is the cornerstone of national structure, and the system of laws is based upon the Constitution, which James Bryce said made the American people a nation and William Ewart Gladstone called "the most wonderful work ever struck off at a given time by the brain and purpose of man." Article VI of the Constitution provides that "This Constitution and the Laws of the United States which shall be made in Pursuance thereof . . . shall be the supreme Law of the land."

The concern of the framers of the Constitution was not to prescribe the formula for administration of this "supreme Law." That was left to the elected representatives of the people. Thus, Congress created the law enforcement machinery that centers in what is now known as the Department of Justice.

Hesitating to vest in the executive branch enforcement powers that might be used unjustly to deprive citizens of hard-won freedoms and rights, legislators of those early years were reluctant to create a strong central legal system. They had known what it was to suffer under laws rigidly enforced by centralized authority not always concerned with even-handed administration of justice. Understandably, in their desire to avoid centralization, they contrived machinery for the administration of federal laws that was rudimentary even by eighteenth-century standards.

Quite naturally, American law and jurisprudence derived from British common law and practice. That Americans should borrow freely from the country whose yoke they had thrown off was inevitable. Thus, the British system supplied the blueprint of what was to be built, but the American founders erected the structure they believed best designed to support their ideas and purposes. The British did not have a department of justice, but they had—and still have—an attorney general. The new nation borrowed that title for the first federal law officer named by an act of Congress.

COLONIAL ATTORNEYS GENERAL

The title and office of attorney general had existed in the colonies before the Revolutionary War, but it was part of a purely colonial operation, under sanction of the British Crown, and not part of a centralized legal system. In 1643, Richard Lee was appointed the first attorney general of Virginia, and Edmund Randolph (who was to become the first Attorney General of the United States) was Virginia's attorney general in 1776, when the colonies went to war against the mother country. The General Court of Rhode Island appointed an attorney general and solicitor for the colony in 1650, and in 1704 the Assembly of Connecticut directed the appointment in each county of "a sober, discreet and religious person . . . to prosecute and implead the laws." Other colonies had officials with comparable duties. Thus, the creation of a federal Office of Attorney General was not a new departure. Rather, it was an adaptation to the federal system of procedures prevalent throughout the colonies.

Nor was the Office of Attorney General a constitutional creature. The Constitution established the legislative, executive, and judicial branches as independent but coordinate units of the federal government; Congress was left the job of creating suitable administrative agencies to carry out the functions of the three branches. At its first session, the national legislature distributed the administrative duties of the executive branch among three departments—Foreign Affairs, War, and Treasury. Viewed in the light of today's vast and complex setup, this was an embryonic establishment, but the United States itself was then an embryonic nation, barely embarked upon its experiments in representative government.

THE JUDICIARY ACT OF 1789

The Judiciary Act of 1789, one of the first enactments of the law-making branch of the new U.S. Government, established the federal judicial system of the United States and the Office of Attorney General. In providing for the appointment of "a meet person, learned in the law, to act as Attorney General for the United States," it is evident that Congress was thinking more in terms of a legal counselor for the government—an official to interpret and expound the law—than of an official whose long arm would reach out to punish those who transgressed the law. The machinery for enforcement was not entrusted to the Attorney General.

Article III of the Constitution provided that "The judicial Power of the United States, shall be vested in one Supreme Court, and in such inferior courts as the Congress may from time to time ordain and establish." Congress performed its initial responsibility under this clause with the Judiciary Act, providing for a Supreme Court with a chief justice and five associate justices, a district court and a district judge for each of the states, and three circuit courts. Judges of these circuit courts would be two members of the Supreme Court and the district judge in whose jurisdiction the court happened to be sitting.

Although the system has been expanded so that now there are nine Supreme Court justices, including the Chief Justice, ten judicial circuits (which have become the first-line federal courts of appeal), and ninety-two U.S. district judges, the basic pattern of the judicial branch has not changed appreciably in almost two centuries. Congress has exercised its constitutional authority to "ordain and establish" inferior courts such as the Tax Court, the Court of Claims, the Customs Court, the Court of Customs and Patent Appeals, and the Court of Military Appeals to deal with controversies in special fields of law, but the effect has been more to reduce the work load than to limit the jurisdiction or powers of the Article III courts.

Unlike the courts, the Office of Attorney General, set up by the same act, was destined to change markedly in nature, although it was to operate as an agency under that name for almost a century before Congress yielded to the urging of the executive branch and the demands of the times and transformed it into the Department of Justice. As prescribed by the Judiciary Act, the duties and powers of the Office of Attorney General were few and vaguely defined and reflected the legislators' concern lest the office become a center of federal power that would infringe upon the prerogatives of the states. Although the statute assigned to the Attorney General the duty to "prosecute and conduct all suits in the Supreme Court in which the United States shall be concerned" and to give opinions upon matters of law, when requested, to the President and heads of departments, it is noteworthy that the Attorney General assumed thereby a role touching the policy-making functions of government only where legal opinions given executive officers might influence policy decisions.

Moreover, the law, in effect, perpetuated the colonial system of county attorneys and of deputy attorneys general by providing, in addition to the Attorney General, additional district attorneys for the United States in the lower courts to prosecute "all delinquents for crimes and offenses cognizable under the authority of the United States, and all civil actions in which the United States shall be concerned." This provision meant that the real law enforcement power rested in lesser officials over whom the Attorney General, in theory the government's top lawyer, had virtually no control.

Although the act of 1789 did not assign to the Attorney General the obligation to act as lawyer for the legislative branch, Congress for some years looked upon the Attorney General as its *de facto* counsel. Feeling their way through the law-making process, and not always sure that the legislation they were considering was legal or constitutional in form or purpose, the legislators asked the Attorney General for his opinion upon all manner of bills and procedures, particularly in regard to their constitutionality. There were many skilled lawyers in the Senate and House who had participated in drafting the Constitution, but they continued to seek the advice of the Attorney General even while exercising the prerogative of disagreeing with his opinions. Over the first thirty years of the Office of Attorney General's existence, requests from Capitol Hill for advice became so numerous that they constituted a large part of the Attorney General's regular work. Incumbents found this situation irksome, but none did anything definite about it until 1819, when William Wirt, the ninth Attorney General, put a stop to it.

YEARS OF FRUGALITY

Having created the Office of Attorney General and an embryonic system of law enforcement, Congress proceeded for most of the next 100 years to practice frugality, if not parsimony, in the matter of funds. At first, the salary of the Attorney General was fixed at $1,500 per year, and he was given no funds for office rent, clerk hire, stationery, postage, candles, oil for his lamps, or coal for his stove. Any expenses involved in the operation of the office were paid for out of his own pocket. Requests for salary increases, office help, and office facilities were transmitted from one Attorney General after another to Congress by Presidents, but the legislature was slow to respond. Reasons of economy probably predominated. However, the fear of strengthening sinews that might be flexed to menace states' and individuals' rights and liberties was often reflected in Congressional debates. A less than lavish increase in salary to $1,900 was granted in 1791, and a more substantial advance to $3,000 was forthcoming in 1799. Still, there was no appropriation for clerk or contingent expenses. Congress loosened the purse strings a little more in 1819, when the salary was raised to $3,500, with an allowance of $1,000 for a clerk and a contingent fund of $500 for stationery, stamps, fuel, and "a boy to attend to menial duties." The office ran on that basis for more than ten years, until, in 1831, the salary became $4,000, with $500 for contingencies, $733 for an office, and $500 for books—the first appropriation for what was to become, eventually, a splendid library. In 1840 and again in 1850, Congress appropriated more money for law books. And, in 1850, at the same time the salary of the Attorney General was increased to $6,000, Congress also granted an additional clerk. Even so, after sixty years' existence, the nation's chief law office still had a staff of only four—the Attorney General, two clerks, and a messenger. When Caleb Cushing became Attorney General in 1853, he found the work of the office so far behind that he appealed to President Franklin Pierce for help and received Presidential authorization to employ three temporary clerks. Soon afterward, Congress authorized four permanent clerks, and record-keeping finally became current and efficient.

Although Presidents and Attorneys General had often recommended legal assistants for the office, Congress did not adopt any such recommendations until Jeremiah S. Black became Attorney General, succeeding Cushing. Black was deluged with California land cases and other litigation. In 1858, heeding his pleas for help, Congress authorized two legal assistants. The Office of Attorney General finally became more than a one-man job as far as the exercise of its legal functions was concerned.

By 1861, the U.S. Government had four chief law officers. They were the Attorney General, an assistant attorney general, the solicitor of the Court of Claims, and the solicitor of the Treasury Department. At that, the solicitors were not under direct control of the Attorney General—although he was obligated to handle much of the litigation that arose out of their offices. Business grew so heavy while the authorized staff stayed so small that it became necessary to employ outside counsels to represent the U.S. Government, and, between 1861 and 1867, fees of these outside counselors cost $475,190. When Congress took note of what seemed such large expenditures to handle the nation's law business, it appointed the Joint Committee on Retrenchments to study the situation. Out of this study came a resolution by Representative William Lawrence of Ohio to consolidate all law offices in one department. Although not new, this proposal strongly appealed to those congressmen interested in governmental economy. However, the appeal was not strong enough to procure passage of the resolution, and it was not until several years later that the basic proposal was enacted into law.

From the beginning, Presidents were aware that the low salary paid the Attorney General made it difficult to attract high-grade men to the office. They baited the hook with the lure of remunerative private practice. George Washington was the first to make use of that enticement.

President Washington wanted Edmund Randolph, who had been his aide in the Revolutionary War and was his personal attorney, as the first Attorney General. Randolph was burdened with heavy financial obligations and was reluctant to accept, but Washington pointed out that the office would "confer pre-eminence" upon the incumbent and accord him a "decided preference of professional employment." Randolph took the bait and the job. During his tenure, he substantially augmented his income by representing private clients. Twenty-two of his successors followed his example, some of them appearing as counsel in the most noted cases of their times. Caleb Cushing was the first to abandon private practice and devote all of his time to the government's legal business.

Cushing was also the first Attorney General to reside full time in the national capital. There was no requirement that the Attorney General live at the seat of government but only that he be present while the Supreme Court was in session. That gave incumbents ample time to devote to personal affairs and private law offices. Wirt, for instance, maintained an office in Baltimore during his entire incumbency and William Pinckney, President Madison's Attorney General, threatened to resign when the President proposed in 1814 that a law be passed requiring the Attorney General to "keep his office at the seat of government during the session of Congress." The law was not passed, but when Pinckney resigned for other reasons, Madison extracted a pledge from Richard Rush, his successor, to live in the capital at least while Congress was sitting. Between Rush and Cushing there were fourteen incumbents who lived in Washington only part of the time.

As has been related, the jurisdiction and duties of the Attorney General were sketchily defined in the Judiciary Act of 1789. One of the earliest legislative measures to increase the duties of the office was to put Randolph on the Patent Board with the secretaries of State and War, and that action was followed by making him a member of the Sinking Fund Commission. As the years went on, Congress and custom added piecemeal to the Attorney General's responsibilities and tasks, such as prosecuting and defending all suits in the Court of Claims in which the United States was involved and inquiring into the status of all funds held in trust by the United States for Indian tribes. The chores given the Attorney General were increasingly numerous and varied, but Congress steadfastly continued to withhold approval of proposals to give him control over all the government's legal business.

As early as Randolph's day, thoughts of some officials and legislators turned toward making the Office of Attorney General into a unified law office, the head of which would have control of all officers and activities concerned with the administration of justice. Indeed, that was one of the proposals made by Randolph when he was asked to suggest improvements in the 1789 Judiciary Act, and President Washington included it in the proposals to amend the Act that he sent to Congress. But no action was taken.

PROPOSALS FOR A DEPARTMENT OF LAW

The first proposal to create a department of law was sent to Congress by President Andrew Jackson with his annual message of 1829. In 1820, Congress had provided that the President designate an official of the Treasury Department to direct proceedings to recover money or property due the United States. The district attorneys were to take orders from that official. By 1828, the Treasury was supervising more than 3,000 lawsuits. Jackson thought the Treasury was not doing the job very well and that it should not be the Treasury's job, anyway. He therefore recommended that these duties be transferred to the Attorney General, at the same time asking that all criminal proceedings involving violations of federal law, which were then conducted by the district attorneys over whom the Attorney General exercised little or no control, be placed under supervision of the nation's chief law officer.

The Senate Judiciary Committee brought in a bill embodying the main points of President Jackson's proposals, but Daniel Webster, then one of the most powerful men in the Senate and hence in the nation, said that to place these functions in the Office of Attorney General would be to make the Attorney General a fractional monstrosity "a half accountant, a half lawyer, a half clerk, a half everything and not much of anything." As a substitute, Webster, still reflecting earlier fears of a strong law enforcement agency, proposed a home department to handle the Patent Office, certain functions of the Treasury, and other items of the Jackson program. A compromise was worked out which created a solicitor of the Treasury who would advise with the Attorney General but who would instruct the district attorneys, marshals, and clerks of the lower courts in all matters and proceedings in which the United States was concerned. President Jackson renewed his proposals in a second message, saying that it would be in the public interest to give the Attorney General superintendence over the law officers and legal interests of the government. Congress ignored the message.

In 1845, President James K. Polk recommended creation of a law department. Congress tabled his proposals.

By 1851, the Department of Interior had been established, and Alexander H. H. Stuart was Secretary. Convinced that his department was performing duties that properly belonged in the hands of the Attorney General, Stuart was next to suggest the formal creation of a department that would perform all law enforcement functions and conduct all legal business of the government. Again, there was no legislative action.

Three years later, the Committee on Retrenchment and Reform, brought in its bill to establish a department of law. The measure was debated, but no action was taken. From then on, however, legislative skirmishing continued, and, at various times, Congress took steps that pointed toward eventual creation of a unified legal department. It acceded to requests of several departments to establish their own legal sections and created the solicitor and naval judge advocate general, the solicitor for the War Department, Post Office solicitor, solicitor for the State Department, an assistant solicitor for the Treasury, and a solicitor of Internal Revenue. As each of these proposals came before it, Congress was told that it would be impossible for the Attorney General to perform legal work for the entire government and that unless these offices were created, the department would have to resort to the expensive device of employing special counsel. Senator Lyman Trumbull, of Illinois, opposed these measures, stating that he did not believe it was "in harmony with the organization of our system of government to have an Attorney General's office" in each department of government. If that were to be done, he asserted, "we might as well abolish the Attorney General's Department." He contended that the Attorney General's office should be an independent department that would construe the laws for all departments, secure uniformity of administration, and eliminate "difficulty, expense and uncertainty."

Congressional interest in the establishment of a coordinated agency for administration and enforcement of federal laws was building up. In 1867, Attorney General Henry Stanbery, asked for his opinion as to what might be done to bring about a more efficient and economical operation of the federal legal machinery, advised that it would be to the advantage of public service if the various law officers attached to other departments were transferred to the Office of Attorney General, "so that it may be made the Law Department of the Government, and thereby secure uniformity of decision, of superintendence, and of official responsibility." In both the Senate and House, appropriate committees kept the subject under advisement and, after three-quarters of a century, the legislative processes were moving toward definite action to establish that which the founders had feared—a centralized agency to administer a growing body of federal law.

During these years before the establishment of the Department of Justice, twenty-nine men occupied the Office of Attorney General (one man served twice, under different Presidents, so that there were thirty appointments in all). The part played by one Attorney General after another in the affairs of the nation before and through the Civil War is revealed in the biographies of some of the outstanding men who filled the post during the first eighty-one years.

OUTSTANDING ATTORNEYS GENERAL, 1789–1870

Edmund Randolph, who reluctantly accepted appointment as the first Attorney General, came to the post with a distinguished record of public service. He had been an aide-de-camp to General Washington, a member of the Continental Congress, the state of Virginia's first attorney general (an office he assumed in 1776 at the age of twenty-three, and, like his father in the colony of Virginia, held for ten years), and governor of Virginia. As a member of the Virginia Convention of 1776, which advised the Continental Congress to declare independence, he had presented to the Constitutional Convention the Virginia Plan, a formula for a federal union that he had helped George Mason draft.

Two issues were paramount in Washington's Administration. One was the maintenance of neutrality in wars between other nations; the other, the advisability of creating a national bank. Attorney General Randolph advised Washington to proclaim a national policy of neutrality, and, in collaboration with Chief Justice John Jay, drew up a proclamation that, when issued by Washington, became the policy of neutrality to which the United States adhered for more than a century. Although he was on the side of Alexander Hamilton in favoring a strong federal government, Randolph was apprehensive that Hamilton's pet project, a national bank, would vitiate the system of checks and balances that was a peculiar virtue of the federal government. So, as a matter of policy, but also of constitutional interpretation, he advised Washington that Congress lacked constitutional power to incorporate a bank. (Thomas Jefferson, then Secretary of State, was also opposed to the bank proposal but, when Congress passed the law incorporating it, Jefferson advised Washington to sign the bill unless he was clearly convinced it was unconstitutional. Washington signed it, and thereafter the bank was a controversial issue in American politics until President Andrew Jackson killed it.)

After he had been Attorney General two years and had formulated his ideas on what the functions of the office should be and how it should operate, Randolph submitted to President Washington three basic recommendations. They were that the Attorney General be authorized to represent the federal government in lower courts as well as the Supreme Court, be given control of the U.S. district attorneys, and be authorized to hire a clerk. Washington transmitted these suggestions, and others, to Congress but no action was taken at that time.

Randolph was appointed Secretary of State in December, 1793, when Jefferson left that office. William Bradford, of Pennsylvania, was then appointed Attorney General. Bradford served only four months.

Charles Lee, the third Attorney General, would have scuttled the young nation's neutrality policy, but Washington did not follow his advice. Controversies had arisen between France, which was at war with England, and the new American Government, and Charles Maurice de Talleyrand suggested that matters might be adjusted more readily if the United States contributed $250,000 to the French treasury. Lee, a fiery Virginian, was outraged. He proposed a declaration of war, an embargo on French shipping, revocation of the exequaturs of French consuls, the opening of American ports to British privateers, and the arming of American merchant ships. Owing to Washington's prudence and policies, Lee's *de jure* war never became *de facto* and ended when, in 1800, a treaty of peace and friendship was negotiated with France. Lee continued to serve as Attorney General under John Adams until 1801, when he was succeeded by Levi Lincoln, of Massachusetts, a Jefferson appointee who held the post until 1805.

Jefferson also appointed the fifth occupant of the office, John Breckenridge, of Kentucky, who served a little over a year, and the sixth, Caesar Rodney, of Delaware.

Rodney did not have a distinguished record as Attorney General, but, in other capacities, stamped his name firmly on the annals of his times. During the first two years he served in Congress as a representative from Delaware, he was one of the House managers in the impeachment trials of Judge John J. Pickering, of the U.S. District Court for New Hampshire, and Associate Justice Samuel Chase, the only Supreme Court Justice ever tried on a bill of impeachment. A dozen years later Rodney was again elected to Congress on a platform opposing extension of slavery into the territories. After serving a year of that term, he was elected by the Delaware legislature to fill a vacancy in the U.S. Senate, and, a year later, left the Senate to become minister to Argentina. Rodney already had served as a member of a commission appointed by President James Monroe to survey the political situation of South American republics, and the commission's report was a factor in the subsequent enunciation of the Monroe Doctrine.

William Pinckney, of Maryland, who followed Rodney as the seventh Attorney General, was one of the most eloquent men of his time. He never wrote his speeches but could pour forth classical oratory whether arguing in the Supreme Court or debating in the Senate. Arguing in the high court in the case of the *Nereide,* involving neutrality violations during the War of 1812, Pinckney scorned the contentions of his opponents and declaimed:

> Can a neutral surround himself "with all the pomp and circumstance of war?" The idea of our opponents exhibits a discordia rerum—an incongruous mixture of discordant attributes; a centaur-like figure—half man, half ship, a phantasmic form, bearing in one hand the spear of Achilles, in the other the olive branch of Minerva; the frown of defiance on her brow, and the smile of conciliation on her lip, entwining the olive branch of peace around the thunderbolt of Jupiter, and hurling it, thus disguised, indiscriminately at friends and foes.

Chief Justice John Marshall praised Pinckney's skill in painting a portrait "exhibiting this vessel and her freighter as forming a single figure, composed of the most discordant materials of peace and war," but said it "required the exercise of that cold investigating faculty which ought always to belong to those who sit on this bench to discover its only imperfection; its want of resemblance." Nonetheless, Marshall called him "the greatest man I have ever seen in a court of justice."

Not as Attorney General but in private practice, Pinckney was a busy lawyer before the Supreme Court, appearing as counsel in seventy-two cases. Elected to the Senate in December, 1819, he remained a Senator until his death in February,

1822, and was known as a foremost interpreter of the Constitution.

Richard Rush, son of Benjamin Rush, the famous physician, and himself a man who was to play an important part in American history as a diplomat, was the eighth Attorney General. The Pennsylvanian's principal contribution in that office was to edit the *Laws of the United States* covering the years 1789 to 1815, published in five volumes as the Bioren and Duance Edition, Philadelphia, 1815.

William Wirt, of Virginia, who followed Rush, held the Office of Attorney General from November 13, 1817, to March 3, 1829—more than eleven years. No other incumbent has served in the post that long. During his tenure, he did more to increase its prestige and define its functions and authority than any of his predecessors.

The day Wirt took office he sought the records of those predecessors; he was astounded to find there weren't any. On the fly-leaf of the earliest record book of the Office of Attorney General this inscription appears in Wirt's handwriting:

> Attorney General's Office,
> 13, Novr. 1817.

Finding on my appointment, this day, no book, document or papers of any kind to inform me of what has been done by any one of my predecessors, since the establishment of the Federal Government, and feeling strongly the inconvenience, both to the nation and myself, from this omission, I have determined to remedy it, so far as depends upon myself, and to keep a regular record of every official opinion I shall give while I hold this office, for the use of my successor.

To make the arrangements as perfect as I can I have prevailed upon the heads of Departments to furnish me with copies of all documents on which I shall be consulted and which will be found, filed and numbered, to correspond with the numbers in the margin prefixed to each opinion. A copius index to this book is also given, with reference, under various heads, to each case for greater facility in using this book.

Wm. Wirt.

Wirt's hand-kept records became the nucleus of a vast system that now makes use of every modern mechanical device to preserve official documents and correspondence.

Wirt, a Latin scholar, when traveling carried a pocket edition of Horace. He was also an author and his *Sketches of the Life and Character of Patrick Henry* was published in 1817, shortly before he became Attorney General. In private practice, Wirt participated in several of the most famous trials of his day. In the treason trial of Aaron Burr, he was counsel for the government. With Daniel Webster and William Pinckney, he was on the winning side in *McCulloch* v. *Maryland* in which the Supreme Court upheld the power of Congress to charter a national bank; in *Trustees of Dartmouth College* v. *Woodward,* in which the issue was whether the legislature of New Hampshire could change the name to Dartmouth University and alter its charter, he represented the legislature and Webster the college. Webster won.

Wirt's most important contribution as Attorney General was to construe the law under which the office was established and relate his activities to the statute. Two months after he took office, he sent to President Monroe a historic letter, now in the Archives of the United States, in which he defined the duties of the Attorney General and his obligations to other branches of the government. The gist of what he called "republican orthodoxy" was that in a government of laws it was important that "the influence of every office should be confined within the strict limits prescribed for it by law." Since the Judiciary Act of 1789 required that the Attorney General should "give his advice and opinion upon questions of law when required by the President of the United States, or when requested by the heads of any of the departments, touching upon any matters that may concern their departments," Wirt decided to operate within the confines of that law. Thus, he ceased giving opinions to Congress and restricted opinion to heads of departments strictly to matters of law, becoming the first Attorney General to lay down a policy his successors, with few deviations, have followed.

Although he restricted his opinion-giving function, Wirt wrote plenty of opinions. They filled 500 pages of the first volume of *Official Opinions of the Attorney General;* none of his predecessors had more than eight pages in the 1,471-page volume. Wirt's opinions ranged over a wide field of subjects: for example, he advised the Secretary of the Navy on methods of distributing prize money from the Lake Erie victory in the War of 1812, gave opinions to President Monroe and his cabinet on questions of neutrality arising from revolutions against Portuguese and Spanish rule in Latin America, and dealt with the vexing problem of the sale of public lands to private companies and the litigation that arose out of it.

As the 1828 elections approached and it became evident that Andrew Jackson would be the next President, the question arose whether Cabinet officers were required to resign. Monroe believed that all should resign except the Attorney General. He wrote to Wirt: "Your duties are different. The President has less connection with them, and less responsibility for them." However, Wirt resigned, and the only record of his participation in politics thereafter was his nomination, in 1832, as the Anti-Masonic Party's candidate for President. He received Vermont's electoral vote.

Roger Brooke Taney, the eleventh Attorney General, was involved in events that shaped the United States, but not especially as Attorney General. His most important participation was as Secretary of the Treasury and as Chief Justice of the United States. As Attorney General, however, he supported President Jackson, implacable foe of the Bank of the United States, and drafted Jackson's veto message of the bill to recharter it. In the message, Taney disagreed with the argument that the Supreme Court's ruling in *McCulloch* v. *Maryland* settled the question of constitutionality of the bank and said that the authority of the Court must not be permitted "to control the Congress or the Executive when acting in their legislative capacities, but only have such influence as the force of their reasoning may deserve."

On January 15, 1835, Jackson sent to the Senate the nomination of Taney for associate justice of the Supreme Court. The Senate, still angry over Taney's position on the bank bill, refused confirmation. Later that year, however, an election removed enough of the Jackson-Taney foes so that when, on December 28, 1835, the President nominated Taney to be Chief Justice succeeding John Marshall, the nomination was confirmed. Taney remained Chief Justice until 1864.

The nine men who followed Taney in the Office of Attorney General were, in many cases, very distinguished—but more for their activities before or after they took the post, or for their private activities while occupying the office, than for what they contributed in the position. (Their names, along with those of all the Attorneys General from 1799–1967 are listed in Appendix II.)

John Jordan Crittenden, of Kentucky, served both as fifteenth and twenty-second Attorney General. During his second term, he advised President Millard Fillmore that a revised Fugitive Slave Act did not conflict with the constitutional guarantee of habeas corpus.

The twenty-first Attorney General, Reverdy Johnson, of Maryland, was one of the most unusual men to occupy the office. His services as Attorney General were not noteworthy, but his other activities during a national career stamped him as a foremost lawyer, diplomat, and citizen. His national career began in 1845 when Maryland sent him to the United

States Senate. He left the Senate in 1849 to become Attorney General and resigned in 1850 upon the death of President Zachary Taylor. As an attorney, Johnson took part in many cases involving constitutional issues. One was the Dred Scott case in which he was of counsel for the defense. He was a Southern sympathizer, but regarded secession as treason. As a member of the Maryland House of Delegates, he worked hard to keep his state from withdrawing from the Union. And, during the Civil War, he approved Lincoln's suspension of habeas corpus, although it applied most rigidly to his fellow Marylanders. After he left public office, he defended many Southerners charged with disloyalty to the Union and was attorney for several defendants in the Ku Klux Klan trials in South Carolina.

In 1863, Crittenden (serving his second term) was succeeded by Caleb Cushing, of Massachusetts. In Essex County, Cushing had grown up at home in a distinguished company that included Rufus Choate, Nathaniel Hawthorne, William Lloyd Garrison, and John Greenleaf Whittier. His legal education consisted of a year at Harvard Law School and intermittent study in the office of a Newburyport attorney. He was admitted to the Massachusetts bar in 1821, and his political career began in 1834 with his election to Congress. He served four consecutive terms until 1843, when he was appointed United States Commissioner to China by President John Tyler. When President James K. Polk declared war on Mexico on May 13, 1846, Cushing, an enthusiastic supporter of the conflict, spent $12,000 to raise and equip a regiment, of which he was named colonel. Before the war ended, in 1848, he had risen to the rank of brigadier general. Five years later, in March, 1853, he became Attorney General and an outstanding figure in the Cabinet of President Franklin Pierce.

Ambitious and versatile, Cushing reached out for new duties and was never appalled by an avalanche of work. He was careful to confine his official activities to the administration of justice, but he brought into the Office of Attorney General functions that had been performed by other government agencies, such as the accounts of the federal judiciary, which had been kept in the Department of Interior, and the issuance of commissions to law officers, which had been done by the Department of State. He also took over from the State Department (where they had been dealt with since George Washington's Administration) the handling of pardons and petitions for executive clemency.

Cushing sent President Pierce two reports in which he outlined his conception of the duties of the Attorney General and suggested modification and enlargement of the entire judicial system. Cushing believed that his office should conduct the legal business of the United States and, to that end, recommended that the Attorney General have charge of all litigation in the lower courts that involved the interests of the federal government. His chief recommendation for the judiciary was that the system be enlarged by the establishment of intermediate courts of appeal. President Pierce sent these reports to Congress. But, sixty-five years after the passage of the Judiciary Act, the legislators were still reluctant to expand the authority of the Attorney General and did not act upon them.

Cushing was called upon to give more official opinions than any of his predecessors. His judgments filled three volumes of the early *Opinions of the Attorney General.*

The dark cloud of secession was looming on the national horizon when Jeremiah Sullivan Black, of Pennsylvania, became the twenty-fourth Attorney General, and his most significant opinion advised President James Buchanan on his powers to deal with states threatening to withdraw from the Union. Black told Buchanan that, in their respective spheres, the federal and state governments were supreme, and each was powerless to go beyond the limits set by the Constitution. He advised that if a state should declare its independence, the President could not recognize that independence or absolve the state from its federal obligations. The Constitution, Black declared, did not give the federal government power to make war on a state, and to attempt to do so would amount to expulsion from the Union, but the federal government might lawfully repel direct aggression on its property. It might not, Black asserted, carry on an offensive war to punish the people of a state for the political misdeeds of their government.

Foes called Black the author of "Buchanan's secessionist doctrine," and when Buchanan nominated him to be an associate justice of the Supreme Court, the Senate rejected him. Following his term as Attorney General, Black resumed the practice of law in York, Pennsylvania.

The term of Edwin McMasters Stanton, of Ohio, who followed Black, lasted only seventy-two days—the shortest of any incumbent before or since. He was appointed December 20, 1860 by President Buchanan and resigned March 3, 1861, when Lincoln became President. Lincoln named him Secretary of War, and he filled that post during the Civil War and into the Administration of Andrew Johnson.

Edward Bates, of Missouri, was a candidate for President in the convention that nominated Lincoln. Lincoln appointed him Attorney General, and he remained in that office until November 24, 1864. Bates, a Virginian by birth, and anxious to avoid war with the South, advised Lincoln not to send provisions to Fort Sumter because he believed that to do so would make war inevitable. He thought the South could be subjugated by closing its ports.

During the war, Marylanders rioted to prevent the passage of Union troops through Baltimore. Many were arrested and held in military custody. When Chief Justice Taney issued writs of habeas corpus, Lincoln refused to honor them. On the advice of Attorney General Bates, who told him his power arose out of his obligation to suppress insurrection, Lincoln suspended habeas corpus, and Congress upheld the suspension as a wartime measure. Bates consistently opposed extension of military jurisdiction into fields of civilian authority. He gave Secretary of State William H. Seward an opinion that freemen of color, if born in the United States, were citizens—something of a modification of the Dred Scott doctrine.

James Speed of Kentucky, followed Bates and held over, after the assassination of Lincoln, into the Administration of Andrew Johnson. He wrote many opinions, including the shortest on record—twenty-eight words—relating to the trial of Lincoln's assassins. It read:

> SIR: I am of the opinion that the persons charged with the murder of the President of the United States can rightfully be tried by a military court.

Speed also gave an opinion that the treason trial of Jefferson Davis, President of the Confederate States, must be in civilian courts. (Davis was indicted but not tried and, on Christmas Day, 1868, President Buchanan pardoned him and all who had participated in the Confederacy.)

Henry Stanbery, of Ohio, the twenty-eighth Attorney General, resigned to become an attorney for President Johnson in his impeachment trial. After the trial, Johnson sought to reappoint him, but the Senate rejected the nomination. The Senate also refused confirmation when the President nominated him as an associate justice of the Supreme Court.

William M. Evarts, of New York, one of the most distinguished lawyers of his day, had a brief tenure as Attorney General unmarked by any distinctive accomplishments. He was succeeded by Ebenezer Rockwood Hoar, of Massachusetts, the last man to hold the office of Attorney General before it became the Department of Justice.

Hoar was another who failed of confirmation when President Grant named him to the Supreme Court, largely because he insisted that a number of new federal judgeships be filled on the basis of character and fitness, not for political reasons, thereby earning the enmity of patronage-minded Senators.

"A PREPONDERANCE OF LAWYERS"

Gideon Welles, Secretary of the Navy in the Cabinet of President Andrew Johnson, so acutely disliked William M. Evarts, the New York lawyer who was Attorney General for eight months from July, 1868, to March, 1869, that he believed lawyers in government generally were a nuisance.

"It is unfortunate for the country," Welles wrote in his diary, "that there is such a preponderance of lawyers in our public councils. Their technical training and extensive, absorbing practice unfit them to be statesmen."

The record shows this to have been an unfair judgment, not only of Evarts, but of thousands of disciples of the law who have served their government with honor and distinction. Although his tenure as Attorney General was brief, Evarts was Secretary of State for four years, counsel in the Geneva arbitration case of 1871–72, a delegate to the Paris Monetary Conference in 1885, and a U.S. Senator, elected in 1891. As a lawyer, he was principal counsel for President Johnson in his impeachment trial, a government attorney in the treason trial of Jefferson Davis, and chief counsel for the Republican Party in the Hayes-Tilden Presidential election dispute. All told, he was one of the most distinguished men of the nineteenth century.

In a government of laws, it is logical that lawyers should participate in enacting, administering, and interpreting the laws. (Today, roughly two-thirds of the members of the U.S. Senate and many members of the House are lawyers, and lawyers predominate, as a rule, in Cabinet posts and administrative agencies.)

Appointment to the Supreme Court is, of course, the highest honor that can be bestowed upon a lawyer. Ten men who served as Attorney General, either before or after the establishment of the Department of Justice, have been advanced to the high judicial tribunal. (There might have been more had not Levi Lincoln, the fourth Attorney General, declined the appointment because of failing eyesight and had not the Senate refused the confirmation of several others.) Those from the early years who accepted and were confirmed were Roger Brooke Taney, Nathan Clifford, and Edwin M. Stanton. Joseph McKenna, William H. Moody, James C. McReynolds, Harlan F. Stone, Frank Murphy, Robert H. Jackson, and Tom C. Clark were Attorneys General in the Department of Justice who were later named to the Supreme Court. Both Taney and Stone served as Chief Justice of the United States.

In earlier years and less frequently in later times, Presidents sometimes chose men who had been Attorney General for diplomatic posts. The first was Caesar Augustus Rodney, appointed in 1823 by President Monroe to be the first Minister of the United States to the Argentine Republic. Others, and the posts they held, were: William Pinckney, Minister to Russia; Richard Rush, Minister to Great Britain and later to France; Hugh Swinton Legare, Charge d'Affaires, Belgium; John Nelson, Charge d'Affaires, the Two Sicilies (Minister to the Court of Naples); Reverdy Johnson, Minister to Great Britain; Caleb Cushing, Minister to Spain; Edwards Pierrepont, Minister to Great Britain; Alphonso Taft, Minister to Austria and later to Russia; Isaac Wayne MacVeagh, Minister to Turkey and later Ambassador to Russia.

Lawyers have always been active in politics and, consequently, have held many public offices. Fourteen Attorneys General, before or after their terms, were elected to the U.S. Senate: John Breckenridge, Rodney, Pinckney, John M. Berrien, Felix Grundy, John J. Crittenden, Isaac Toucey, Reverdy Johnson, Evarts, George H. Williams, Augustus H.

Garland, Philander C. Knox, J. Howard McGrath, and Robert F. Kennedy. Levi Lincoln, Rodney, Pinckney, Grundy, Crittenden, Legare, John Young Mason, Toucey, Clifford, Cushing, Edward Bates, McKenna, Moody, A. Mitchell Palmer, and James P. McGranery were members of the House of Representatives.

Edmund Randolph of Virginia, Levi Lincoln of Massachusetts, Crittenden of Kentucky, Toucey of Connecticut, Garland of Arkansas, Judson Harmon of Ohio, John W. Griggs of New Jersey, Murphy of Michigan, and McGrath of Rhode Island were governors of their states.

Sometimes, Presidents have shifted Attorneys General from one Cabinet post to another. Randolph, Black, Richard Olney, and Knox were secretaries of State; Rush and Taney secretaries of the Treasury; Toucey, Moody and Charles J. Bonaparte, secretaries of the Navy; Stanton and Alphonso Taft, secretaries of War.

No Attorney General has yet become President or Vice President of the United States.

PROTOCOL

The Judiciary Act of 1789 did not accord the Attorney General Cabinet rank; rather he was to serve as counsel to those who were members of the Cabinet. From the outset, however, matters considered by the Cabinet had so many legal aspects that the first President found it expeditious to have his Attorney General present at Cabinet meetings. Attorney General Edmund Randolph attended his first session of Washington's Cabinet on March 31, 1792. Thereafter, the Office of Attorney General was recognized as a Cabinet post and the incumbent sat with the President's inner council.

The Office of Attorney General was the fourth created by the 1789 statute, after the Foreign Affairs (State), Treasury, and War departments, and, under legislation of 1886, the

Attorney General ranked fourth, after the Vice-President, in the line of succession to the Presidency. The incumbent held that rank until Congress passed a law making the Speaker of the House and the president pro tempore of the Senate next in line of succession after the Vice-President. For protocol purposes, such as seating at the Cabinet table, the Attorney General still ranks fourth, after the Secretary of State, Secretary of Defense, and Secretary of the Treasury.

THE SEAL

As has been noted, the Department of Justice was, in essence if not in form, an offshoot of the English office of attorney general. In England, the title first appeared in the reign of Edward IV; the principal functions of the incumbent were to give legal advice to the King and his ministers and to conduct prosecutions in important criminal cases. Not only did the American law office take its title from its English counterpart, but it borrowed, or perhaps adapted, its motto from a Latin phrase commonly used in the courts in the time of the first Queen Elizabeth.

Seals and mottoes had been adopted early by other departments, and the Great Seal of the United States was emblazoned on treaties and other solemn documents. The Attorney General, however, had no emblem to imprint upon official papers.

Congress appears to have been the first to become concerned about the situation. On February 22, 1849, it passed an act that instructed the Attorney General to cause to be devised for his office a seal "with such device as the President of the United States shall approve." (The files of the Department today do not disclose when the seal was designed, when the President approved it, or precisely when it came into use. There may have been several types contrived before the one now officially in use was adopted.)

For many years, the legend was that the seal was devised by Attorney General Jeremiah S. Black and the motto chosen by him. Black served from March 6, 1857, to December 17, 1860. That some form of seal preceded those dates, however, is attested by a report from Caleb Cushing to the President on March 6, 1854, that the Attorney General's Office "has an official seal, and all copies of records authenticated under this are declared to be evidence equally with the original record or paper."

Reverdy Johnson was Attorney General when Congress passed the law. The assumption is that the seal that Cushing used was devised and approved by President Zachary Taylor during Johnson's tenure. It is quite probable that the motto was chosen by Black and added to a redesigned seal, showing an eagle arising from the United States shield with outspread wings, bearing in his right talon an olive branch and, in his left talon, arrows. When first designed, the outer circle bore the inscription "The Attorney General's Office" and the inner circle the motto *Qui pro domina justitia sequitur*. (The design is preserved in the present seal, adopted in 1872, except that in the outer circle the words "Department of Justice" appear.)

Where did the motto come from? What does it mean? To what function of the Attorney General does it apply? Answers provided by fact or legend are not precise.

The tradition is that Attorney General Black took the motto from a passage in Coke's *Institute*, Part 3, Folio 79: "And I well remember when the Lord Treasurer Burleigh told Queen Elizabeth, Madam, here is your Attorney General (I being sent for) *qui pro domina regina sequitur*, she said that she would have the records altered: for it should be *attornatus generalis qui pro domina veritate sequitur*."

In Elizabeth's time, all pleadings were in Latin. Translated, they began: "Now comes (the Attorney General) who prosecutes on behalf of our Lady, the Queen." Elizabeth substituted *veritate* (truth) for *domina regina.*

Adapted in whatever year it was by Black or whoever made the further change, *veritate* became *justitia.* Since the word "sue" comes from *sequor,* there is no distortion in the translation given many years later by Roscoe Pound, who said that the "seal asserts that the Attorney General prosecutes on behalf of justice," which has become the generally accepted meaning of the motto.

As it has evolved from the simpler original concept of an official to interpret and expound the law, the function of the Attorney General (and the Department he now heads) is to sue, or prosecute, on behalf of justice. Conversely, he has an obligation to prevent injustice being done citizens under color of law. He is the lawyer for the blindfolded lady with the scales, engraved upon the emblem that symbolizes equal justice under law.

Injustice can arise from maladministration of laws. Whether laws are applied justly or unjustly must be decided by the courts. Before the federal judicial tribunals, the Attorney General prosecutes *pro domina justitia.* The official concept of success is expressed today in the inscription over the door of the Attorney General's office:

"The United States wins its case whenever justice is done one of its citizens in the courts."

II

Who Sues for Justice:
The Attorney General After 1870

Today, the Attorney General is head of the largest law office in the world. But he has only one client. That single client is the government of the United States.

The basic function of the Department of Justice, which the Attorney General heads, remains the same as the function of the Office of Attorney General from 1789 to 1870—to represent the interests of the United States in the courts. Another principal function of the modern Department is to provide means for the enforcement of federal laws. To perform these monumental tasks requires an increasingly vast and complex organization.

The growth of this operation from the original one-man Office of Attorney General has been slow but persistent; it has kept pace with the development of the United States from a loose federation of thirteen states along the Atlantic seaboard into an increasingly centralized union of fifty states, spanning the continent and reaching out into the Pacific Ocean, with interests and obligations in every part of the globe. At each stage in the process of development, an Attorney General has stood by to counsel the President, Congress, and the courts in matters of law and national policy. In war and peace, the Attorney General has played a vital role, not just in enforcement and administration of the laws, but on the whole broad stage of executive management of federal affairs.

THE OPINIONS OF THE ATTORNEY GENERAL

As written over the years at the request of the President and heads of executive departments, the opinions of the Attorneys General are as varied as the refractions of a prism. They involve domestic problems, international issues, pet plans of bureaucrats, the application of the Constitution and the laws to administrative policies and procedures, the powers and jurisdictions of departments and agencies, the advisability of contemplated actions; trivial matters, momentous matters. Hardly a demand is made upon the Attorney General that does not involve some interpretation of civil, common, international, commercial, or municipal law. His opinions officially define the law in a multitude of cases, and they remain authoritative until withdrawn by the Attorney General or his successors or overruled by the courts. As such, they have become a body of legal precedent and exposition invaluable to lawyers in the preparation of their cases and to judges in reaching their decisions.

The first compilation of opinions was prepared by Henry Dilworth Gilpin, of Pennsylvania, who was appointed Attorney General on January 11, 1840, by President Martin Van Buren. Until that time most, but not all, of the formal rulings of Attorneys General had been in the files of the Department of Justice or the National Archives. Gilpin combined all those available in a volume entitled *The Opinions of the Attorney General of the United States from the Beginning of the Government to 1841*. President Van Buren sent this compilation to Congress, and it was printed as a House document. For the first time, opinions of the Attorneys General became accessible to the public. On July 24, 1850, the House passed a resolution calling for opinions since 1841 and had them published. They included all those up to and through the second incumbency of Attorney General John Jordan Crittenden.

After 1851, the opinions were published privately until 1890. Benjamin F. Hall, a New York author and lawyer, combined all opinions since 1790 into five volumes, and they were published commercially until 1852. Others were added until the privately printed volumes numbered sixteen. Beginning with Volume XVII, all have been published by the Government Printing Office, and, by 1966, the total number reached forty-two.

Some Attorneys General wrote many opinions; for example, those of Charles Devens, of Massachusetts, a learned man who was regarded as one of the strongest members of a strong Cabinet in the Administration of President Rutherford B. Hayes, filled 900 pages in three volumes. Edmund Randolph, the first Attorney General, wrote eight opinions. John Breckenridge, of Kentucky, who was Attorney General in the Cabinet of President Jefferson from August 7, 1805, to December 4, 1806, produced only three opinions, the smallest output on record.

Some of the opinions of Attorneys General still provide beacons for the ship of state; others are embalmed in the pages of history. But at the time they were written, they dealt with important issues and hence touched upon the official life of the nation and the individual lives of its people.

ESTABLISHMENT OF THE DEPARTMENT

Some eighty years after the Office of Attorney General was established, the Joint Committee on Retrenchment and Reform of the Congress reported a bill to establish a department of justice. It was passed by the Senate and the House, and President Ulysses S. Grant signed it on June 22, 1870.

Formally, the Department of Justice came into existence on July 1, 1870, with an appropriation of $67,320 for its first year of operation. The simple days of Randolph, Wirt, and Cushing were gone, and the nation's legal business was statutorily centered in a single federal organization, with a single head in the Attorney General of the United States.

The "Act To Establish the Department of Justice" (for full text, see Appendix I) made little change in the statutory duties of the Attorney General. His salary and tenure were to be the same as before. However, the law created a new office, that of solicitor general, which was to become an important cog in the administrative machinery. The main provisions of the new statute:

Fixed the salary of the solicitor general at $7,500 per year and designated him as acting attorney general in the absence or disability of the head of the Department, and in case of a vacancy;

Provided two assistant attorneys general at salaries of $5,000 per year each;

Gave the Attorney General supervision over law officers of the other departments, such as solicitor of the Treasury and solicitor of Internal Revenue;

Provided that the Attorney General might refer to his assistants or subordinates any questions except those involving construction of the Constitution and that their opinions, when approved by him, would have the same effect as his own;

Gave the Attorney General and the Department control over all criminal prosecutions and civil suits in which the United States was interested;

Provided that the Attorney General might require the solicitor general or any other officer of the Department to conduct and argue in the Supreme Court, the Court of Claims, or in any federal or state court, any case in which the United States might be involved;

Gave the Attorney General supervision of U.S. attorneys and other counsel employed on behalf of the United States, and supervision of the accounts of district attorneys, U.S. marshals, and clerks and other officers of the federal courts.

Those remain the basic functions and responsibilities of the Attorney General. By law or by Presidential direction, other duties have been assigned him, and his administrative work load has increased as the Department has grown in size and importance. But the framework erected by the 1870 act still supports a Department with sweeping powers that would have astounded statesmen of the post-Revolutionary War era.

Ebenezer Rockwood Hoar, of Massachusetts, who was Attorney General when the Department was created, might have been named the head of it. As discussed in Chapter I, President Grant had nominated Hoar to be a justice of the Supreme Court, but the Senate had rejected the nomination because of certain opinions the Attorney General had given, which displeased influential politicians, and because of his failure to consult Senators about candidates for appointment as district attorneys and judges. While the Justice Department bill was progressing toward enactment, Grant, in need of Southern support for certain of his policies, had recognized that political advantage could be gained from having in the Cabinet some person from the South. So it was that he asked Hoar to resign—and appointed a Georgian to head the new Department. The thirty-first Attorney General of the United States, Amos Tappan Akerman, was a native of New Hampshire who had moved to Georgia in early life and served with the Confederate Army in the Civil War. Politically, however, he remained an old-line Whig, and, when the war was over, aligned himself with the Republicans. Because he had served voluntarily in the military forces of the Confederacy, he was not able to take the test oath required of federal officials until Congress granted him special relief.

Akerman was confirmed by the Senate and served from July 8, 1870, to January 10, 1872. It was he who organized the new Department and launched it on its course. His task was made difficult by the fact that, while his official duties were defined and centralized, departmental facilities were not. The staff was scattered in offices in various buildings in many parts of Washington. (Not until more than sixty years later was adequate housing provided for a unified department.)

As with salaries in the early days, Congress was frugal in providing money for housing for the new Department of Justice. Although when Akerman took office the Attorney General and his clerks occupied limited office space in the Treasury Building, for the next thirty years, or thereabouts, the Attorneys General had to pay office rent out of their salaries. From the start, the new solicitor general, Benjamin H. Bristow, of Kentucky, and one assistant attorney general occupied rented quarters, and the other assistant attorney general had his office in the basement of the Capitol. In the second year of Akerman's incumbency, two floors of the Freedman's Bank Building on Pennsylvania Avenue were leased; the Department was housed there in cramped quarters, often without heat in the winter and offended by foul air from a sewer beneath the building in hot weather, until 1899.

Upon his appointment to the Attorney Generalship, Akerman was plunged into the Credit Mobilier controversy, a scandal of the Grant Administration. His opinions supporting the government's position earned him the enmity of entrenched financial interests with powerful friends in Congress. The resulting pressures led the President to request the Attorney General's resignation, offering him his choice of federal judgeships in Florida or Texas. Akerman declined and retired to private life.

THE ERA OF THE "TRUST-BUSTERS"

In the late nineteenth century, protection of the rights of citizens under law extended to suits on behalf of the United States against large business and industrial "trusts" designed to monopolize or restrain trade. Under the Sherman Act of 1890, antitrust activities became a principal responsibility of Attorneys General. (See Chapter V.)

The first of a line of "trust-busters" that continues to this day was William Henry Harrison Miller, of Indiana, who was Attorney General from March 5, 1889, to March 6, 1893. Under the newly enacted Sherman Act, Miller sued the so-called Sugar Trust to test the constitutionality of the law and break up an alleged monopoly. Richard Olney of Massachusetts, Miller's successor, carried the Sugar Trust case to the Supreme Court, and the pace of antitrust enforcement was stepped up in the incumbency of Philander Chase Knox, of Pennsylvania, who served from April 5, 1901, to June 30, 1904. Knox was an attorney for Andrew Carnegie in the formation of the Carnegie Steel Company and a successful lawyer representing large business interests, but within a year after he became Attorney General he initiated suit under the Sherman Act against the Northern Securities Company to prevent a merger of the Great Northern, the Northern Pacific, and the Chicago, Burlington, and Quincy railroads. He argued the case in the Supreme Court and won a decision on April 9, 1903. (See Chapter V.)

While Attorney General, Knox was sent to Paris to examine the title of the New Panama Canal Company, a French concern that offered to sell its interests in the Isthmus to the United States. Upon Knox's certificate of title, the French company's offer was accepted. Knox also drafted the legislation that created the Department of Commerce and Labor in 1903, and participated in drafting the law that gave the Interstate Commerce Commission control of railroad rates. He resigned in June, 1904, to fill an unexpired Senate term and subsequently was elected to a full term in the Senate, resigning in 1909 to become Secretary of State under President William Howard Taft.

Trust-busting reached its height in the Administration of President Theodore Roosevelt. William Henry Moody, of Massachusetts, succeeded Knox and not only successfully argued the "Beef Trust" case (*Swift & Co. v. United States*), but instituted prosecutions alleging restraint of trade against combinations in the paper, fertilizer, salt, tobacco, oil, and lumber industries. Moody moved on to the Supreme Court, and his successor, Charles Joseph Bonaparte, of Maryland, instituted twenty antitrust suits, eight of which eventually were decided in the government's favor, and won a decree dissolving the tobacco trust in a suit that had been instigated by Moody. (For more detailed treatment, see Chapter V.)

Few Attorneys General have been more active than George Woodward Wickersham, the forty-seventh, a New Yorker who held office from March 5, 1909, to March 5, 1913, in the Administration of President Taft. An outstanding Wickersham accomplishment was the drafting, in collaboration with Senator Elihu Root, of the income tax amendment to the Constitution, adopted in 1913, but enforcement of the antitrust laws also engaged much of his time and he made the closing arguments in the Supreme Court in the Standard Oil and American Tobacco Company cases and in the government suit for dissolution of the Union Pacific–Southern Pacific merger. The device of the consent decree, in which defendants agree to negotiated settlements without resort to court trials, came into use in Wickersham's administration; nineteen of forty-seven suits begun by Wickersham ended in that way.

James Clark McReynolds, of Tennessee, who afterward became an associate justice of the Supreme Court by appointment of President Woodrow Wilson, also was active in the antitrust field. Some achievements of his Attorney Generalship were the decree requiring the American Telephone and Telegraph Company to relinquish its monopoly of wire communications; the dissolution of the United States Thread Association; an injunction restraining the National Wholesale Jewelers' Association from a conspiracy to restrain trade; and the decree requiring the New Haven Railroad to relinquish a monopoly of transportation in New England.

Thomas Watt Gregory, of Texas, who followed McReynolds, served during World War I and wrote many opinions related to American participation in that struggle. The Clayton Act, the Federal Trade Commission Act, measures supplementing the Sherman Act, and other regulatory statutes were passed in Gregory's administration. Gregory opposed proposals to put aside for the duration of the war antitrust actions pending against several large corporations (but was overruled by President Wilson), and he presented in the Supreme Court motions to suspend suits against combinations in shoe machinery, farm machinery, steel, and other products.

Although A. Mitchell Palmer, a Pennsylvanian who became the fiftieth Attorney General, continued departmental activities in the fields of antitrust and business regulation, including establishment of price-fixing committees to curb the cost of living, the high light of his law enforcement program came with the so-called Red Raids. Alleged anarchist plots and seditious activities were a matter of concern in the wake of World War I. Terrorists sent bombs to the homes of many prominent persons, and one exploded while being carried up the steps of Palmer's house, damaging the dwelling and blowing the bearer to bits. Similar acts of violence occurred in other cities, and the Justice Department intensified its hunt for the persons responsible. The climax came when, in a series of dramatic raids, more than 5,000 persons were arrested. Palmer was both praised and denounced for those raids and other anti-Radical activities, but he was a pioneer in enforcement of laws pertaining to internal security.

EXPANDING RESPONSIBILITIES, 1924–45

Gradually, as the Department of Justice itself evolved, the duties of the Attorney General multiplied. Some of the achievements of a sampling of men who held the post in the 1920's and 1930's reflect certain of the changes.

Thus, Harlan Stone, later to become Chief Justice of the United States, during his period as Attorney General (a position to which the distinguished New York lawyer and dean of Columbia Law School had been appointed by Calvin Coolidge) reorganized the Federal Bureau of Investigation and chose J. Edgar Hoover to head it.

William DeWitt Mitchell of Minnesota, who was solicitor general in the Coolidge Administration and was elevated to the Attorney Generalship by President Herbert Hoover, followed Wirt's historic precept by refusing to give the Senate an opinion regarding proposed railroad mergers, but he advised the President that proposed legislation authorizing Congress to make final decision on tax refunds of more than $20,000 would be an unconstitutional transfer to the legislative branch of a function of the executive branch. Enforcement of Prohibition was a burdensome duty of Mitchell's term and reorganization of the federal prison system one of his accomplishments.

Homer Stillé Cummings, of Connecticut, the fifty-fifth Attorney General, took office March 4, 1933, as Franklin D. Roosevelt became President. The nation was in economic distress, and repeal of Prohibition had brought new problems of law enforcement. Cummings was Roosevelt's legal adviser in the banking crisis and throughout the recovery program that changed traditional patterns of the country's economy

and brought a new era in labor relations. He argued successfully in the Supreme Court the so-called Gold Clause cases
that absolved the government of obligation to redeem its
securities in gold. Cummings proposed, and Congress enacted, a series of laws widening the federal government's
power to combat the criminal elements that became bold
when the dry laws were repealed. Cummings found the
record-keeping operations of the Department in disarray,
and he modernized the system Wirt had begun and brought
it up to date.

Frank Murphy, of Michigan, who followed Cummings,
was an energetic foe of official wrong-doing. He prosecuted
corrupt political machines in Missouri and Louisiana and
indicted U.S. District Judge Martin Manton in New York
for "selling justice." During the year he served before President Roosevelt elevated him to the Supreme Court, Murphy
set up a civil rights section, the first such unit in the Department of Justice.

Robert H. Jackson, of New York, who also went to the
Supreme Court, served as general counsel of the Bureau of
Internal Revenue, assistant attorney general in charge of the
Tax and Antitrust Divisions, and solicitor general before
becoming Attorney General. When he took office, the United
States was moving toward deeper involvement in World War
II; one of his most notable opinions was that President
Roosevelt's deal with the British to exchange fifty over-age
destroyers for offshore naval and air bases in the Atlantic
did not exceed the President's constitutional powers.

Francis Biddle, of Pennsylvania, the fifty-eighth Attorney
General and a direct descendant of Edmund Randolph, the
first, was solicitor general and had won fifteen of the sixteen
cases he argued in the Supreme Court when Roosevelt appointed him Attorney General. He was the wartime law enforcement officer and, immediately after Pearl Harbor, ordered the internment of aliens who were citizens of the Axis

powers. When eight Nazi saboteurs were captured and tried before a military commission in 1942, Biddle directed the prosecution and argued successfully in the Supreme Court in opposition to their petitions for habeas corpus. Six of the eight were executed, one sentenced to life imprisonment, and the other to thirty years.

FROM CLARK TO CLARK, 1945–67

Thomas Campbell Clark, of Texas, followed Biddle. He had been coordinator of Alien Enemy Control of the Western Defense Command and chief of the Civilian Staff for Japanese Relocation in 1942, and, before becoming Attorney General, he had served as head, first of the Antitrust Division and then of the Criminal Division of the Department.

President Harry S. Truman appointed Tom Clark, as he prefers to be called, to the Supreme Court in August, 1949, and named a Senator from Rhode Island, J. Howard Mc-Grath, to the post of Attorney General.

In the early days of the Truman Administration, there was much talk of scandal and corruption in Washington. Truman ordered a government-wide investigation under the supervision of the Department of Justice, but he brought in Newbold Morris, a silk-stocking New York lawyer, to conduct it. This action on the President's part outraged McGrath, a former solicitor general—especially when Morris announced that the Justice Department would be the first target of the investigation. Truman settled the ensuing and bitter McGrath-Morris feud by dismissing both men. Afterward, a House Judiciary subcommittee inquired into the operations of the Department and found some things to criticize, but produced no general condemnation of McGrath's official conduct.

Internal security, civil rights, and organized crime and racketeering were national problems when Herbert Brownell, Jr., became the sixty-second Attorney General.

Brownell, a Nebraskan turned New Yorker, instituted proceedings under the Internal Security Act of 1950 to compel the Communist Party to register with the Attorney General as a Soviet-dominated organization; added some 200 other groups classified as totalitarian, Fascist, or Communist to the list of organizations required to register as Communist fronts, and set up an Internal Security Division in the Department to prosecute violations of the internal security laws. After the school segregation cases were decided by the Supreme Court in 1954, the first lawsuits to implement those judgments were filed by Brownell. He also intensified the Department's drive on crime, and several notorious racketeers were sent to jail while he held office. Departmental antitrust policies were studied and redefined and a vigorous program of enforcement instituted during his incumbency.

William Pierce Rogers, Brownell's deputy attorney general succeeded to the top job when Brownell resigned in November, 1957. Under Attorney General Rogers, the Civil Rights Division was established in 1958, and suits to enforce provisions of the Civil Rights acts, especially those pertaining to voting rights, were instituted in Southern states. Rogers advised President Eisenhower about his constitutional authority to send troops to Little Rock, Arkansas, to enforce compliance with school desegregation orders of the federal courts and assigned an assistant attorney general to counsel troop commanders and civilian officials on the legal phases of the Little Rock operation. Rogers also strengthened the Organized Crime and Racketeering Section of the Criminal Division and directed investigation and prosecution of the overlords of crime, some of whom were aliens and subsequently deported. During Rogers' term, the FBI tracked down several spies—the most important being Rudolph Abel, a Soviet agent, who was convicted and given a thirty-year prison sentence. In the antitrust field, indictments were obtained against General Electric Company, Westinghouse Electric Corporation, and twenty-five other corporations in the heavy electrical equipment industry on charges of illegal price-fixing; their convictions resulted in the imposition of heavy fines and jail sentences for some officials.

In 1961, President John F. Kennedy's appointment of his younger brother and campaign manager as Attorney General was widely criticized, chiefly on two grounds: nepotism, and Robert F. Kennedy's lack of legal experience. The younger Kennedy was active and vigorous, however, especially in the areas of civil rights and organized crime. He directed legal aspects and policies involved in the effort to compel the University of Mississippi to admit James Meredith, a Negro, as a student and, when federal laws were involved, the prosecution of persons charged with acts of violence against civil rights demonstrators. Kennedy was particularly persistent in prosecution of alleged illegal activities of labor leaders, including James Hoffa, powerful president of the Teamsters' Union. The Attorney General was a close adviser of President Kennedy in international crises, especially those involving Soviet Russia and Cuba. After the assassination of President Kennedy, Robert F. Kennedy resigned from the Cabinet of President Lyndon B. Johnson and, although a resident and voter in Massachusetts, ran for Senator in New York and was elected.

Nicholas deBelleville Katzenbach, of Illinois, was Kennedy's deputy attorney general and, as his successor, carried out many of the Kennedy policies. He played an important role in drafting the Civil Rights Act of 1964 and was the Department official in command on the scene during desegregation crises at the University of Mississippi and the University of Alabama. In the 1962 missile crisis, Katzenbach drew up a lengthy brief in support of the Kennedy Administration's decision to blockade Cuba, and—moving into the jet age—was the principal drafter of legislation establishing the Communications Satellite Corporation.

On October 3, 1966, President Johnson, in a surprise move, switched Katzenbach's responsibilities in government and named him to the post of under secretary of State. Ramsey Clark, the son of Tom Clark, and a Texan like his father, served as acting Attorney General for five months. Then, on February 28, 1967, the President announced that he was nominating him to be Attorney General and head of the Department of Justice, which his father had run for four years a generation earlier. To avoid any possible conflict with his son's duties, the elder Clark announced that he would step down from the Supreme Court. Ramsey Clark's appointment was confirmed by the Senate on March 2, and he was sworn in on March 10, 1967.

FUNCTIONS OF THE ATTORNEY GENERAL TODAY

Whoever is Attorney General of the United States performs functions that touch the basic concerns of citizens in their security at home and abroad, in their rights and freedoms, and in their protection under the even-handed administration of the law. He counsels statesmen and sues for justice on behalf of the government and the people. In addition to performing these functions, he is also responsible for the over-all administration of the Department of Justice, including the divisions charged with enforcement of laws.

Separate chapters of this book describe the organization of the Department the Attorney General now heads, and the organization and functions of its individual divisions, boards, and bureaus. Before turning to the first of these chapters, it is necessary to sum up the broad responsibilities the Attorney General now exercisis as counsel to the executive branch and chief lawyer for the United States.

A Judge of Judges

The judiciary is an independent branch of the government over which neither the Attorney General, nor the President, has control once judges are appointed. Prior to appointment, however, the Attorney General and his assistants are, in effect, the judges of who shall become judges, and thus exercise greater influence upon the character and personnel of the federal courts than many other officials of the government. The procedure is not statutory, but administrative.

When a vacancy occurs, on the Supreme Court or lower tribunals, names of a possible appointee may reach the Attorney General in various ways. They may come from the individual who wants the job, from national or local bar associations, from individual lawyers or judges, from members of Congress, from political leaders, from the White House, from civic organizations, from other members of the Cabinet. The Attorney General may even have ideas of his own; in fact, he often does.

Once a name is in the hopper, the nominee is thoroughly investigated by the FBI, which sets forth his qualifications and record in a factual investigative report to the Attorney General. This report is not a judgment of fitness for appointment. The American Bar Association is asked for its appraisal of the character and abilities of the person under consideration, and it grades him from highly qualified to not qualified, as its judgment warrants, and gives the reasons for its rating. If the appointment is regional, as for a district judgeship or the elevation of a district judge to a higher court, the opinions of bar groups in the area also may be requested. And, since all judicial appointments must be confirmed by the Senate, it is important that Senators representing the state from which the prospective jurist comes be consulted. (Because of all these inquiries, the potential nominee knows he is under consideration for appointment, but it is the policy of the Department not to make public announcements nor to confirm reports about possible appointments, lest any stigma attach to the records or reputations of those nominees who fail.)

When the investigations are complete, the reports and other data are carefully screened in the office of the deputy attorney general, and some persons who are obviously unqualified or otherwise ineligible are eliminated there. The Attorney General, of course, is kept informed of these proceedings, and when the time comes to consider those who are regarded as qualified, the Attorney General and his deputy, perhaps with other officials of the Department, go over the list carefully. One by one, names are eliminated, until a single aspirant is left. The Attorney General then sends that name to the President, with a statement on the individual's qualifications and a recommendation that he be appointed. At this stage of the proceedings, of course, additional Presidential considerations enter in. But once the choice is final, the White House announces the appointment, and the nomination is sent to the Senate, where it is considered by the Judiciary Committee. The committee may or may not hold hearings; if it does, the Attorney General usually attends and testifies. (In any case, at no time are the names of those passed over for appointment publicly disclosed.)

In theory and largely in practice, the federal judiciary is independent of politics, and its judgments are based on law. But politics creeps into the appointive process. Patently, consideration must be given to the political affiliation of the aspirant and his standing with the party of the Administration in power. When Democrats hold the White House, or a majority in the Senate, more Democrats than Republicans will be named to the federal bench, and vice versa. The result is that a political imbalance always prevails; in recent years, because Democrats have been so often and so long in power, the balance has favored their party. When General Eisenhower became President, the ratio of Democrats to Republicans sitting in federal courts was, roughly, 80 per cent to 20 per cent. There was only one Republican on the Supreme Court, and he had been appointed by President Truman, a Democrat.

The Eisenhower Administration, through Attorney General Rogers, pledged itself to create and maintain a fifty-fifty balance, if the Democrats would do likewise. Obviously, the Democrats could not commit a future President to such a policy, hence no pledge was given. The Eisenhower Administration then appointed three Republicans and one Democrat to the Supreme Court, and several Democrats to lower courts, but it was not in power long enough to correct the imbalance, which continues in favor of the Democrats.

Appointment of District Attorneys and Marshals

Like federal judges, U.S. attorneys and marshals are also appointed by the President upon the advice of the Attorney General and subject to confirmation by the Senate. The procedure is much the same as with judges. However, politics enters in even more strongly since these are local offices aspired to by men whose support is valued by the Senators from their state and the Congressman from their district. Often, these aspirants are political leaders themselves in their area. It is, therefore, sometimes more difficult for the Attorney General to satisfy politicians in the appointment of a U.S. attorney or a marshal than a justice of the Supreme Court. (See Chapter III.)

Applications for Pardon

It is also the Attorney General's duty to determine when clemency should be extended to those sentenced to imprisonment for breaking federal laws. Countless men in federal prisons have thus found that, in one sense, their fate rested in the hands of the Attorney General. Under the Constitution, the pardoning power is vested in the President, but applications for pardon or other forms of executive clemency are received by the Attorney General. After investigation, the pardon attorney prepares for the Attorney General a letter of advice to the President and, if clemency is recommended, an appropriate warrant. Upon these documents, the President bases his decision, and the recommendations are usually, though not invariably, followed.

The parole function is exercised by an eight-member body appointed by the President upon recommendation of the Attorney General, of which the Attorney General designates the chairman. The Parole Board has sole authority to release federal prisoners on parole and to determine the conditions under which parole is granted.

Influence on National Policy

Although not statutorily a policy-making official, the Attorney General, through his membership in the Cabinet, can—and often does—exercise great influence upon national policy. Foreign and domestic policies emerge from the White House—and from Congress—as the product of consultative processes, and Presidents since George Washington have relied upon their Attorney General for guidance in charting the courses of their administrations, not only to avoid legal shoals but in the wider fields of politics and statesmanship. The extent of the Attorney General's influence in policy-making depends chiefly upon his own wisdom and the receptivity of the chief executive to advice.

Today, as throughout the history of the United States, the opinions of the Attorney General guide the President and other executive officials as to their statutory and constitutional powers and the legality of contemplated actions. In most cases, opinions rendered by the Attorney General have been accepted as the authoritative basis for executive actions. Sometimes they have been disregarded by those to whom they have been given. And, although they carry weight in the courts, as Justice Felix Frankfurter once said, judges do not "always take the interpretation by the Attorney General." In essence, the function remains what it was when Attorney General Jeremiah S. Black described it in a letter of 1857 to the Secretary of the Navy. Black wrote:

> The duty of the Attorney General is to advise, not to decide. A thing is not to be considered as done by the head of a department merely because the Attorney General has advised him to do it. You may disregard his opinion if you are sure it is wrong. He aids you in forming a judgment on questions of law; but the judgment is yours, not his. You are not bound to see eye to eye, but only to use the light which he furnishes in order to see better with your own.

The Attorney General will not give opinions involving administrative judgment, or on matters of propriety and expediency. Abstract questions are not answered. (Attorney General Wirt laid down the rule that questions of law must be specifically propounded.) Questions pending in the courts are to be left to the courts. Most Attorneys General have avoided passing upon the constitutionality of acts of Congress in advance of challenges in the courts, although they may have expressed doubts in testimony before Congressional committees.

The practice of giving formal opinions to Congress was discontinued in Attorney General Wirt's day, but the legislators were not to be completely deprived of the advice of the chief law officer. The practice developed, and is increasingly in use, of requiring the Attorney General to testify before Congressional committees when legislation in his domain is under consideration. Often this takes place when hearings are held on proposed new laws or revisions of existing statutes that have been drafted in the Department of Justice and represent Administration policy. In these circumstances, the Attorney General or other official of the Department must explain and defend the proposals and the policies that gave rise to them. Questions of constitutionality are often involved, but when Attorneys General express doubts about the constitutionality of bills, or certain provisions of them, their views are in no way binding upon Congress. Congressional disagreement may be expressed by enactment of the measures. Then it remains for the courts to decide if constitutionality is challenged. The appearances of Attorneys General before Congressional committees have come to be mostly as protagonists of measures favored by the executive branch or as opponents of bills—of which there are many—that do not meet with Administration approval. They no longer serve as lawyers for the legislative branch; Congressional committees and subcommittees now employ their own legal counsel. But when a federal law is attacked in the courts, the Department of Justice must defend it.

As evident from the foregoing pages, the decisions of the Attorney General lie predominantly in the domestic field, but he also gives counsel to the President and the Cabinet on matters affecting national security. He sits in on meetings of the National Security Council, the high-level body that consults with the President in time of national or international crisis, and here shares in policy-making on a much broader basis than when only domestic laws and situations are involved. In recent years, his voice has been heard on what to do about the Bay of Pigs and Viet-Nam.

III

The Department as Now Constituted

On the pediment above the center entrance to the building that occupies the block of land between Pennsylvania and Constitution avenues and Ninth and Tenth streets in Washington, D.C., is enscribed: "The Place Of Justice Is A Hallowed Place."

This principal building of the Department of Justice, completed in 1935, is also a remarkably busy place. And, although it is seven stories high and has a gross floor area of 1,237,000 square feet, it is by no means large enough to house all of the headquarters activities of the Department. The Immigration and Naturalization Service, the Bureau of Prisons, the Board of Parole, the Office of the Pardon Attorney, and some sections of other divisions occupy other buildings in the city, or space in them. Congress has authorized construction of a $65 million building for the Federal Bureau of Investigation, which now uses more than half the space in the parent building.

The problem of space alone tells something about the magnitude of today's Department, and gives a hint of the complexity of its organization. Other statistics are additionally revealing: for fiscal year 1967, the total budget for the Department of Justice was approximately $407 million, and at present count, the Department employs more than 33,000 people, some 15,000 of them in the FBI.

DEPARTMENT OF JUSTICE

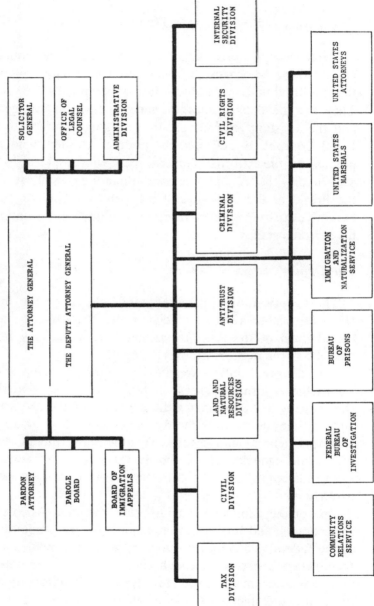

THE RIGHT-HAND MEN AND THEIR FUNCTIONS

Three men comprise what might be called the "inner circle" of those who assist the Attorney General in conducting the multitudinous affairs of the government's law office. They are the deputy attorney general, the solicitor general, and the assistant attorney general in charge of the Office of Legal Counsel. In addition, the pardon attorney, who is appointed by the Attorney General, performs a specialized service under the Attorney General handling applications to the President for pardon, and the Attorney General has an executive assistant and a director of Public Information on his personal staff.

The Deputy Attorney General

The deputy attorney general stands closest to the throne. He is the second ranking official in the Department, and, in the absence of the Attorney General or a vacancy in that post, he is the acting Attorney General.

The deputy's duties are largely administrative, and he assists the Attorney General in the over-all direction of the Department. He coordinates the activities of the Department and, in many matters, is the first to be consulted by assistant attorneys general and officials of other government departments and agencies. His authority extends to decisions, subject to the approval of the Attorney General, in many administrative matters.

One of the deputy's most important functions is to screen applications and make recommendations for appointments to the federal judiciary. No man or woman is named to the federal bench until a thorough check of his or her qualifications has been made under the deputy's direction; qualities of diplomacy, tact, political astuteness, and the ability to appraise the character and capabilities of men are requisite to the effective performance of this function. There are very few judges nominated by the President who do not owe their selection to the judgment of some incumbent deputy attorney general.

The deputy also recommends appointments of legal personnel to the Department and is thus responsible for the employment of qualified lawyers to staff the various divisions and bureaus. (See Appendix IV.)

The Executive Office for United States Attorneys and the Executive Office for United States Marshals are units of the deputy's organization, and he recommends appointment of candidates for those posts in the 92 judicial districts into which the country is divided for administrative purposes. There are 184 U.S. attorneys and marshals all told, and they are the field forces—the "grass roots" staff, as it were—of the Department of Justice, in the front line of law enforcement. The direction of their activities sometimes transcends the routine and escalates into virtual command of fighting forces on the battlefields of law and order. (See page 67.)

The deputy is the Department's liaison with Congress. Proposed legislation prepared in the Department or in which the Department has an interest is transmitted to Congress through his office, and he frequently testifies before Congressional committees in support of or in opposition to measures under consideration.

In the exercise of his functions and responsibilities, the deputy attorney general combines policy-making with administration of policy. He participates in the formulation of departmental policies and, as a principal consultant of the Attorney General, indirectly, and to a limited extent, in those domestic and international policies that evolve from the Attorney General's role as legal adviser to the President and his Cabinet.

Prior to the administration of Attorney General Herbert Brownell, Jr., the deputy ranked third in the official hierarchy. The solicitor general was in the Number Two spot and was acting Attorney General in case of a vacancy or in the absence of the Department head. Even in third place, however, the deputy's role in the management of the Department was, in practice, that of first assistant to the Attorney General.

Even though the incumbent is seldom in the public eye, the deputy attorney general's job is prestigious. Several deputies have become Attorney General—recent examples being William P. Rogers, who succeeded Brownell; Nicholas deB. Katzenbach, who succeeded Robert F. Kennedy; and Ramsey Clark, who replaced Katzenbach when the latter went to the State Department. At least one deputy, Stanley F. Reed, went from that office to be associate justice of the Supreme Court.

The deputy attorney general is selected by the Attorney General, but his nomination is sent to the Senate by the President and must be confirmed by the Senate.

The Solicitor General

The solicitor general of the United States appears more often in the Supreme Court than any other lawyer. He is the government's advocate in cases brought by the Justice Department or other federal agencies; he is the government's defender when private litigants carry cases involving federal interests to the high court. Since a majority of cases heard by the Court involve government interests, the solicitor general has more business before that tribunal than any private attorney.

The office was created by the Act of June 22, 1870, which established the Department of Justice and was the only new office created by that Act, which specified that the incumbent must be "learned in the law." Since that time, with rare exceptions, incumbents have been selected because of their legal attainments and effectiveness in presenting to the Supreme Court the government's arguments.

In 1870, and until 1952, as noted, the solicitor general was the second ranking official of the Department, serving as acting Attorney General when occasion required. He was relieved of that responsibility in 1952 and now is free from administrative duties except those of his own office. This enables him to devote his time more fully to acting as the government's Supreme Court lawyer. Although third in the official line, he would be acting Attorney General only in the unlikely event of both the Attorney General and the deputy being unable, for any reason, to perform their official duties.

Except for such higher authority as might be exercised by the Attorney General in rare circumstances, the solicitor general has sole jurisdiction to decide which government cases are appealed to the Supreme Court or other appellate courts. If a lower court decision is adverse to the government, it is the solicitor's function to determine whether the issues are important enough to justify an appeal and whether the government's case is good enough to afford reasonable chances of an appellate victory. If he says no appeal, there is none.

When an appeal is taken, the preparation of briefs and other documents is supervised by the solicitor. He is assisted by a small staff and collaborates with other departmental lawyers having special knowledge of the pertinent law and issues.

The solicitor general supervises all oral arguments in the Supreme Court and personally argues the more important government cases. He may assign other members of his staff, other departmental lawyers, or counsel for other Departments or agencies, but the responsibility to see that the government's case is effectively presented is his. He may conduct and argue in any court in the land any case in which the federal government is interested, but, as a practical matter, such cases are handled by U.S. attorneys in the districts, or by departmental counsel especially assigned.

The solicitor wears the traditional morning coat and striped trousers when he appears in the Supreme Court. Thus clad, he stands before the lectern and presents the Department's arguments and answers the questions of the justices. On most days when cases are being heard, he is present at the table where participating lawyers sit. There is always a quill pen on the table in front of him, but not since the earliest days has a solicitor been known to use one.

Like the deputy attorney general, the solicitor general is chosen by the Attorney General, nominated by the President, and confirmed in his office by the Senate.

The Office of Legal Counsel

The assistant attorney general in charge of the Office of Legal Counsel is often described as "the Attorney General's lawyer," because of his responsibility for preparing the formal opinions of the Attorney General, rendering informal opinions and legal advice to the various government agencies, and assisting the Attorney General in the performance of his functions as legal adviser to the President and the Cabinet.

Opinions originating in the Office of Legal Counsel have guided Presidents in many famous executive decisions. For example, in 1940, the "Lend-Lease" opinion of Attorney General Robert H. Jackson gave President Roosevelt legal authority to transfer American destroyers to England in return for the right to establish naval and air bases in British possessions. In 1957, the Office of Legal Counsel justified the use of federal troops in Little Rock, Arkansas, to enforce a court order that the schools be segregated. And in 1963, the Office devised the basis for the quarantine of Cuba during the missile crisis.

All proposed executive orders and proclamations are reviewed and revised for form and legality in the Office before final submission to the President. It also reviews and revises regulations that require the approval of the President or the Attorney General. Also, it performs the legal work entailed by gifts and bequests to the government.

American participation in the United Nations and related international organizations requires coordination with other government departments, and this work is done for the Department of Justice in the Office of Legal Counsel. In the domestic area, the Office is responsible for supervision of studies and recommendations for the improvement of administrative procedures of the various federal agencies. In addition, it has direct supervision over the handling of all conscientious objector cases, other than criminal prosecutions.

The Office was established in 1933, pursuant to an Act of Congress. It was first headed by an assistant solicitor general. In 1951, Attorney General J. Howard McGrath gave it division status with an assistant attorney general in charge, and named it the Executive Adjudications Division. This was changed to Office of Legal Counsel in an administrative order by Attorney General Brownell, issued April 3, 1953.

THE PRINCIPAL PARTS

Maintenance of law and order is the most essential function of government. Since the Department of Justice is not only the government's law office, but also the government's central agency for enforcement of the federal laws, its responsibilities are heavy. To discharge them, in addition to the officials described above, there are under the Attorney General's direction eight assistant attorneys general (each the head of a division), the director of the Federal Bureau of Investigation, the director of the Bureau of Prisons, and the commissioner of Immigration and Naturalization.

All of these men, some of whom direct very large numbers of employees, are responsible to the Attorney General for the conduct of their offices. The assistant attorneys general are his personal selections, and—as in the case of the deputy attorney general and the solicitor general—their nominations are sent to the Senate by the President, and they must be confirmed by the Senate. The directors of the FBI and of the Bureau of Prisons and the commissioner of Immigration and Naturalization are appointed by the Attorney General and do not require Senate confirmation.

Two boards complete the roster of principal parts of the Department. The Board of Immigration Appeals is a quasi-judicial body in the Office of the Attorney General. It has jurisdiction to review cases certified by the Immigration and Naturalization Service (see Chapter X). The Board of Parole has sole authority to grant, modify, or revoke paroles of all U.S. prisoners. Its eight members are appointed by the President with the advice and consent of the Senate.

Including the assistant attorney general in charge of the Office of Legal Counsel, whose special place in the organization as "the Attorney General's lawyer" has already been described, there are nine assistant attorneys general in the Department of Justice today.

One of them, the assistant attorney general in charge of the Administrative Division, occupies the top Civil Service position in the Department. He is the Department's housekeeper and business manager, responsible for the preparation of the budget; recruitment, replacement, training and classification of personnel; disbursement of and accounting for all expenditures; collection and compilation of statistics; purchase of supplies and equipment; allotment and utilization of space and services; transportation; receipt and distribution of mail; maintenance and disposition of records; and supervision of the library, which contains more than 200,000 volumes on law and related subjects.

THE DEPARTMENT AS NOW CONSTITUTED

The other assistant attorneys general head the following divisions, the organization and functions of which will be detailed in subsequent chapters:

Civil Rights, which enforces the Civil Rights acts of 1957, 1960, and 1964 and the Voting Rights Act of 1965;

Antitrust, which administers the Sherman Act, the Clayton Act, and other laws to preserve the competitive nature of the free enterprise system;

Tax, which acts as counsel for the Internal Revenue Service in controversies between the government and citizens over the payment of taxes;

Civil, which represents the rights and interests of the U.S. Government in all of its litigation other than criminal;

Land and Natural Resources, which protects the federal government's ownership, conservation, and use of land and related natural resources;

Internal Security, which enforces all laws relating to treason, espionage, sedition, and sabotage;

Criminal, which enforces several hundred federal criminal statutes, especially in the field of organized crime and racketering.

In 1964, Attorney General Kennedy established the Office of Criminal Justice, a special section headed by a director, and in 1966, Congress transferred from the Department of Commerce to the Justice Department the Community Relations Service, a special agency set up to supplement the Civil Rights Division in dealing with problems that arise locally as a result of efforts to enforce the civil rights laws.

Arms of the Law

The Judiciary Act of 1789 divided the country into judicial districts and provided that in each district "a meet person learned in the law" be appointed to "act as attorney for the United States." His duties were "to prosecute all delinquents for crimes and offenses cognizable under the authority of the United States, and all civil actions in which the United States shall be concerned."

Section 27 of the Act provided for a marshal in each district to execute "all lawful precepts directed to him and issued under authority of the United States."

That was more than 175 years ago, and the jobs were relatively easy. Today, the U.S. attorneys in the 92 districts into which the country is divided file more than 60,000 cases a year and receive more than 120,000 criminal complaints. The marshals, during an average year, will have in custody at different times a total of more than 80,000 prisoners and serve nearly 1 million "lawful precepts." Only the most farseeing could have envisioned the time when these two arms of the law would deal with the lives and affairs of so many citizens.

Very early in the history of the United States, the offices of district attorney and marshal became political plums. Support of a candidate for federal office frequently was rewarded by appointment to law enforcement posts, and incumbents usually were men of stature and political influence in their districts. Almost invariably, they were stalwarts of the party in power, and, to a lesser degree, this is still true; no district attorney or marshal is likely to be appointed or removed without the approval of his Senator or Congressman. Incumbents seldom appoint deputies or clerks without consulting local political leaders.

Before 1896, district attorneys were paid by fees, which, in busy districts, could produce a substantial income. They were also allowed to engage in private practice, but they were required to keep regular hours in their public offices and could not transact private business there. Marshals also were paid by fees. The fee system was abolished and salary scales graduated to the volume of business in the district—the incumbents in the southern district of New York, for example, get larger salaries than in Alaska—but it was not until after

1950 that all federal attorneys were forbidden private practice. Control of district attorneys and marshals was not centralized in the early days. Those officials were chiefly directed by the district judges, who themselves were subject to few rules of procedure and ran their courts pretty much as they pleased. Federal judges now must conform to rules of procedure prescribed by Congress and the Judicial Conference of the United States which attorneys and marshals must also observe, as well as regulations promulgated by the Attorney General of the United States. They were brought under control of the Attorney General by an act of August 2, 1861, in which Congress directed that:

> The Attorney General of the United States be, and he is hereby, charged with the general superintendence and direction of the attorneys and marshals of all the districts of the United States and territories, as to the manner of their discharging their duties; and the said district attorneys and marshals are hereby required to report to the Attorney General an account of their official proceedings and the state and manner of their respective offices at such time and manner as the Attorney General shall direct.

As described above, direction of the activities of U.S. attorneys is under the supervision of the deputy attorney general. Work of the U.S. marshals is directed by a chief marshal and an assistant to the deputy attorney general.

District attorneys and marshals are appointed by the President for terms of four years, subject to confirmation by the Senate. A district attorney is responsible for the prosecution of all offenses in his district against the United States and prosecutes or defends all civil actions or proceedings in which the government is concerned. A marshal's duties include attendance at the terms of U.S. courts in his district; custody and transportation of prisoners; execution of warrants and judgments of the courts; and disbursement of funds appropriated to his office, including payment of his own salary, salaries of his staff, and the salaries of the judges in his district. In a sense, the marshals are the administrative officers of the district courts.

That the Peace Be Kept

"There is a peace of the United States," the Supreme Court said in 1890, in the case of *in re Neagle*. "We hold it to be an incontrovertible principle that the government of the United States may, by means of physical force exercised through its official agents, execute on every foot of American soil the powers and functions that belong to it."

Marshals are federal guardians of the peace. Attorney General Homer Cummings called them "the first line of defense on occasions of public disturbance." In that role, they have earned a place in history. They have been called upon to act in such labor disputes as the Pullman strike in 1894, to deal with hostile Indians, and to cope with the bad men of the West in frontier days.

Many of the disturbances of the Wild West were between individuals, and the six-shooter was the instrument of pacification. But there were lone bandits and gangs of outlaws, who robbed the mails, stole the gold being transferred by Wells-Fargo, held up trains, rustled horses and cattle, and even despoiled the wagon trains of settlers. Marshals shared the peace-keeping responsibilities of those lawless times with federal troops, but they were the civilian enforcement officers whose horses were always saddled and whose lives depended on being quicker on the draw than the desperado.

During that period, competent district attorneys were hard to find. Most of them found it necessary to derive income from sources other than the fees they were paid by the government. Unscrupulous actions were reported to Washington but received little attention; after all they were isolated cases in a land that was far away. When Brigadier

General Garland, commanding troops in New Mexico, demanded the removal of one district attorney, he described the official as "notoriously the greatest liar and blackguard in New Mexico."

The 1789 Judiciary Act provided that marshals might summon troops in their district to aid them in quelling disorders. They used that authority in the South in Reconstruction days to an extent that annoyed citizens and the military; in 1878, Congress rescinded it. Since then, marshals have cooperated with soldiers in restoring order and preserving peace, but no civilian officer has commanded federal troops. If federal forces are needed now, they are ordered out by the President.

Civil Rights Enforcement

As officers of the courts, district attorneys and marshals have a duty to enforce the judgments of the courts. In recent years, this duty has involved them in "occasions of public disturbance" arising from resistance to court orders in civil rights cases. When it became evident that state authorities would offer forcible resistance to enrollment, under a court order, of James Meredith at the University of Mississippi, marshals were sent to effect his registration. They were reinforced by border patrolmen and Bureau of Prisons personnel and troops. In his 1962 report, the deputy attorney general stated laconically that "after quelling a riot with the assistance of the United States Army, Mr. Meredith's registration was effected."

In June, 1963, marshals assisted three Negroes in gaining admission to the University of Alabama; in 1964, deputy marshals were stationed at the University of Mississippi and the University of Alabama to ensure the safety of Negro students. Earlier, the widely publicized enforcement of court orders to admit Negroes to a segregated public school in Little Rock, Arkansas, saw the Justice Department dispatching a force of marshals recruited from other areas and President Eisenhower reinforcing them with federal troops. Confronted with this array of federal force and bulwarked by legal actions instituted by the district attorney under the supervision of an assistant attorney general, the governor of the state retreated from his position, and Negroes entered the school unmolested.

In 1964, deputy marshals were assigned to protect a federal judge in Montgomery, Alabama, whose life had been threatened. They maintained order during hearings conducted by the Subversive Activities Control Board in Portland, Oregon, by the House Committee on Un-American Activities in Chicago, and by the United States Commission on Civil Rights in Jackson, Mississippi. Marshals also guard witnesses and their families in trials of members of crime syndicates, and witnesses who testify before grand juries; in 1964, they maintained order and security control in a trial of fourteen defendants in a narcotics case in New York.

The chapters that follow, describing the work of the separate divisions, tell more of the civil rights and other Department activities in which the U.S. attorneys and marshals serve.

IV

The Civil Rights Division

The civil rights of all citizens of the United States are protected by the first ten amendments to the Constitution (the Bill of Rights), by the Thirteenth, Fourteenth, and Fifteenth amendments, and by various laws passed by Congress to enforce these amendments. The enforcement agency for constitutional and statutory rights is the Department of Justice, acting through its Civil Rights Division.

Newest of the Justice Department's legal divisions, Civil Rights is one of the most active, owing to the accelerated drive by and for Negroes, launched full scale in the decade of the 1950's, to attain full equality of citizenship under the Constitution and the laws and to abolish all forms of racially motivated discrimination.

The Civil Rights Division was established on December 9, 1957, in an executive order issued by Attorney General William P. Rogers under authority vested in him by the Civil Rights Act of 1957. Functions assigned to the assistant attorney general in charge of the new Division included:

Enforcement of all federal statutes affecting civil rights, and authorization of such enforcement, including criminal prosecutions and civil actions and proceedings on behalf of the government; and appellate proceedings in all such cases;

Requesting, directing, and reviewing of investigations arising from reports or complaints of public officials or private citizens with respect to matters affecting civil rights;

Coordination within the Department of Justice of all matters affecting civil rights;

Consultation with and assistance to other federal departments and agencies and state and local agencies on matters affecting civil rights;

Research on civil rights matters, and the making of recommendations to the Attorney General as to proposed policies and legislation therefor.

The Attorney General's order also transferred to the new Division all functions, records, property, positions, and funds of the Civil Rights Section of the Criminal Division, which hitherto had administered the civil rights statutes.

The Division thus began with a comprehensive charter of responsibilities in the enforcement and policy-making fields. It took over from the Criminal Division a backlog of 143 cases, and a small staff of attorneys. Its rapid growth is evidenced by the information in the Attorney General's 1965 report, eight years after the Division was created, that it employed eighty-six lawyers and received in that year more than 3,000 matters (matters being the term used to refer to all items of business, including—but not limited to—cases taken to court).

The Division was first organized along functional lines. The Voting and Elections Section handled registration and voting matters as well as election frauds and Hatch Act violations arising under the criminal statutes. Criminal matters involving deprivation of civil rights, such as denials of due process and equal protection of the laws, were assigned to the General Litigation Section; litigation was conducted by the Trial Staff, and the Appeals and Research Section handled appellate and Supreme Court cases and research matters. The Administrative Section served the operating units.

In the summer of 1964, because of new duties imposed by the Civil Rights Act of 1964, the Division was reorganized into geographical units. Four new sections were created—the Eastern, Western, Southeastern, and Southwestern—to handle the broad spectrum of civil rights enforcement, each in its own geographical area. Jurisdiction in election frauds and Hatch Act matters was transferred back to the Criminal Division. (See Chapter XI.) The Voting and Elections Section, the General Litigation Section, and the Trial Staff were abolished; the Appeals and Research and Administrative sections were retained.

Because of the concentration of civil rights problems in the South, the Southeastern and Southwestern sections embrace fewer states than the other two. South Carolina, Georgia, Florida, and Alabama are in the Southeastern Section; Mississippi and Louisiana in the Southwestern. Field offices are maintained in Jackson, Mississippi, and in Selma, Alabama. The Eastern Section includes all other states east of the Mississippi River except Indiana, Illinois, and Wisconsin, which are grouped with states west of the Mississippi in the Western Section.

The assistant attorney general in charge is aided by a first assistant, a second assistant, and an executive assistant.

THE RIGHTS OF ALL CITIZENS

The Constitution, as amended, guarantees the rights of all citizens, regardless of race, creed, or color. The Mexican citizen in Arizona, the Japanese citizen in California, or the Indian in Alaska has the same right to equal protection of the laws as the Negro in Alabama or the Puerto Rican in New York. The right to vote has been a constitutional privilege for citizens since the federal government was founded.

However, the guarantees of equal protection and due process became part of the Constitution before racial problems plagued law enforcement officers. The principal laws that the Civil Rights Division is responsible for enforcing now are of recent origin and were aimed basically at the protection of the rights of Negroes.

After the Civil War, Congress passed several laws designed to enable newly enfranchised Negroes to exercise their functions and responsibilities as citizens. Some of these laws, especially the Enforcement Act of 1870 designed to cope with problems of the Reconstruction Era, remain on the statute books. It may be remembered that the first ten amendments to the Constitution were adopted before Negroes were considered to have any civil rights; they were slaves, not citizens. The Bill of Rights that had become part of the Constitution on December 15, 1791, protected freedom of religion, speech, the press, and the right to peaceable assembly; the right to keep and bear arms; the right to a public trial by an impartial jury; against unreasonable search and seizure; and other privileges of *citizens* and *free men.* The Fifth Amendment contained a clause that no persons shall "be deprived of life, liberty, or property without due process of law;"—a broad interdiction to protect the person and property of individuals, which was also applied specifically, in the Fourteenth Amendment, to state laws or actions that would "abridge the privileges or immunities of citizens."

The Thirteenth Amendment abolished slavery. The Fourteenth made citizens of "all persons born or naturalized in the United States," and the Fifteenth protected the right to vote of all citizens regardless of "race, color, or previous condition of servitude." Each of those amendments, adopted in the years immediately after the Civil War, took effect before the Department of Justice replaced the Office of Attorney General. In his book *Federal Justice,* former Attorney General Homer Cummings wrote that the establishment of guarantees to protect the newly acquired civil and political rights of Negroes was to be "the most difficult, the most dramatic and the most sordid task to be performed by the new Department of Justice."

A month before the new Justice Department came into existence, the Enforcement Act of May 31, 1870, became effective. Its purpose was to prevent or punish the disenfranchisement of Negroes by force or intimidation. Amos T. Akerman, the first head of the new Department, had the responsibility of enforcing it. The Senate gave him $50,000 to cover expenses of investigations to acquire evidence of violations. On April 20, 1871, Congress passed the second of the so-called Ku Klux Klan acts; it created civil and criminal liability for violence against individuals and authorized the President to employ the Army and the Navy to suppress violence.

KU KLUX KLAN, THE NUMBER ONE ENEMY

Armed with these weapons, the Justice Department spent the earliest years of its existence in warfare with the forces in the Southern states that refused to accord Negroes those rights bestowed upon them by the Constitution and the laws. United States attorneys, marshals, and federal troops were the forces the Attorney General led into battle. The so-called carpetbaggers from the North, who held civil offices in the Southern states, were deeply resented by the Southerners, and their presence and actions complicated the Justice Department's problems. Depredations against the Negroes and the carpetbaggers made the Klan the Number One enemy.

Federal troops were used freely in Alabama, and, at one time, more than 100 Klansmen were arrested. Large numbers were indicted in Mississippi for outrages attributed to the Klan, and the governor notified President Grant that violence prevailed beyond the power of the state authorities to suppress. Grant consulted with Edwards Pierrepont, then Attorney General, and made troops available, but, because both Republicans and Democrats opposed an invasion by Northern soldiers, the troops were withheld.

There were serious disorders, too, in South Carolina. Habeas corpus was suspended, and troops were sent in. In the November, 1871, term of court, 420 persons were indicted, and at one time there were more than 1,000 indictments pending. Attorney General George H. Williams, who went to South Carolina to make a personal survey of the situation, recognized that it would be impossible to try all the cases and that it would cost the federal government at the rate of $300,-000 a year to prosecute all the offenders. He therefore suspended prosecutions in all but the most flagrant cases.

Louisiana provided two outstanding instances of violence.

On election day, 1870, in Baton Rouge, an armed mob attacked the commissioners of election as they were counting the votes. The Republican candidate for the legislature and others were killed. The marshal arrested sixty-four persons, but few were tried and none convicted.

In 1873, at the small town of Colfax, in Grant Parish on the huge estate of William Calhoun, a Republican friendly to the colored people, many of whom had been his father's slaves, a dispute arose over local officials. Opposing factions claimed the offices of sheriff and judge. Governor William Pitt Kellogg commissioned a man named Shaw as sheriff. Shaw organized a posse of Negroes and seized Calhoun's brick warehouse, which served as the courthouse of the parish. The Negroes were beseiged, burned out of the courthouse, and shot down. The Justice Department sent J. J. Hoffman, an investigator, to obtain evidence, and, on the basis of his report, ninety-six persons were indicted under the Enforcement Act of 1870. There were difficulties in making arrests in a land of bayous, lakes, and rivers, but, finally, nine men were brought to trial. After deliberating three days, the jury acquitted one defendant, but could not agree on the other eight. A new trial was ordered for May 18, 1874.

At this second trial, Justice Joseph P. Bradley, of the U.S.

Supreme Court, sat with District Judge W. B. Woods. The defendants were acquitted on the murder counts of the indictments, but convicted on the conspiracy counts. On a motion for arrest of judgment, Justice Bradley wrote an opinion holding that the indictments were poorly drawn because they did not state that the offenses were committed because of race, color, or previous condition of servitude. Neither the Fourteenth Amendment nor the Enforcement Act, Justice Bradley said, were to be interpreted so broadly as to include the general protection of persons or property. The Justice Department then appealed to the Supreme Court, where Bradley was one of the justices to hear the case. Pending a Supreme Court decision, the defendants were released on bail. The Supreme Court, in *United States* v. *Cruikshank*, upheld Justice Bradley's position that the indictments were faulty in not alleging racial discrimination and reversed the convictions. The Court found an additional fault in that the indictments did not allege state action to deprive Negroes of lives or property without due process of law.

From the beginning, the Justice Department's efforts to protect Negro rights in the South encountered frustrating resistance. Witnesses were hard to find, juries were reluctant to convict, and citizens resented the use of federal troops and carpetbagger marshals to arrest civilians or otherwise protect Negroes.

Finally, in 1877, President Rutherford B. Hayes withdrew all troops from the South, and Congress, in an appropriation act of June 18, 1878, forbade the use of any part of the U.S. Army as a marshal's *posse comitatus*—in effect, ending federal protection of Negro rights in the South during the post-Civil War years. The constitutional amendments and the civil rights statutes remained, but there was little effort on the part of the Justice Department to enforce them.

LANDMARK CASES, 1875–1954

Despite the setbacks of the Reconstruction Era, cases involving civil rights continued to come to the Supreme Court. and the Justice Department participated in them. In 1875, several cases arising under the civil rights amendments were decided, among them one in which the Court held that the Fifteenth Amendment did not confer the right of suffrage but protected those citizens entitled to exercise the elective franchise from discrimination. In another case, the Court ruled that Congress had not provided appropriate legislation for the punishment of an inspector of a municipality for refusing to receive or count the vote of a citizen of African descent.

Civil rights cases came to the Court in 1883 from Kansas, California, Missouri, New York, and Tennessee, basically involving the question of full and equal enjoyment of accommodations in theatres, public conveyances, restaurants, hotels, and the like. In these cases, the Court ruled that the applicable sections of the Civil Rights Act of 1875 were unconstitutional enactments as applied to the several states, not being authorized by either the Thirteenth or Fourteenth amendments.

Negroes were systematically excluded from juries in many states, and they considered such exclusion to be racial discrimination prohibited by the Constitution. They won an early victory in 1879 when the Supreme Court, in *Strauder* v. *West Virginia,* decided that a West Virginia statute making Negroes ineligible for jury duty was discrimination forbidden by the Fourteenth Amendment. This landmark case is still cited as grounds for reversing convictions of Negroes by juries from which members of their race are excluded.

The most famous case of the era was *Plessy* v. *Ferguson,* decided in 1897. That decision established the "separate but equal" doctrine under which racial segregation was maintained in the South and in border states for nearly sixty years. The case involved only racial discrimination in public transportation—by a railroad, to be exact,—but when the Court held that if a railroad provided accommodations for Negroes equal to those supplied white passengers it was not guilty of constitutionally prohibited discrimination, segregationists applied the doctrine to public schools, restaurants, hotels, street cars, buses, golf courses, parks, swimming pools, and bathing beaches—indeed, to every phase of community activity in which intermingling of the races could be prevented. A "way of life" developed in the belief that it was sanctioned by the Constitution and the courts.

Thus, *Plessy* v. *Ferguson* set the stage for the shocked and angry reaction that ensued when, on May 17, 1954, the Supreme Court scrapped the "separate but equal" formula as applied to public schools.

Cases challenging state school segregation laws came to the Court from Kansas, Virginia, South Carolina, Delaware, and the District of Columbia. For decision purposes, they were combined under the title of *Brown* v. *Board of Education*, the name of the Topeka, Kansas, case. The decision the Court reached, after twice hearing arguments, was that, regardless of quality or equality of facilities, Negro children were denied equal protection of the laws when they were barred from attending with white children schools maintained by states or their political subdivisions. The doctrine of "separate but equal," Chief Justice Earl Warren said for the unanimous Court, had no place in the field of public education.

Brown v. *Board of Education* was an outstanding Negro victory in a resurgent movement to attain full equality of citizenship. It placed upon the Justice Department the responsibility for enforcing integration orders issued by federal courts and led to the establishment of the Civil Rights Division.

NEW STATUTORY WEAPONS

Congress enacted the Civil Rights acts of 1957, 1960, and 1964, and the Voting Rights Act of 1965 to provide the Justice Department with statutory weapons to wield in the continuing battle for the elimination of racial discrimination in all areas protected by the Constitution.

When the Civil Rights Division was established, its first cases were related to rights of citizens—but not specifically to Negroes. The Division's first brief prepared for the Supreme Court involved the question of whether a soldier serving a sentence after a dishonorable discharge was subject to court martial. The case of *Madsen* v. *Kinsella* raised the question of military jurisdiction over civilian dependents of military personnel—specifically, whether a wife who killed her soldier husband could be tried by a military court. Police brutality, later to become a virtually inevitable charge whenever Negro demonstrators clashed with officers of the law, was involved in cases from Texas, Alabama, and Illinois, respectively, wherein a police chief, a sheriff, and prison guards were accused of beating prisoners. It was not long, however, until the Division was deeply occupied with cases that stemmed from the 1954 school decision.

TROUBLE AT LITTLE ROCK AND ELSEWHERE

In compliance with *Brown* v. *Board of Education,* the Little Rock, Arkansas, school board prepared a plan of integration of a city high school, and a federal court ordered the admission of Negroes in accordance with the school board's plan. In September, 1957, Governor Orval Faubus, on the pretext that they were needed to prevent public disorder, assigned state officers to guard the school and prevent the Negroes from entering. This was state defiance of a federal court order the Justice Department was obligated to enforce.

The U.S. Government reinforced a detachment of U.S. marshals with federal troops to insure safe conduct of the Negroes into the school, and the Justice Department locked horns with Governor Faubus' attorneys in a legal test of federal versus state power.

The Civil Rights Division was successful in three moves. First, it obtained an injunction prohibiting the governor and other officials from interfering with the federal district court's order; second, it procured dismissal of a suit brought to enjoin interference of federal troops with the state's efforts to apply its own laws to the conduct of its public schools; and, third, by obtaining a federal injunction, it thwarted a segregationist attempt to prevent the opening of partially integrated schools in Little Rock. The first skirmish in the desegregation battle had been won by the Justice Department.

Prelude though it was to other legal triumphs, total victory is yet to be attained.

Verbal defiance of court orders to admit Negroes to schools in Alabama brought Governor George C. Wallace publicity in 1962 and 1963, but again victory went to the Justice Department. When the governor proclaimed that he would "stand in the school-house door" and prevent Negroes from entering, the Civil Rights Division obtained an injunction restraining him from blocking the entrance of Negroes to the University of Alabama. The President federalized the Alabama National Guard, thus depriving the governor of use of his own militia, and used the state soldiers to see that the injunction was obeyed and that court orders to integrate schools in Birmingham, Huntsville, and Tuskegee were carried out. The governor did not stand in the doorway, and Negro students entered without molestation.

The Civil Rights Division was deeply involved in the events of late September, 1962, surrounding the admission of James Meredith, a Negro, to the University of Mississippi.

United States marshals were assigned to assist in preserving order, and to protect Meredith. Federal officers were attacked and fought back in riots that attended Meredith's enrollment; some were injured. Marshals served as bodyguards for Meredith, escorting him to classes, to the dining room where he ate, and to the dormitory where he lived. Criminal and civil contempt proceedings were brought in federal court against Governor Ross Barnett and Lieutenant Governor Paul B. Johnson, Jr., alleging failure to comply with court orders, but the cases were dismissed in 1965 after Governor Barnett's term of office ended and Meredith had completed his courses at the University.

Meredith was to be a spotlight figure in another violent episode. He joined a "freedom march" of Negroes and white civil rights workers in Mississippi and was shot from ambush as he trudged along a highway. He was not seriously wounded. His assailant was apprehended, pleaded guilty, and received a five-year prison sentence.

SCHOOL DESEGREGATION SUITS

School desegregation suits initially were brought by individuals—in most cases, the parents or guardians of minor children. The role of the Justice Department was to appear in support of them as *amicus curiae*. The 1964 Civil Rights Act, however, gave the Department authority to take a direct part in school cases, and, in 1965, the Civil Rights Division participated in seven original school suits in response to parent's complaints and in eighteen interventions in cases already filed by private litigants. All of the original suits were against school officials in Tennessee, Alabama, Mississippi, Louisiana, Arkansas, and South Carolina. In a 1966 report, Attorney General Nicholas deB. Katzenbach said that "the principal purpose of the Department's school actions has been to assure that school districts desegregate at least as fast as required by the Office of Education, whether or not they were accepting federal financial assistance and whether or not earlier court orders approved slower progress."

Katzenbach's reference to requirements of the Office of Education was to guidelines issued early in 1965 by the Department of Health, Education, and Welfare requiring that public school systems desegregate at least four grades in the fall of 1965 and be completely desegregated by the fall of 1967 in order to qualify for federal financial assistance. The 1964 Civil Rights Act required the cutoff of federal funds from discriminatory systems.

In implementing its 1954 school decision, the Supreme Court said that lower courts should proceed with "all deliberate speed" to bring about total integration, but left it to the courts to determine, in the light of prevailing conditions, what constituted "deliberate speed." The Office of Education was the first nonjudicial agency to set time limits. In ordering desegregation of at least four grades in Jackson, Mississippi, a federal court of appeals proclaimed its determination to keep pace with Office of Education schedules. "The time has come," the court stated, "for foot-dragging public school boards to move with celerity toward desegregation."

Only if all school districts received federal financial assistance, and desegregated rather than lose it, could total integration have been achieved by 1967. Recognizing that thirteen years after *Brown* v. *Board of Education,* integration is only token in many places, the Department of Justice is devoting strong efforts to induce "foot-dragging" boards to substitute "celerity" for "deliberate speed."

THAT NEGROES SHALL VOTE

Since its inception, a major activity of the Civil Rights Division has been protection of the constitutional right of citizens to vote. The Civil Rights Act of 1957 authorized the

Attorney General to seek injunctions against public and private interference with the right to vote. Perfecting amendments in the Civil Rights Act of 1960 permitted the joinder of states as party defendants, gave the Attorney General access to local voting records, and authorized courts to register voters in areas of systematic discrimination. The Civil Rights Act of 1964 outlawed some of the tactics, such as discriminatory literacy tests, used to disqualify Negroes from trying to vote in federal elections. The Voting Rights Act of 1965 fashioned specific remedies, applicable to particular localities where discrimination is most flagrant—a key provision authorizing the Attorney General to assign federal poll watchers to assure that lawfully registered Negroes are allowed to vote and that their votes are counted.

The constitutionality of those laws was challenged in the Supreme Court, when South Carolina and other states asked an injunction against certain provisions of the Voting Rights Act on the ground that they exceeded the powers of Congress and encroached on an area reserved by the Constitution to the states. On March 7, 1966, in an opinion by Chief Justice Warren, the Court ruled that Congress had exercised its powers under the Fifteenth Amendment in an appropriate manner with relation to the states and that the Act was constitutional.

Assured of its constitutional position, the Justice Department began a drive to register Negroes in the principal Southern states. Federal examiners were sent to 42 counties and registered 111,500 new nonwhite voters in the first 9 months after the Voting Rights Act became effective. At the beginning of 1965, in the 11 states of the old Confederacy, only one-third of 5 million voting-age Negroes were registered; in Alabama, Georgia, Louisiana, Mississippi, and South Carolina, barely a quarter of the 2.5 million Negro eligibles were registered voters; in many rural counties in the South, less than 10 per cent of the eligibles were enrolled. By

May 1, 1966, Attorney General Katzenbach was able to report that in Alabama, Georgia, Louisiana, Mississippi, and South Carolina more than 1 million Negroes were registered, compared with 680,000 when the Voting Rights Act was signed by President Johnson on August 6, 1965.

Selma, Alabama, was a focus of activity for Justice Department representatives and civil rights groups seeking to add Negroes to the polling lists. Literacy tests were the device chiefly used to reject Negro applicants. Between January 18 and August 10, 1965, when the first federal examiners went to Selma, at least 100 Negroes appeared at the office of the Board of Registrars every registration day, but in a single month the Board rejected 24 with college degrees, 97 with at least a high school education, and 337 with records of at least 6 years' school attendance.

During this period, violence arising out of civil rights enforcement added to the Division's case load. The conviction, in Montgomery, Alabama, of Collie LeRoy Wilkins, Jr., William Orville Eaton, and Eugene Thomas for the murder of Mrs. Viola Liuzzo, a civil rights worker from the North, was the first in modern times under the 1870 statute outlawing conspiracies to deprive citizens of their civil rights. Two other murder cases tried under the same law were lost in state courts but won when taken to the Supreme Court.

One was the indictment in Jackson, Mississippi, of eighteen men, including the sheriff of Neshoba County, Lawrence A. Rainey, and his deputy, Cecil Ray Price, for conspiring to deprive three civil rights workers, Michael Schwerner, James E. Chaney, and Andrew Goodman, who were killed during the summer of 1964 near Philadelphia, Mississippi, of life and liberty without due process of law. A U.S. district judge dismissed the indictments on the grounds that general Fourteenth Amendment rights are not protected by the federal criminal code.

Indictments against six Klansmen accused of murdering

Lemuel Penn, a Washington, D.C., school official, as he drove through Georgia were dismissed by another district judge on the same grounds, namely, that violation of civil rights by private action did not come under the due process clause of the Fourteenth Amendment.

The Civil Rights Division appealed both cases. They involved the delicate issue of federal versus states rights, and Solicitor General Thurgood Marshall (who later became the first Negro appointed to the Supreme Court) argued that the federal criminal code did protect Fourteenth Amendment rights of due process whether violated by state or private action. The court found that both cases alleged some state involvement, thus providing grounds for federal action, and held that the indicments should not have been dismissed. It ordered the cases tried.

PEONAGE AND POLITICS

During its relatively brief existence, the Civil Rights Division has dealt with violations in many fields, sometimes successfully, sometimes not.

In January, 1959, a federal grand jury at Mobile, Alabama, indicted a foreman and an employee of a factory because they forced a man and his wife to return to work to discharge a debt owed the company. A charge of peonage was sustained against a Connecticut chicken raiser who held a Mexican family he had brought to this country in involuntary servitude by refusing to permit contact with outsiders and attendance at church, refusing to pay wages due, and threatening deportation.

Two National Guard officers were prosecuted, but acquitted, for soliciting political contributions from federal employees in a federal building. Democratic Party officials in York County, Pennsylvania, were indicted on vote-buying charges in the 1958 general election. Labor unions in St. Louis and in

Edmund Randolph of Virginia, the first U.S. Attorney General, 1789–94.

William Wirt was the Attorney General during the administrations of James Monroe and John Quincy Adams. His handwritten records became the nucleus of the Justice Department's vast collection of official documents.

Attorney General Roger B. Taney served under President Andrew Jackson and was one of ten men who held the office later to be appointed to the Supreme Court.

Associate Justice of the Supreme Court Tom C. Clark, a former Attorney General, swears in his son Ramsey as Attorney General. President Lyndon B. Johnson stands at the far left; Vice-President Hubert H. Humphrey is to the right of Ramsey Clark; and Solicitor General Thurgood Marshall, later appointed to the Supreme Court, looks on at the far right.

The first building occupied by the Department of Justice after its founding in 1870.

The present Justice Department Building, in Washington, D.C.

During the depression of the 1930's, the Federal Art Project commissioned many artists to decorate public buildings. As a result interesting and unusual murals appear in various parts of the Department of Justice Building. Two such paintings—depicting the signing of the Magna Charta (opposite, above) and of the American Constitution (opposite, below)—were done by Boardman Robinson. The mural (top) "Law Versus Mob Rule, by John Curry, is painted above the library entrance in the Justice Department Building; and (below) George Biddle has illustrated with scenes of his times the famous statement of Justice Oliver Wendell Holmes.

THE LIFE OF THE LAW HAS NOT BEEN LOGIC IT HAS BEEN EXPERIENCE

An FBI agent photographs a heel print at the scene of a crime.

FBI technicians prepare a scale model for use in court.

Serology laboratory of the FBI's physics and chemistry section.

Identifying a piece of cloth from a crime scene.

Minimum security prison at Seagoville, Texas.

September 26, 1962. Assistant Attorney General John Doar (center), James Meredith, and James J. P. McShane (right) confront Governor Ross Barnett of Mississippi on the University of Mississippi campus after racial disturbances over Meredith's enrollment.

Anchorage, Alaska, were indicted under laws that prohibit political contributions and expenditures by corporations and labor organizations. Under a provision of the U.S. Code, that makes it a crime to distribute campaign literature without disclosing those responsible for its publication, two men were indicted in Arizona for distributing a leaflet during the 1962 campaign bearing a cartoon of Joseph Stalin with the caption "Why Not Vote for Goldwater?"

In West Virginia, a constable went to the home of a Republican election official shortly before the polls opened in the general election of 1962 and arrested him on a fictitious charge of rape, preferred in a warrant signed by the wife of the constable, who was a justice of the peace. The couple was charged with conspiring to deprive an election official of his freedom to officiate at the polls in an election in which the constable was a candidate. Prison sentences were imposed upon both man and wife.

Prosecution of fourteen custodians of the Florida State Prison at Raiford on charges of systematic mistreatment of prisoners failed when the court granted motions of acquittal at the close of the government's case.

The Division was uniformly successful in actions to desegregate places of public accommodation and to eliminate all-white, discriminatorily selected state and federal juries. It was victor in suits to outlaw the poll tax as a requisite to voting in federal elections and in upholding the provision of the Voting Rights Act, which absolved citizens educated in "American Flag" schools in a language other than English from the obligation to pass a literacy test in English before qualifying to vote.

Despite the failure of the Johnson Administration to obtain passage of a new Civil Rights Act in 1966 (largely because of the opposition to the "open housing" clause forbidding discrimination in rental or sale of houses) the Civil Rights Division, at this writing, has a heavier-than-ever case load. Initiating actions, investigating complaints, maintaining close and necessarily complex relationships with the FBI and other divisions of the Department, the Civil Rights Commission, and citizens' groups, it is central to the continuing effort to effect what President Johnson, in 1965, reviewing the first year of accomplishments under the Civil Rights Act of 1964, called "the next step . . . to achieve compliance in spirit."

V

The Antitrust Division

The general objective of the antitrust laws is the promotion of competition in open markets. This policy is the primary feature of private enterprise. Most Americans have long recognized that opportunity for market access and the fostering of market rivalry are basic tenets of our faith in competition as a form of economic organization.

This opening paragraph of the introduction to the report of the Attorney General's National Committee to Study the Antitrust Laws, issued March 31, 1955, defines the underlying purposes of the laws enacted by Congress to encourage the growth of a competitive economy and protect it from monopolists. The Committee stated that those laws "have helped release energies essential to our leadership in industrial productivity and technological development." "Antitrust," it said, "is a distinctive American means for assuring the competitive economy on which our political and social freedom under representative government in part depend."

THE LAWS

The laws are the Sherman Act of 1890, the Clayton and the Federal Trade Commission acts, both passed in 1914, and several supplemental statutes. They are the laws administered principally by the Department of Justice but shared in specific areas with the Federal Trade Commission. The Sherman Act is a criminal statute, under which conspiracies to restrain or monopolize trade, price-fixing, and predatory practices such as boycotts may be prosecuted. Companion civil cases may be filed where, in addition to criminal penalties, injunctive relief is sought.

The Clayton Act is intended to stop, while incipient, undue concentration of economic power. It is, primarily, the anti-merger statute. As amended, it makes illegal the acquisition by one corporation of, the stock or assets of another company "in any line of commerce in any section of the country" if acquisition would substantially lessen competition or tend to create a monopoly.

The Federal Trade Commission was created as an auxiliary of antitrust enforcement that largely deals with unfair methods of competition, such as exclusive dealing arrangements that foreclose competitors from a substantial market.

A supplemental law, known as the Miller-Tydings Act, passed in 1937, exempted from the antitrust laws

> contracts or agreements prescribing minimum prices for resale of a commodity which bears, or the label or container of which bears, the trade-mark, brand, or name of a producer of such commodity and which is in free and open competition with commodities of the same general class produced or distributed by others, when contracts or agreements of that description are lawful.

Several states had laws permitting resale price-fixing on brand name products and the purpose of Miller-Tydings was to avoid conflict between federal statutes and state laws the Supreme Court had sustained as constitutional.

In order to prevent the use of standard brands as "loss leaders" to drive out competition, Congress enacted the Mc-Guire Amendment to the Federal Trade Commission Act, which made all distributors—signers as well as nonsigners of resale price maintenance agreements—exempt from antitrust prosecution.

Congress has shielded various business activities from the rigors of competition by authorizing regulatory bodies to approve certain private conduct, control market entry, eliminate existing competition, and fix rates or prices when a judgment is made that the public interest will be promoted.

The Transportation Act of 1920 encouraged railroad combinations and provided antitrust exemption for consolidations approved by the Interstate Commerce Commission. The Shipping Act of 1916 authorized the Maritime Board to approve agreements "fixing or regulating transportation rates or fares," which are not found to be "unjustly discriminatory or unfair" or to the detriment of the commerce of the United States. No specific exemption from the antitrust laws has been granted the petroleum industry, but Congress periodically renews approval of the Interstate Compact to Conserve Oil and Gas, which involves price-making on domestic and imported petroleum.

The Clayton Act declares that "the labor of a human being is not a commodity or article in commerce." That Act was passed after the famous Danbury Hatters case in which, in 1908, the Supreme Court held that a union-inspired boycott of nonunion-made hats restrained interstate commerce and violated the Sherman Act. The Clayton Act sheltered standard activities of labor unions by providing that unions might not be "held or construed to be illegal combinations or conspiracies in restraint of trade under the antitrust laws." Unions are vulnerable to antitrust, however, when they engage in fraud or violence and intend, or achieve, some commercial restraint; combine with a nonlabor group to bring about some direct commercial restraint; or engage in activities not involved in a labor dispute.

The Clayton Act, in Section 6, gave blanket exemption to agricultural cooperatives conducted for mutual help and not for profit. Under the Capper-Volstead Act, the Secretary of Agriculture is empowered to enter cease and desist orders against a cooperative if he finds it monopolizes or restrains commerce to the enhancement of the price of any agricultural commodity. The Attorney General institutes court proceedings to enforce those orders.

THE TASK OF ENFORCEMENT

Enforcement of the antitrust laws is the responsibility of the Attorney General and no antitrust suit may be brought without his authorization. In simpler times, the Attorney General gave much of his attention to antitrust matters. Several Attorneys General argued important cases in the Supreme Court, and almost all of them dealt personally with procedures and policies involved in the application of the antitrust statutes to the operations of corporate business. A special assistant to the Attorney General actively conducted the antitrust business of the Department, however, directing the preparation of cases, pretrial negotiations, trial strategy, and appellate procedures. Outside counsel was often engaged—sometimes men who were noted lawyers in private practice. Until the solicitor general took over appellate matters, the special assistant or outside counsel usually argued cases in the Supreme Court.

The task of enforcement is complicated by intricate corporate structures and skilfully managed intercorporate relationships. With the growth of corporate enterprise, served always by batteries of skilled lawyers, it became evident that the Justice Department must have its own corps of specialists in antitrust law to cope with an increasingly complex enforcement situation.

Consequently, the Antitrust Division was established in 1933. It is headed by an assistant attorney general, nominated like all Division heads, by the President upon recommendation of the Attorney General, and requiring Senate confirmation. It is customary for the head of the Division to resign when there is a change of Administration, but members of his staff continue in office, and many are career lawyers who retain their positions until retirement. Thus, a staff of experts, familiar with the laws and cognizant of the ways of corporate business, is permanently available.

The assistant attorney general has a first assistant, a director of Operations, a director of Policy Planning, and a special assistant as his personal aides. There are ten section chiefs, each in charge of a particular field. The sections are Administrative, Appellate, Economic Evaluation, Foreign Commerce, General Litigation, Judgments and Judgment Enforcements, Special Trial, Special Litigation, and Trial. Besides the headquarters organization, there are seven field offices in various parts of the country. The number of lawyers employed varies, but some 275 generally comprise the legal staff.

Possible violations of the antitrust laws are called to the attention of the Division in various ways. A competing manufacturer, a merchant, a banker, an exporter or importer, a railroad, a steamship line, a labor union—anyone who feels that he is being menaced by a monopoly or illegally deprived of his right to trade in a competitive market may call the situation to the Division's attention. And hundreds of them do, each year. Newspaper accounts of proposed mergers may provide leads on situations that require looking into. Other agencies of the government may become aware of collusive actions, such as identical bidding, and report their information to the Justice Department.

Not all complaints require investigation, but those that indicate a substantial or willful violation of the laws are investigated. In the early days, the investigative facilities of the Department were inadequate. When President William McKinley appointed Philander C. Knox as Attorney General, Knox recommended establishment of a commission to

gather facts to supplement the Department's inquiries. Mc-
Kinley supported the idea, and a Bureau of Corporations was
created—not in the Justice Department but in the new Department of Commerce and Labor. Relations between the
Department and the Bureau, which soon manifested its intention to proceed independently, became strained during
the Theodore Roosevelt Administration and continued so
for years afterward. The Bureau of Corporations subsequently disappeared, and investigations in the antitrust field
eventually came under the direction of the Antitrust Division
and associated units of the Justice Department. Today, most
of the investigating is done by lawyers in the field offices or
on the staffs of U.S. attorneys, working under headquarters
supervision, and the services of the FBI may be called upon,
or those of the Federal Trade Commission.

Evidence produced by the investigations is sifted and analyzed by the Division's experts. If a violation that would
invoke criminal penalties is disclosed, the customary procedure is to present the evidence to a grand jury and ask an
indictment. If criminal charges are not involved, a civil suit is
instituted. Before any action is taken, however, the Attorney
General reviews the case and decides whether prosecution
should be undertaken. Attorneys General do not relish defeat, nor do they believe in squandering time, effort, and
money on inherently weak cases. The government doesn't
win all its antitrust cases but, when possible, it avoids suits it
patently might lose.

In a year, the Division may conduct as many as 250 new
investigations and close as many as 200. There are usually
between 400 and 500 investigations pending.

Because the actions of other government bodies may affect
free competition, the Antitrust Division is required to participate in some regulatory proceedings before the Interstate
Commerce Commission, the Federal Communications Commission, the Civil Aeronautics Board, the Federal Maritime

Board, and other agencies. Orders issued by these bodies are sometimes challenged in the courts, and it becomes the Justice Department's obligation to represent the government in enforcement proceedings.

Another duty imposed upon the Division by statute is making surveys and preparing periodic reports for the President and Congress on possible anticompetitive factors involved in operations under the Defense Production Act, the Small Business Act, and the Interstate Compact to Conserve Oil and Gas. Annual reports on competition in the synthetic rubber industry are also prepared by the Division.

The Department has no authority to give advisory opinions but, under the so-called railroad release, it may bind itself not to prosecute criminally under certain conditions. Section 7 of the Clayton Act provides procedures under which the Department of Justice and the Federal Trade Commission may assure corporations that they will not oppose contemplated mergers. However, the Department may sue to void a merger that has been approved by another government agency if it believes that the antitrust laws have been violated.

EARLY CONCERN OVER MONOPOLY

The spectre of monopoly haunted the country throughout the closing decades of the nineteenth century as vast wealth accumulated in the hands of corporations and individuals who used their power to create an economic and political climate conducive to their private growth. The demand for a federal law to curb their power was first heard in the Presidential campaign of 1884 that carried Grover Cleveland into the White House. Seven states had already passed antitrust laws, but it became evident that state legislation alone was not adequate to deal with a situation involving restraints on interstate commerce. Congress exercised its constitutional power to regulate commerce by passing the Interstate Commerce Act of 1887 and, as agitation for federal action in the antitrust field continued, moved closer to the view expressed a century before by Edmund Randolph, the first Attorney General, that in the field of commerce the central government must hold the reins. Finally, the Sherman Act was passed and signed by President Benjamin Harrison on July 2, 1890.

Even before the antitrust laws were enacted, a target of antimonopolists was the industry that developed out of the invention of the magnetic telegraph, by Samuel F. B. Morse in 1837, and the telephone, by Alexander Graham Bell in 1876. The outcome, in this case, was not the breaking up of a monopoly but the sanctioning of the formation, under federal regulation, of a monolithic public service corporation, which today is one of the most profitable giants of American industry.

In those days, there were no laws to regulate competition and the only way the federal government could attack the developing telephone trust was through its control of patents. Telephone patents were awarded Bell on March 7, 1876, and January 30, 1877, and the manufacture and leasing of telephones quickly became a profitable business. The National Bell Telephone Company, later reorganized as the American Bell Telephone Company, was formed. Other inventions were acquired by the Western Union Telegraph Company, already operating profitably on patents granted Morse, in 1844, and Western Union challenged the validity of the original Bell patents. However, the litigation was settled out of court, and the telegraph company made a deal that left Bell dominant in the burgeoning industry. As Bell's business grew, and the value of its stock went up, the obvious attraction of large profits lured others, and new companies were formed to exploit additional inventions, some claiming priority to Bell.

One of these new competitors was the Pan-Electric Telephone Company, formed in 1883. It gave stock to several prominent members of the Senate and House of Representatives, among them Senator Augustus H. Garland, of Arkansas, who held one-tenth of the stock and was attorney for the company. Garland became Attorney General in the first-term Cabinet of President Grover Cleveland. Several other shareholders in Pan-Electric held posts in Cleveland's Administration, and they urged Garland to sue to annul the Bell patents as obtained by fraud, cn the ground that Philip Reis of Germany had invented the telephone before Bell, and Bell knew of the invention. The president of another competitor, the National Improved Telephone Company, also charged that Bell was not the inventor of the telephone and petitioned the government to bring suit.

The question was whether the government had statutory power to sue to annul a basic patent. At the urging of the National Improved Telephone Company stockholders, U.S. Attorney H. W. McCorry, of Jackson, Tennessee, assembled evidence and forwarded it to Attorney General Garland with a recommendation that suit be brought in the name of the United States. Garland was on vacation, but Solicitor General John Goode authorized McCorry to sue. When Garland heard about it three weeks later, he immediately issued a statement that he had not granted permission to file the suit.

Threatened with a scandal because of Garland's connection with Pan-Electric, President Cleveland asked Garland for an explanation, and the Attorney General offered to resign if his Cabinet associates thought he had embarrassed the Administration. He was not asked to resign, but Cleveland reprimanded Goode, stating that proper procedure required that patent matters be referred first to the Secretary of the Interior and suggesting that the suit be dismissed. Goode defended his action, but directed dismissal and sent the evidence to the Secretary of the Interior, who, after hearings, decided that, although no statute authorized a government suit to annul a patent, such power existed and the evidence against Bell was sufficient to justify action. The Justice Department made preparations to sue. Garland was disqualified because of his interest in Pan-Electric, and Goode handled the case for the government.

Five years were spent by the government and by Bell in accumulating evidence. Benjamin Harrison succeeded Cleveland, and the second Cleveland Administration came in with Richard Olney as Attorney General. By then, the Sherman Act had been passed. The country was undergoing an economic recession, and public hostility to large corporations was building steadily. Bills were introduced in Congress to investigate the telephone monopoly. Procedural delays multiplied, and legal issues remained unsettled. Meantime, the original Bell patents expired. The case remained on the docket for another ten years and was dismissed at last on January 1, 1906, thirty years after the first suit was instituted.

The Bell interests continued to face, and beat, competition for some years. By 1913, an estimated 20,000 independent companies, by connecting their lines, were providing long distance service; Bell hampered that service by buying up links in the independent chain and cutting off connections. Looking to a merger of all exchanges and lines into one operating company under single ownership, Bell's policy was to amalgamate companies as fast as it could acquire them, and the Justice Department was deluged with petitions to take action against the growing trust. In 1921, Congress authorized merger of telephone properties, if approved by the Interstate Commerce Commission. Thirteen years later, the ICC was superseded in the field of telephone, telegraph, radio, and television by the Federal Communications Commission. Unperturbed by a few competing independent lines, the American Telephone & Telegraph Company continued to dominate the field and became the nearest thing to an absolute monopoly in U.S. corporate business.

FIRST ANTITRUST SUITS

The first Sherman Act case was instigated by District Attorney John Ruhm, in Tennessee. He presented to Attorney General William H. H. Miller evidence of a price-fixing conspiracy in coal and was authorized to file suit against the Jellicoe Mountain Coke & Coal Company. This suit produced the first ruling on the constitutionality of the Sherman Act. In granting a permanent injunction against the Jellicoe Mountain Company, the court ruled that the law was constitutional and the United States had power to sue under it on behalf of the public interest.

Since Miller, every Attorney General but one has instituted some action under the antitrust laws. The exception was Richard Olney, who held office in the second Cleveland administration. Olney, who was described as "stern and dogmatic" and a victim of "lockjaw of the will," regarded the Sherman Act as "an experimental piece of legislation" and advocated its repeal.

One of the most important antitrust cases brought by the government in earlier years was lost during Olney's incumbency. A circuit court ruled that a combination in the manufacture of sugar was not a combination in interstate trade. Olney chose that case to test the applicability of the Sherman Act in the Supreme Court. The government's argument was that the local manufacture of sugar and its interstate distribution to consumers was an integrated operation within the purview of the antitrust law. With only one dissent, the Supreme Court distinguished between the manufacturing process and the distribution in interstate commerce that followed it—and held that the Sherman Act did not apply. Rather gloatingly,

Olney told an associate that "the government has been defeated in the Supreme Court on the trust issue" and that "I always suspected it would be."

Historically, Attorneys General have enforced the antitrust laws in accordance with their concept of their official obligations and the policies of the Administration in which they served. Thus, there have been periods of vigorous prosecution and intervals of comparative inactivity. Some Attorneys General and their assistants have considered numbers to be an indication of zeal and efficiency and "sued everybody in sight," while others have considered it to be in the public interest to invoke the antitrust laws more sparingly. The record shows, however, that since the enactment of the first federal antitrust law the government has moved against offenders ranging from the most powerful industrial interests in the country to lobstermen who conspired to fix prices on crustaceans shipped in interstate commerce.

Addyston Pipe and Steel Co. v. *United States* was the only antitrust action instituted by John W. Griggs, who was appointed Attorney General by President McKinley in 1898. The Supreme Court's decision in that case blunted the point of its ruling in the sugar case. Price-fixing was the issue, and the Court held that, when the direct and immediate effect of a contract or combination among dealers in a commodity was enhancement of its price, such action by the dealers amounted to a restraint of trade forbidden by the Sherman Act. Thus, in a case involving a combination of companies manufacturing and selling pipe, decided five years after the sugar ruling, the Court joined manufacture and selling, or distribution, in circumstances wherein a commodity, although manufactured locally, moved in interstate commerce. The Addyston ruling adopted a concept postulated by Griggs in an opinion he gave President McKinley that, under the commerce clause, the power of the United States to regulate commerce in general was without limit, either as to time, place, or details of exercise, except as to navigable waters lying wholly within the boundaries of a state. Griggs said the power included the right to regulate all means and instrumentalities used in commerce, was not restricted to purchase, sale, or barter, and included navigation and transportation.

MORE "TRUST-BUSTING"

The era of "trust-busting" began in the McKinley Administration, but reached its peak when Theodore Roosevelt occupied the White House. Philander C. Knox, a corporation lawyer who served in both the McKinley and Roosevelt cabinets, was the first of a quartet of Attorneys General who enforced the laws with vigor and success in the years between 1900 and the World War I. The others were William H. Moody, Charles Joseph Bonaparte, and George W. Wickersham, the latter an appointee of President Taft.

The outstanding case begun by Knox, against the Northern Securities Company, a holding company, sought to prevent a merger of the Great Northern, the Northern Pacific, and the Chicago, Burlington and Quincy railroads. Knox argued the case in the circuit court and won, and when an appeal was taken to the Supreme Court he faced alone an imposing array of corporation counsel, including his predecessor, Griggs. Knox argued that the Securities Company's arrangement provided for unified control and would establish a monopoly in restraint of trade although no actual restraint had taken place. Knox won a five-to-four decision. A noteworthy dissent by Justice Oliver Wendell Holmes contended that the antitrust act said nothing about combinations in restraint of competition but only combinations in restraint of trade; to Holmes, competition and trade were not synonymous. President Roosevelt hailed the victory in the Northern Securities case as "one of the great achievements of my Administration."

In 1904, Knox began a suit against the Chicago meat packers, Swift & Company, Armour & Company, and the Cudahy
Packing Company, alleging an illegal agreement to regulate
prices, restrict shipments, establish uniform rules of credit,
make uniform and improper rules of cartage, and get less
than lawful rates from railroads to the exclusion of competitors, with the intent to monopolize interstate commerce in
fresh meats. The Bureau of Corporations had conducted an
investigation; when the Attorney General asked the Bureau
for its information, he was astounded to be told that the
information was confidential, to be used for administrative
purposes, not for prosecutions. Nonetheless, the Justice Department obtained indictments in 1905, but when the case
came to trial the packers claimed immunity because they had
been required to testify before the Bureau, which had exoner-
ated them. To the disgust of Theodore Roosevelt, who was
then President, and Attorney General Moody, who argued
the case in the Supreme Court, the Court accepted the packers' plea. A civil action in 1920, however, produced the historic "Packers' Consent Decree," a ruling that broke up the
so-called Beef Trust. More than forty years later, in 1961, the
packers asked a federal district court to modify the decree,
asserting that under changed economic conditions they would
have no power to monopolize. The court denied the petition.

During his tenure, Moody instituted prosecutions against
alleged combinations in restraint of trade in paper, fertilizer,
salt, tobacco, oil, lumber, and other businesses. Roosevelt
hailed him as the strong man of his Cabinet. Several of the
cases Moody filed did not reach the Supreme Court until
after his term, among them the Standard Oil and American
Tobacco Company cases. Bonaparte, who filed twenty suits
under the antitrust laws, conducted the proceedings that
brought about dissolution of the tobacco trust, although the
decree was issued after Wickersham became Attorney General.

Standard Oil Co. of New Jersey et al v. *United States* was the outstanding case of the era. In that case, the Supreme Court interpreted the general phrases of the Sherman Act to establish an essential standard of "reasonableness"; in other words, the evidence in the case had to establish a reasonable basis for concluding that the formation and operation of a trust would result in illegal monopoly or undue restraint of trade. This became known as the "rule of reason" and still prevails as a guiding principle in antitrust decisions.

The Supreme Court reviewed Standard Oil's history since 1870 and found that after 1899, at least, the company had monopoly power over refined petroleum, its transportation by pipeline, and sale of refined products, inevitably resulting in control of the crude oil market. Standard had achieved this position through partnerships, mergers, and other combinations with competing and complementary interests and had utilized unfair practices, such as local price-cutting, espionage, and procuring preferential rates and rebates.

Applying the "rule of reason" to these circumstances, the Court ordered Standard to transfer its stock in thirty-seven subsidiaries to its stockholders and enjoined both subsidiaries and shareholders from combining with each other or with Standard to bring about further Sherman Act violations.

Moody began another action against a Standard Oil Company, but not under the antitrust laws. He filed suit under the Elkins Act, which forbade rebates by railroads to shippers. That case was tried before Judge Kenesaw Mountain Landis in U.S. district court, and Judge Landis imposed the famous $29 million fine upon Standard Oil of Indiana. Landis was reversed by the circuit court of appeals, and Roosevelt wrote Bonaparte, "I feel pretty ugly over that decision." He said that the ruling amounted to "saying that the biggest criminals in this country should be shielded and the law of Congress nullified."

American Tobacco was found by the Supreme Court to have almost an unchallenged monopoly of the market for leaf tobacco as well as most branches of the trade in tobacco products. This position had been achieved by purchase of control from competitors, often after trade wars and at unusually high prices. The Court noted large expenditures for purchase of plants, soon scrapped, and a policy of requiring covenants not to compete from vendors, stockholders, and employees. To remedy the situation and re-create a "new condition which shall be honestly in harmony with and not repugnant to the law," the Court ordered American Tobacco split into fourteen corporations and provided that "no company will have substantially over 40 per cent in volume or value in any particular line." (Radio and television audiences of today are aware that the Court restored competition in cigarettes and other tobacco products.)

The most important suit filed after the oil and tobacco cases was against the U.S. Steel Corporation. In the Roosevelt Administration, Elbert H. Gary and Henry C. Frick had told the President that, although U.S. Steel did not want to acquire the Tennessee Coal & Iron Company, they were willing, in view of the current economic situation, to buy it in an effort to prevent an industrial crisis. Roosevelt regarded this as a public-spirited gesture and told them to go ahead. Taft's Administration, however, believed the motive was not altruism but monopoly and filed a suit, which was finally decided in 1920 when Woodrow Wilson was President and A. Mitchell Palmer was Attorney General. The significance of the Supreme Court's ruling in that case was its postulate that mere size of a corporation was not proof of illegal monopoly; actual restraint of trade, not merely the capacity to restrain, must be demonstrated.

(Years later, the Justice Department blocked a proposed merger of two major steel companies. In 1959, Judge Edward Weinfeld, in the Southern District of New York, ruled that a union of Bethlehem Steel Corporation and the Youngstown Sheet and Tube Company would violate Section 7—the anti-merger section—of the Clayton Act.)

Although he was Attorney General for only eighteen months prior to his appointment as an associate justice of the Supreme Court, the tenure of James Clark McReynolds was marked by dissolution of the United States Thread Association, an injunction restraining the National Wholesale Jewelers Association from a conspiracy in restraint of trade, and a decree requiring the New Haven Railroad to relinquish a monopoly of transportation in New England.

During World War I, Attorney General Thomas W. Gregory believed that food dealers were "capitalizing upon the misfortune and oppression of our own people by the arbitrary increases of the prices of foodstuffs" and instructed district attorneys to proceed against combinations in the food business wherever evidence warranted action. Twelve suits were filed, but President Woodrow Wilson, disregarding Gregory's advice, instructed the Attorney General to suspend actions pending in the Supreme Court against combinations in various products, such as shoe machinery, farm machinery, steel, and others. As a result of Wilson's policies of cooperating with business in the common cause of winning the war, there was comparatively little antitrust activity during the war years. Once the war ended, however, and during the decade of the 1920's, the Justice Department was active in enforcing the antitrust laws. Approximately 148 antitrust proceedings were authorized, involving oil, sugar, coal, motion pictures, radio, and other products and industries. An important decision was in *United States* v. *Trenton Potteries,* in which the Supreme Court held that an agreement of those controlling 80 per cent of the business of manufacturing and distributing sanitary pottery in the United States to fix and maintain prices violated the Sherman Act, whether the prices themselves were reasonable or unreasonable.

EMPHASIS ON REGULATION

The period of the Great Depression, which had begun before Franklin D. Roosevelt became President, was not an auspicious time for prosecutions of business, nor was the World War II period that followed. There were some antitrust prosecutions, but the emphasis throughout Roosevelt's three terms was on regulation rather than punishment. Agencies such as the National Recovery Administration, the Office of Price Administration, and the War Labor Board were established, operating outside the Antitrust Division—except that when their controversies got into court it was the obligation of the Justice Department to appear on behalf of the government. Some of the regulations promulgated by those agencies sanctioned price-fixing and other collusive actions that were forbidden by the antitrust laws. One of those was the case of *United States* v. *Socony-Vacuum Oil Co., Inc.*, which involved NRA sanction of a regional program of stabilization by a group of major oil companies. When the program continued after NRA had been declared unconstitutional, the government instituted a criminal action and the Supreme Court held that the program was illegal price-fixing prohibited by the antitrust laws.

In the late 1940's, the problem of exclusive dealerships became an issue. The government sued Bausch & Lomb Optical Company to invalidate a manufacturer's agreement not to compete with its exclusive distributor nor sell to other distributors. The product was unpatented pink-tinted optical lenses in active competition with other tinted and untinted lenses. The Supreme Court ruled that since the main purpose of the agreement was to provide a source of supply to a distributor who had spent large sums to develop a market for "a relatively new article of commerce" the Sherman Act had not been violated.

In 1948, in *United States* v. *Columbia Steel Co.*, the Court proclaimed the doctrine that exclusive dealing arrangements were not illegal unless they "unreasonably restrict the opportunities of competitors to market their product." In that case, and in the 1953 New Orleans *Times-Picayune* case, the Court prescribed a formula for determining reasonableness that would take into account the percentage of business controlled, the strength of the remaining competition, and whether the action springs from business requirement or purpose to monopolize. Since the *Times-Picayune* case, this formula has been applied by the Justice Department in several instances involving mergers and acquisitions in the newspaper field. It has not opposed such mergers as that of the United Press Association and International News Service, wherein a showing of substantial money losses over an extended period revealed a precarious financial situation.

ACTIONS SINCE 1950

Antitrust moved into the field of international agreements in 1953 when it filed a civil suit to break up an alleged petroleum cartel in which five major United States oil companies allegedly had participated. The suit asked a permanent injunction to restrain the companies from continuing to carry out an alleged conspiracy to control the price, production, and distribution of most of the petroleum and petroleum products marketed in the free world. The cartel, it was charged, controlled 81.5 per cent of the world's estimated crude oil reserves.

The five American companies were Standard Oil of New Jersey, the Socony-Vacuum Oil Company, the Texas Company, Standard Oil of California, and the Gulf Oil Corporation. The Justice Department asserted that the conspiracy had begun in 1928 with the formation in London of a "pool association" with Royal Dutch Petroleum, the Shell Transport Company, and the Anglo-Iranian Oil Company, Ltd.

Subsequent agreements with French, German, Turkish, Mexican, Brazilian, and Venezuelan companies, and other United States producing and distributing companies, broadened the conspiracy to involve virtually all the oil-producing areas of the free world.

A grand jury investigation looking toward criminal indictment was begun by Attorney General James P. McGranery after President Harry S. Truman had authorized release of a Federal Trade Commission report on the cartel. McGranery's successor, Herbert Brownell, Jr., terminated the grand jury proceedings and filed the civil suit, as less likely to disturb sensitive international relations.

The pace of antitrust enforcement stepped up in the Eisenhower Administration under the direction of Attorney General William P. Rogers. Fifty-three new cases were filed in 1958, sixty-two in 1959, and eighty-six in 1960. Major actions in 1958 were the indictment of the Radio Corporation of America on charges of conspiracy to restrain manufacture, sale, and distribution of radio apparatus and to monopolize the licensing of radio patents; a civil suit charging that the B. F. Goodrich Rubber Company and the Dayton Rubber Company had conspired with an English group to allocate world markets in sponge rubber products; and the indictment of five leading manufacturers of polio vaccine on price-fixing charges.

In 1959, the Division challenged corporate mergers in a number of areas. An outstanding one was the case against Firstamerica Corporation, the largest bank holding company in the United States, which had acquired control of 48 banks with 645 offices in 5 Western states. The government asserted that the company was "moving toward a monopoly in banking in the five states," but the court found the charge unsupported by the evidence. Another merger case was a suit to require the Hertz Corporation, the country's largest motor vehicle renting company, to divest itself of the stock and assets of companies it had acquired over a period of five years at a cost of approximately $40 million. The cumulative effect of those acquisitions, the Justice Department alleged, was to eliminate competition.

Another cartel case was filed against General Electric Company, Westinghouse Electric Corporation, and a Netherlands electronics firm alleging restraint of trade by the formation of a patent pool that, operating through Canadian subsidiaries, prevented the importation into Canada of radio and television receiving sets manufactured in the United States.

Price-fixing cases were filed in 1959 against dealers in automobiles, food, milk, clothing, construction, tools, electrical appliances, furniture, mattresses, fences, and the printing trades.

The 1960 enforcement program was highlighted by the indictment of twenty-seven corporations, and many of their officials, on charges of price-fixing in the heavy electrical equipment industry. Among the corporations were the General Electric Company, the Westinghouse Electric Corporation, and the Allis-Chalmers Manufacturing Company. The total volume of commerce accounted for by the various products subject to the price-fixing conspiracy was approximately $2 billion annually. The defendants pleaded guilty. Heavy fines were imposed upon the companies, and several of the officers served prison sentences.

Antitrust activity was carried on at a comparatively normal pace during the term of Attorney General Robert F. Kennedy, with more than sixty new cases filed annually. An outstanding case in 1961 was the indictment of General Motors Corporation on charges of monopolizing the production and sale of Diesel locomotives. Kaiser Aluminum and Chemical Corporation's purchase of the wire and cable facilities of the United States Rubber Company was challenged under the antimerger section of the Clayton Act, as was Aluminum Company of America's acquisition of the stock of an independent manufacturer of aluminum windows and other aluminum products. In 1963, eleven corporations were indicted on charges of price-fixing in the sale of brass mill tube and pipe. Alcoa was one of six corporations indicted for price-fixing in the sale of aluminum conductor cables. In April, 1963, United States Steel and four other corporations were charged in an indictment with price-fixing in sales of wrought steel wheels. United States Steel and seven other major steel companies were indicted for conspiring to eliminate price competition in carbon sheet steel, widely used in automobile bodies, washing machines, refrigerators, kitchen cabinets, and office furniture. Twelve flour milling companies, including General Mills and Pillsbury, were indicted for a price-fixing conspiracy that allegedly resulted in artificially high and noncompetitive prices for commercial buyers of flour. In July, 1963, the United Fruit Company was indicted for conspiring to monopolize the importation and sale of bananas in seven Western states. The Justice Department's objection, in April, 1964, to acquisition by Humble Oil & Refining Company of Western properties of Tidewater Oil Company was challenged by the Justice Department, and Humble withdrew from the sale.

Enforcement dropped off in the first year of the administration of Attorney General Nicholas deB. Katzenbach, with only thirty-three cases filed. Mergers and acquisitions in the fields of automobile trucks, newspaper publishing, scientific supplies, and packaged candy were among those opposed by the Antitrust Division.

Mergers proliferate in the business world, and a new type appeared to gain acceptance in the 1960's. Whereas mergers used to be of direct competitors in the same fields, they are new conglomerate; a corporation in one industry will acquire a business in an entirely different field.

An example was the 1965 purchase of the New York Yankees baseball team by the Columbia Broadcasting System—a union the Justice Department did not oppose.

VI

The Tax Division

The first tax law passed by Congress led to the first rebellion against the federal government and the first trial of civilians for treason. The insurrection was suppressed, and the men convicted of treason were pardoned. But tax laws multiplied. Their enforcement now, almost two centuries later, engages one of the most important—since it protects the income of the United States—and busiest divisions of the Department of Justice.

THE WHISKEY REBELLION

In 1790, the old federal debt had been refunded, and the Revolutionary War debts of the states had been assumed by the federal government. Alexander Hamilton, Secretary of the Treasury, proposed that Congress raise money to pay the debts by levying an excise tax on distilled spirits. Congress levied the tax, and the Whiskey Rebellion ensued.

Several of the states opposed the tax, but forcible resistance developed in Western Pennsylvania. A petition sent to Congress by Pittsburgh citizens said that commerce in the area was carried on more by barter than by sale and that "there is not among us a quantity of circulating cash for payment of this duty alone."

The first violence came when Robert Johnson, an excise

110

collector, was tarred and feathered, and robbed of his horse and money. A district court issued writs against three persons of the mob that had mauled Johnson, but a deputy sent to serve the writs came back saying that if he had tried to serve them he would have been killed.

Aware of the temper of people in the states, Hamilton sought to mollify it by reducing the tax on stills and their products. But cutting the tax rate was not enough. Mob threats increased. On September 15, 1792, President Washington issued a proclamation stating his intention to execute the laws and warning all persons against combining to obstruct enforcement of the excise tax. He also urged all courts, officers, and magistrates to exert their powers to enforce the tax. Reluctant to use other force, the government adopted a policy of prosecuting delinquents, seizing the product of noncomplying distilleries on the way to market, and limiting purchases for the Army to spirits upon which the tax had been paid. These pressures did not work, however, and in June, 1794, Congress gave the President full discretion to organize such enforcement machinery as he deemed necessary.

The actual Whiskey Rebellion broke out on July 17, 1794. An armed force took forcible possession of an excise inspector's house, although it was guarded by federal troops. U.S. Marshal David Lennox, who had gone to Pittsburgh to summon recalcitrant distillers to Philadelphia and serve warrants on persons who had participated in the attack on Collector Johnson, was seized and held until he promised to serve no more writs. Eastbound mail was robbed to intercept reports of federal officers. Washington sent a commission to Pittsburgh to attempt conciliation, but when it reported failure, the President announced that the militia of New Jersey, Pennsylvania, Maryland, and Virginia, under command of Governor Henry Lee of Virginia, was on its way to Pittsburgh. Hamilton went along, and so did a federal judge and a district attorney.

The militiamen routed out suspects, and, after hearings, eighteen prisoners were sent to Philadelphia, where prosecutions began in April, 1795. Only two of those indicted for treason were convicted. They were sentenced to be hanged, but President Washington pardoned them.

Not all tax resistance in Pennsylvania ended with the Whiskey Rebellion. On March 7, 1799, a mob attacked a U.S. marshal and his posse at Bethlehem and released thirty prisoners who had resisted efforts of federal officials to enforce the provisions of the Direct Tax Act of 1798. President John Adams saw in this a new threat of treason and sent the militia, which rounded up many prisoners. Three men were indicted for treason, convicted by a jury, and sentenced to be hanged. Emulating Washington's compassion, President Adams pardoned them.

RESPONSIBILITY FOR TAX COLLECTING

Enforcement of the tax laws no longer requires the militia, and no longer involves treason. It has to deal, however, with citizens who don't like to pay taxes, who cheat and evade and falsify their tax returns—and also with thousands of honest taxpayers who disagree with their assessments. It requires tedious and painstaking preparation of civil and criminal cases and long days in court. It calls for the exercise of skill, vigilance, and judgment to protect the internal revenue of the United States.

For more than a century, enforcement of the tax laws was primarily a function of the Treasury Department. In 1820, Congress made the Secretary of the Treasury responsible for directing suits for the recovery of debts due the United States. When the Secretary authorized a suit, however, the U.S. attorneys in the several districts handled the cases. As early as 1828, President Andrew Jackson recommended to Congress that all litigation regarding government revenues be transferred to the Office of Attorney General (see Chapter I), but Congress did not accept the recommendation. Not until June 10, 1933, was such a step finally taken and the Tax Division of the Department of Justice established. This separation from the Treasury Department was done by an executive order of President Franklin D. Roosevelt pursuant to a general plan of government reorganization.

FUNCTIONS OF THE DIVISION

The Tax Division represents the United States and its officers in civil and criminal litigation arising under the internal revenue laws in all federal and state courts except the Tax Court of the United States. The Tax Court is an independent executive agency created primarily to permit review of asserted tax deficiencies prior to payment.

In civil litigation, it is the duty of the Tax Division to prepare and try cases in courts of original jurisdiction and to prepare briefs and conduct oral arguments in appellate courts, including the Supreme Court on assignment by the solicitor general. Civil litigation includes refund suits brought against the United States by taxpayers or by district directors of the Internal Revenue Service of the Treasury Department to recover taxes alleged to have been erroneously paid; lien suits brought by individuals to foreclose mortgages or to quiet title to property in which the United States is named as a party defendant because of a federal lien on the property; collection suits brought by the United States to foreclose tax liens, to take judgments against delinquent taxpayers, to enforce tax claims in bankruptcy, receivership, probate proceedings, and similar types of collection matters; and intergovernmental immunity suits in which the United States resists attempts to apply a state or local tax to an activity or property of the United States.

Offenses within the jurisdiction of the Tax Division under

the criminal provisions of the revenue laws include attempts to evade and defeat taxes; willful failure to file returns and pay taxes; filing false returns and other documents; making false statements to revenue officials, and miscellaneous offenses involving internal revenue matters, excluding liquor and narcotics taxes and offenses under the Wagering Tax Act. Cases involving the liquor, narcotics, and betting taxes are handled by the Criminal Division. (See Chapter XI.)

WHAT THE DIVISION DOES NOT DO

The Tax Division does not formulate basic policy in revenue matters, nor does it participate in tax controversies at the administrative level. Those are exclusive functions of the Treasury Department and the Internal Revenue Service. Only when a matter reaches the litigation stage does it come within the jurisdiction of the Tax Division to defend the government's interests in the courts and to provide an independent appraisal of the government's position from the point of view of litigating strategy and uniformity in application of the tax laws. What that means is that when the Internal Revenue Service refers a case to the Justice Department for prosecution the Tax Division decides whether the facts and the applicable laws warrant legal action.

In a recent annual report, the head of the Tax Division described the relationship between the Internal Revenue Service and the Tax Division as "exceptionally constructive, friendly and free of friction." The Division, he said, "sought to be as fully responsive as possible to the policy direction of the Internal Revenue Service, and to maintain the highest professional standards in the conduct of trials and the disposition of litigation without trial." He added that "the division of responsibility has proved fruitful because it affords an opportunity for a fresh, intensive and intelligent reexamination of the government's position in each tax controversy at the point in time when that controversy emerges from the administrative level into full public view in federal court." When the Tax Division is convinced that it would be a mistake to argue the position advanced by the Internal Revenue Service, the assistant attorney general stated, "we are often able, from our independent vantage point, to persuade Revenue that from the standpoint of litigation certain positions ought not to be pursued in court."

ORGANIZATION AND STAFF

The assistant attorney general in charge of the Tax Division has a first assistant, a second assistant, an executive assistant, and an assistant for Civil Trials as the top members of his staff. For functional purposes, the Division is subdivided into six sections: Appellate, Review, Criminal, General Litigation, Court of Claims, and Refund Trial, each with a section chief to head it. The Refund Trial Section is further subdivided into three units, each headed by a section chief.

More than 200 lawyers comprise the legal staff. Many are career men who remain in the Division and become specialists in certain branches of tax law. They try cases in district courts in every part of the country and argue appeals before appellate tribunals. In a typical year of the 1960's, Tax Division attorneys conducted 94 per cent of all tax trials and arguments; the remaining 6 per cent—mostly criminal cases—were handled by U.S. attorneys in the districts. Even when a district attorney tries a case, a Division lawyer almost always assists in its preparation and stands by at the trial to give the benefit of his specialized knowledge and experience.

Not all tax cases reach the courts. It is an axiom of lawyers that a poor settlement is better than a good lawsuit. Compromises are often reached, thus avoiding long and expensive court proceedings. When a taxpayer offers to settle a civil suit, the offer is studied in both the Internal Revenue Service and the Tax Division. If an agreement is reached after proposals and counterproposals are considered, the head of the Division authorizes acceptance.

Pretrial procedures also eliminate many court trials. Often, after a suit is filed, lawyers for each side confer with the judge in an effort to agree upon a settlement that satisfies all parties and saves the time of the court. If the judge approves the settlement, the suit is dismissed, the court's work load is lightened, and time and expense conserved by all concerned.

The volume of tax litigation has grown steadily. In the first 30 years of the Division's existence, it received more than 117,000 civil and criminal cases in which more than $3.6 billion was in controversy. During those years, the Division collected $381 million in delinquent taxes and saved the Treasury $1.3 billion in refunds. In 1965, the assistant attorney general in charge of the Division reported that tax litigation had increased 33⅓ per cent in 3 years. In fiscal 1964 alone, more than 10,000 cases were commenced in the courts.

One reason there are so many more tax cases now is because there are so many more taxpayers. The Sixteenth Amendment, which became part of the Constitution on February 25, 1913, gave Congress the power "to lay and collect taxes on income." The laws enacted under that authorization added millions of names to the tax rolls—and the rolls swell every year. The number of federally taxable businesses likewise has increased and excise taxes multiplied. Auditing returns to detect deceits and deficiencies is a monumental task of the Internal Revenue Service; if the IRS fails to uncover false or inaccurate returns, the United States loses money. In recent years, the IRS has added thousands to its staff and kept abreast of the times by installing electronic equipment that processes tax data automatically. Thus, a clerk or a computer may check a return and determine whether the taxpayer falsified or merely miscalculated. In either case, litigation may result or be threatened, and the work load of the Tax Division grows accordingly. There are no indications that either the volume of work or the size of the staff will shrink in the future.

CONSTITUTIONAL QUESTIONS

Some tax cases that are carried to the Supreme Court involve constitutional questions, the powers of Congress, and governmental policies. In 1870, more than half a century before the income tax amendment was passed, the Court ruled that Congress did not have power to tax the salary of a judicial officer of a state. In 1895, the Court held that a tax on income from bonds issued by a municipal corporation was a tax upon the power of a state and its instrumentalities to borrow money and, constitutionally, could not be imposed. In 1897, and again in 1903, the Court upheld the tax on oleomargarine (since repealed). In 1911, in fifteen cases, it ruled that a corporation tax imposed by the Tariff Act of 1909 was an excise tax upon the privilege of doing business in a corporate capacity and was constitutional. Eleven years later, the Court decided that the Act of August 21, 1921, known as the "futures trading act," exceeded the taxing power of Congress, and, in the same year, it upheld the right of the United States to tax income of American citizens domiciled abroad from property situated abroad. The tax status of charitable foundations is frequently questioned; in 1961, the Court ruled that a foundation established by comedian Bob Hope was tax exempt.

SOME FAMOUS TAX CASES

The glamorous—or notorious—cases, however, do not involve questions of whether a corporation overpaid or underpaid its tax. The rule in such cases is to "pay first and litigate later"; that is, pay and avoid the penalties and then sue for a refund. Refund suits, even when they relate to large corporations and huge sums of money, get scant attention and modest headlines compared with tax cases involving the vice lord, the racketeer, the corrupt official. Tax laws have been the weapons used to put many shady characters in jail.

One of the most famous, of course, was Al Capone. As head of a powerful guild of gangsters that throve in the Prohibition Era, Capone got away with bribery, robbery, extortion, and murder—until auditors examined his tax returns. Crime paid handsomely for Capone. But he cheated on his income taxes, and not all his wealth nor the wiles of his lawyers could keep him out of the federal penitentiary at Atlanta.

Paul (the Waiter) De Lucia, alias Paul Ricca, one of the heirs of Capone's notorious empire, got nine years for tax evasion. Peter Licavoli, reputed leader of Detroit's "Purple Gang," was convicted of tax evasion, as was John Diogardi, known as Johnny Dio, New York racketeer. Meyer Harris "Mickey" Cohen, California gambler and racketeer, got fifteen years in prison and a $30,000 fine for intentional miscalculation of how much tax money he owed the government.

Millionaire industrialists, too, have gotten into trouble because they tried to beat the tax collector. One who received wide publicity was Bernard Goldfine, New England textile manufacturer and friend of Sherman Adams, Assistant to the President in the Eisenhower Administration. After auditing Goldfine's corporate and individual returns, the Internal Revenue Service charged him with eleven counts of tax evasion, to which he pleaded guilty. A $15,705,387 suit to foreclose tax liens on the estate of Lee Shubert, Broadway theatrical producer, was filed in 1964, and, in the same year, the Tax Division claimed $12,289,316 from Texan Billie Sol Estes. Estes was bankrupt, and the trustee in charge of his affairs contended that the government's claim was based on levies against loans that were not taxable income. The government's position was that Estes' wealth was the fruit of a swindle or embezzlement and hence taxable under a 1961 ruling of the Supreme Court that funds obtained by embezzlement were subject to income tax.

Major and minor labor union officials also have been punished for tax evasion. The most noted case was that of Dave Beck, president of the International Teamsters' Union, who was sentenced to five years for tax fraud in 1959. In 1960, eight Teamsters' Union organizers were convicted of tax evasion in Pennsylvania.

Lester Maddox, the Georgia restaurateur turned politician who won election as governor in 1966, deducted political advertising as a business expense. The government said it was not deductible, and a jury agreed. Many public officials have run afoul of the tax laws. A former mayor and two other officials of Gary, Indiana, went to prison for evading taxes, and Frank Keenan, Assessor of Cook County, Illinois, was sentenced to two years and fined $57,000 for flagrant tax evasion. In 1964, thirty-two indictments and convictions of rackets figures or corrupt public officials obtained by the Tax Division included Oklahoma Supreme Court Justice Earl Welch, who was fined $13,500 and sentenced to three years in prison.

The only political party ever sued was the Communist Party. The Tax Division sued it in 1963 to collect $381,-544.88, which the IRS claimed the Communists had failed to pay.

Almost everybody pays taxes. Most people grumble, but avoid getting into legal difficulties. Since the Tax Division was founded, however, more than 150,000 persons have been parties to civil or criminal cases arising out of the taxing power of the United States.

VII

The Civil Division

The duties and responsibilities of the Civil Division of the Department of Justice are heavy. The laws it administers are multitudinous; its activities are kaleidoscopic; its impact upon the affairs of citizens is incalculable.

The Division represents the rights and interests of the U.S. Government in all of its general civil—that is, noncriminal—litigation. The essentially commercial activities in which the government engages—buying, selling, constructing, shipping, lending, insuring, employing, etc.—give rise to law suits. The Civil Division defends all suits against the government and prosecutes all suits in which the government is plaintiff. Sums of money involved are often very large; the legal issues complex.

Broadly speaking, the Division is the claims lawyer for the government. It used to be called the Claims Division. Claims against the government stem from such things as floods, plane accidents, explosions, underground nuclear tests, sonic booms generated by military aircraft, auto collisions, the dynamiting of an ice jam in an Alaskan river, and personal injuries suffered by exposure to radiation or falling down a hatchway aboard a government-owned steamship.

The scope and variety of the Division's activities are constantly expanding. The volume of work involved is illustrated by the fact that at the end of 1965 the Division had

12,453 cases in federal district courts and more than 220 petitions and protests by importers in the U.S. Customs Court. The amount of money involved is reflected in the fact that in 1965 nearly $2 billion was claimed in suits against the government.

Until 1855, the Treasury Department, rather than the Attorney General, dealt with claims by and against the government. Such matters were the responsibility of the solicitor of the Treasury, who supervised the U.S. attorneys in the conduct of court cases. The Attorney General's role was to act as legal adviser to the solicitor (who often was not a lawyer) in the same way that he gave legal advice and opinions to other departments, agencies, and officers of the United States.

In 1855, however, President Franklin Pierce, by executive order, placed all civil legal business of the country in the hands of the Attorney General. He ordered that all cases arising in any of the departments be conducted by the Attorney General unless he delegated the task to the respective head. In either case, the Treasury solicitor was directed to assist, but no longer had supervision.

CIVIL WAR LITIGATION

In a few years, the Attorney General was deeply involved in civil litigation generated by the Civil War. International problems as well as domestic policies and actions were embodied in cases that produced significant court decisions.

The most famous were the so-called prize cases, arising out of the letters of marque issued by the Confederacy empowering privately owned vessels to prey upon Union shipping. A large number of privateers were fitted out and roamed American coastal waters seeking to capture the ships of the North. The statutory penalty, under United States laws, was death.

In July, 1861, the first privateer commissioned, the *Savannah,* was captured by Union forces and sailed into New York, where the officers and crew were taken in irons to the Tombs to await trial by jury. President Jefferson Davis offered to exchange an equal number of captured Union soldiers for the privateers, but the offer was rejected. He then threatened to retaliate against an equal number of Northern captives if the crew of the *Savannah* was put to death. The prisoners were tried in federal court, but the jury disagreed and there were no executions. The *Jefferson Davis* was another privateer captured. It was taken to Philadelphia, but, although the cases were kept on the docket until the end of the war, they were never tried and eventually were dismissed and the prisoners released.

A series of prize cases tried in New York and Boston reached the Supreme Court and were consolidated for decision purposes. They were argued for twelve days by some of the ablest lawyers of the time. A major contention of the defense was that the Civil War was an "insurrection" rather than a war between independent nations and, since the right of prize and capture arose under the laws of war, the blockade of Southern ports and the seizure of ships that ran the blockade were illegal. The decision of the Court was that it was not necessary that both parties be acknowledged as an independent nation or a sovereign state in order to constitute a war and that the blockade, imposed under the laws of war, was legal.

The Attorney General's participation in these cases was chiefly to give opinions on the legal questions involved. The actions were military. Legislation enacted by Congress under which property of Confederate citizens and sympathizers was seized involved much more work for the Attorney General and his staff, over a much longer period, than did the prize cases.

The First Confiscation Act and the Captured and Abandoned Property Act constituted a broad license to take virtually any property that belonged to any Confederate officer or state official, or others engaged in the rebellion, and zealous adherents to the Union cause took full advantage of it. The position of the Attorney General was that they were civil laws to be enforced by civil authority. Some military commanders thought otherwise and regarded the civilian processes as too slow. Provost courts were set up to facilitate military appropriation of enemy property, and the Army continued a ruthless campaign of seizure until President Lincoln, approving a protest by Attorney General Bates, stopped it by executive order.

With the end of the war, claims for restoration of or compensation for seized property were filed by thousands of persons and for thirty years afterward the Department of Justice was engaged in adjustment by negotiation or litigation of those claims.

GENESIS OF THE CIVIL DIVISION

At the time the Department of Justice was established in 1870, as successor to the Office of Attorney General, its work and functions were not delegated to sections and divisions. The Department had few attorneys, and their assignments were general, rather than specific. The practice was, when specialized talents were required to handle momentous cases, to engage outside counsel, often lawyers of national reputation whose fees were much above the salary scale fixed by Congress for the Attorney General and his small staff.

As early as 1868, however, Congress recognized that claims constituted a major part of the work load of the government's law office, and it provided an assistant to the Attorney General whose chief duty was to deal with litigation related to claims, especially defense of suits against the government. This was the progenitor of what is now the Civil Division.

By the Act of March 3, 1891, Congress made it the duty of

the Attorney General to defend suits in the Court of Claims growing out of Indian depredations and authorized the appointment of an "Assistant Attorney General of the United States" to expedite disposition of the cases. That legislative enactment was the first to prescribe specifically the duties to be performed by any assistant attorney general under the supervision of the Attorney General. However, the position was temporary, and ceased to exist when the Indian depredation cases were completed.

Of the same temporary character was the office of the assistant attorney general in charge of Spanish Treaty claims, created by the Act of March 2, 1901. The incumbent was, in effect, the legal adviser to the Spanish Treaty Claims Commission, established by the same Act, and the office lapsed when the Spanish claims were settled.

For a number of years, a unit of the Department operated under the title of the Admiralty and Civil Division, with an assistant attorney general in charge, but this unit was abolished by a departmental order of December 30, 1933. That same order created the Claims Division and defined its functions. Issued by Attorney General Homer Cummings, it established the pattern of organization out of which the present Civil Division has evolved.

Mr. Cummings allocated to the assistant attorney general in charge of the Claims Division responsibility for all civil suits and claims for and against the government not otherwise specifically assigned, patents and copyrights, cases arising out of war transactions, civil bankruptcy matters, the National Bank Act (civil), admiralty and shipping matters, and alien property claims and litigation. Separate sections to handle the work relating to those assignments were set up.

PRESENT FRAMEWORK

The Civil Division today operates in much the same framework, although legislative enactments, the vast expansion of the government's law business, and internal management policies have resulted in shifts of assignments and responsibilities within the Division or to other existing or newly created units of the Department. As currently organized, the Division distributes its work—some of it necessarily overlapping—among nine sections. They are Admiralty and Shipping, Appellate, Court of Claims, Customs, Frauds, General Litigation, General Claims, Patents, and Torts.

Admiralty and Shipping

The Admiralty and Shipping Section is responsible for litigating all matters involving ships, shipping, navigable waters, and workmen's compensation in which the United States is involved. Its normal complement of attorneys is twenty-five, stationed in Washington, New York, and San Francisco. The strange ways of ships and sailors and the complex maritime laws, national and international, which have developed through the centuries since man first launched ships upon oceans, provide the Section's lawyers with cases arising out of the tragic, the prosaic, and the bizarre aspects of seafaring.

One such case involved barratry—a word little known and seldom used. It describes a crime rarely committed, defined as "any wilful and unlawful act by the master or crew of a ship whereby the owners sustain injury." Barratry was an issue in a case with Chinese Communist overtones that set lawyers of the Admiralty Section delving into old law books in 1957. Crews of six ships that had been sold to a Nationalist China company by the United States defected in Hong Kong and turned the ships over to the Communists. The United States held mortgages on the ships, and the mortgages were insured against barratry and other perils. A rider to the policy, however, excluded capture and seizure from coverage. The insurance companies refused to pay the loss, contending that it arose from a political change and was brought about by "seizure" not covered in the policies. Meantime, a seventh ship, the *Hai Hsuan,* was seized at sea by a mutinous crew and sailed into Singapore. As British colonies, Hong Kong and Singapore recognized Communist China, and hence, to the Red Chinese, were available ports for defection. The masters of the Hong Kong vessels had acquiesced in the defections. The master of the *Hai Hsuan* had been seized and held captive by the crew.

The issue of barratry versus seizure was taken to a U.S. district court, which ruled that the six Hong Kong ships had been lost by barratry but that the *Hai Hsuan* had been seized and was not covered by the insurance policies. A Circuit Court of Appeals upheld the ruling on the Hong Kong vessels, but reversed on the *Hai Hsuan,* holding that its loss also was due to barratry. The United States collected $4 million from the insurance companies.

When Texas Tower, No. 4, an Air Force installation off the New Jersey Coast, weakened by storms toppled into the sea, 14 Air Force personnel and 14 civilian repairmen died. Claims totaling $9 million were filed against architects, builders, repair firms, and the United States as the tower's operator. Attorneys of the Admiralty Section participated in settlement negotiations that resulted in a payment of $1.7 million, of which the United States paid $677,000, to satisfy the claims.

Appellate Section

Approximately 50 per cent of the appellate work of the Department of Justice consists of Civil Division cases that involve the disposition of large sums of money and the solution of crucial questions of government law and policy. One interesting, less important question decided in 1958 by a court of appeals related to a bit of pioneer history.

In 1952, a collection of documents was found in an attic in St. Paul, Minnesota. It consisted of notes written in the hand of Captain William Clark of the Lewis and Clark Expedition. A number of claimants asserted interests in the papers and suits were begun to determine rightful ownership. The United States intervened, claiming paramount title on the grounds that the papers were government records of an Army expedition. Appellate courts rejected that claim, holding that the documents were private notes kept by Captain Clark for use in his personal diary, and not official records.

Court of Claims

As early as 1855, the growing number of claims against the United States caused Congress to establish the U.S. Court of Claims to handle various categories of them. Primarily, at that time, the claims evolved from government contracts. A wider field is now embraced, but jurisdiction is still limited to suits against the United States. The Court of Claims Section of the Civil Division is responsible for the defense of all except land, tax, admiralty, and Indian claims. A sampling of Court of Claims cases of recent years gives an idea of its scope:

An agreement between a Swedish corporation and the U.S. Government produced a claim involving the United States' relations with her Allies in World War II. The Bofors Corporation granted the United States a license to use its 44-mm. anti-aircraft gun. In negotiating the license, the U.S. Navy inserted a clause "for the United States use," thinking "use" broad enough to cover anything the United States wanted to do with the guns. Bofors claimed that the license was breached when some of the guns were turned over to the Allies under Lend-Lease. The Court of Claims agreed with the Swedes, in this case, and the American Government settled for $4 million but won an amendment to the license to permit future transfers.

Politics and policies were involved in a famous case that was decided in fiscal 1959—the Dixon-Yates case, which arose out of a contract with the Atomic Energy Commission for construction of a plant at West Memphis, Tennessee, to produce electric energy for the Tennessee Valley Authority. The plant was also to supply additional power to the city of Memphis, then under contract with the TVA to supply all of its power needs. When Memphis decided to build its own power plant and did not renew its contract with TVA, the AEC terminated its contract with the Mississippi Valley Generating Company (Dixon-Yates), which already had expended considerable money on the West Memphis project. The company sued the United States. The government relied for its defense chiefly upon an alleged conflict of interest, based on the fact that Adolph Wenzel, a consultant of the Bureau of the Budget, was also vice-president of the First Boston Corporation, the financial agent of Mississippi Valley Generating. The Court of Claims found that no conflict of interest existed sufficient to affect the contract and gave judgment of approximately $1,800,000 for the company.

Three American soldiers who were captured during the Korean War and refused repatriation after the armistice were dishonorably discharged by the U.S. Army, and their pay and allowances during their period of captivity were forfeited. When they later voluntarily returned to the United States, they sued for their pay and allowances. The government claimed that they had breached their contract of enlistment and abandoned their status as U.S. soldiers by collaborating with the enemy, broadcasting false propaganda, and spreading false reports about the President of the United States, thereby themselves forfeiting their right to compensation while captive. The Court of Claims agreed and dismissed the suit.

Civil Division lawyers were presented with quite a different type of case when a group of mink raisers sued for $1,055,-506.60 for loss of business resulting from feeding their animals a synthetic female sex hormone, contained in a chicken waste preparation, that rendered female minks sterile. The mink raisers claimed that they had relied upon a Department of Agriculture publication dealing with chicken waste as a feed, and that the Department was negligent in not warning that the waste contained the hormone substance. The Court of Claims found that the Department did not know that the waste contained the synthetic hormone when it issued the pamphlet and was not aware that the mink raisers had relied upon free and unsolicited advice. To permit recovery, the court said, would put a damper upon government experimentation and stop approval of worthwhile publications.

Customs Section

The Customs Section represents the United States in all cases in the U.S. Customs Court, including the defense of appeals for reappraisement of imported merchandise, petitions for remission of duties, protests for review of classification of goods, the rate and amount of duties charged, and the handling of appeals in reappraisement cases. With the Appellate Section, the Customs Section handles appeals of customs cases in the Court of Customs and Patent Appeals.

American importers and individuals buy millions and millions of dollars worth of foreign goods each year and bring them to American seaports and airports, where customs collectors appraise their value and assess the duty. An indication of how many times the judgments of the collectors are challenged is afforded by the fact that at the close of fiscal 1965, there were 218,926 cases pending on the Customs Court's docket.

The cases call for decisions and interpretations of the

laws and regulations in a fantastically complex system of tariffs. One case may pose the question of the proper basis for valuation of Japanese electronic tubes and another whether spark plugs are classifiable as parts of internal combustion engines of the carburetor type rather than as parts of automobiles. In 1958, the Customs Court was asked to decide whether a device for determining the sex of day-old chicks was an optical instrument and dutiable, or an agricultural implement which could be imported duty free. The things lawyers in the Customs Section have to know—or find out— are infinite, and they all affect the laws and revenues of the United States.

Frauds

When persons deliberately try to cheat the government, they are likely to run up against the Frauds Section. This unit is responsible for suits under the False Claims Act to recover double damages and civil penalties, suits under the Surplus Property Act to recover double damages or other elective remedies, and others. Cases arise from procurement contracts, various agricultural support programs, storage and conversion of agricultural and other commodities, various programs administered by the Veterans Administration, government employee frauds, housing loan programs, and the sale or distribution of government supplies and property to veterans or other recipients qualified by legislation—a broad field, obviously, and one in which attorneys of the Section may handle 2,000 cases a year and win awards totaling many millions of dollars.

General Litigation and General Claims

Prior to 1963, the General Litigation Section was responsible for litigating in federal and state courts actions by and against the United States. This responsibility involved proceedings to review orders of administrative agencies, suits against agencies and officers of the United States to enjoin action, and suits prosecuted by the Section to implement the carrying out of governmental activities. It included intervention in any action in which the constitutionality of any Act of Congress affecting the public interest was drawn into question, injunctions in labor disputes, renegotiation litigation, judicial review of decisions under the Social Security Act, and kindred matters. In 1963, the Section was split and a new General Claims Section created. General Litigation retained nonmonetary suits; General Claims took over those in which money was involved.

The work of the General Claims Section includes the assertion of all claims in favor of the United States and the litigation relating to them; the recovery of fines and bail bond forfeitures; the defense of civil suits against the United States to quiet title, foreclose a mortgage or other lien upon real or personal property upon which the government claims a mortgage or other lien. The General Claims Section handles the largest volume of cases in the Civil Division. In 1965, its attorneys handled 8,091 cases involving more than $250 million. A year later, the volume was less—4,481 cases—but the claims involved a larger sum of $472 million.

One of the landmark cases handled by General Litigation prior to the separation involved the threatened steel strike in 1959. The Section obtained an injunction to prevent the strike and successfully defended in the Supreme Court the government's authority under the Taft-Hartley Act to use injunctive procedures to halt a threatened labor crisis in the steel industry. Equally important were the "windfall cases" of 1958, in which General Litigation successfully recovered millions of dollars illegally distributed by builders under the insured mortgage loan program of the Federal Housing Administration. An illustrative suit involved a group of New

York corporations that borrowed more than $21 million to build a multifamily rental housing unit in Brooklyn. The mortgage loans insured by FHA exceeded the construction costs by more than $3 million, and that sum was distributed to stockholders as dividends. The government regarded these "windfall" payments as illegal and sued to recover. In a compromise settlement, approximately $2 million was refunded by stockholders. Today, such a suit would be handled by the General Claims Section.

Patents

Litigation involving the rights and liabilities of the U.S. Government in patent, copyright, and trademark cases is handled by the attorneys of the Patents Section. Included are the defense of patent infringement suits involving government contracts; proceedings to establish government priority of invention; suits involving transfer of rights, title, payment of royalties, and cancellation of patents acquired by fraud upon the Patent Office; actions on behalf of the government in the use of trademarks, and so on.

Torts

When Hurricane Audrey hit the Gulf Coast of Louisiana in 1957, the United States was sued for approximately $10 million for the death of 135 persons. The suits alleged that Weather Bureau warnings and advisories were inaccurate in predicting when Audrey would arrive, with the result that residents were lulled into a false sense of security and did not get out of the danger area. The court held that the Weather Bureau's forecasters had not been negligent and that the legal duty of the bureau in reporting on speed, velocity, and direction of hurricanes came under the "discretionary function" exemption of the Tort Claims Act, one of the statutes in the Civil Division's jurisdiction.

When violence accompanied the enrollment of James Meredith, a Negro, at the University of Mississippi, U.S. marshals and representatives of the Attorney General participated in efforts to restore and preserve order. (See Chapter IV.) Suits were brought to establish personal liability of the Attorney General and the Chief U.S. Marshal for injuries to participants in the disorders. The courts ruled that the officials were acting within the scope of their official duties and were immune from personal liability. These suits, too, were brought under the Tort Claims Act.

By definition, a tort is an injury, or wrong. The Torts Section conducts the defense of suits against the United States for damages in torts cases. Today, many such cases arise out of crashes of military and civilian aircraft. The United States is sued as an owner and operator of great fleets of military airplanes, and also because it regulates and controls civilian flights. Plaintiffs win when they can establish that the accidents were caused by negligence of federal employees. In 1965, the Torts Section had pending 2,580 tort claims involving $425 million. Several recent cases have involved suits for damages caused by the sonic boom from jet airplanes breaking the sound barrier. The noise sometimes disturbs sleeping citizens and brings on nervous disorders, or frightens a farmer's cows so that milk production falls off. One of the cases arose in Oklahoma City, Oklahoma, where citizens sought to enjoin supersonic transport tests over the city, claiming they were injurious to health and safety. A court held that little damage to property and no personal injury had resulted from the tests and dismissed the request for an injunction.

UNUSUAL CIVIL CASES

After World War II, a special section was set up in the Civil Division to handle claims against the United States by persons of Japanese ancestry for property damage resulting from their evacuation, under military orders, from their West Coast homes and businesses. The section also conducted litigation involving restoration of citizenship to Japanese who had renounced their American allegiance. Originally, the claims totaled nearly $134 million. In final settlements, the U.S. Government paid out $26,874,240 to indemnify property losses and restored citizenship to 5,034 persons out of 5,790 who had renounced their rights.

Not all the matters dealt with by the Civil Division relate to purely domestic affairs. In 1958, the Division obtained in Lisbon a judgment of $124,000 in favor of the United States as damages for default of a Portuguese firm on a tungsten procurement contract. A case of broader interest evolved from the anti-American riots in Panama in 1964. The Panamanian Bar Association brought to the International Commission of Jurists charges that the United States had violated the United Nations Declaration of Human Rights by depriving Panamanians of the right to life and security, by treating them in a cruel, inhuman, and degrading manner and by denying them the right of freedom of assembly. In May, 1964, after a ten-day trial, the Commission completely exonerated the United States.

That same year, the Civil Division was successful in defending an attack upon the Atomic Energy Act by a group of scientists and citizens with pacifist leanings. Dr. Linus C. Pauling, a scientist who had helped develop the atomic bomb, and 254 others sued the Secretary of Defense and the Atomic Energy Commission to enjoin further nuclear testing. They claimed the Atomic Energy Act did not authorize nuclear testing, or, if it did, the Act was unconstitutional. The court dismissed the complaint. It held that the testing came within the national defense and foreign policy powers of the executive and legislative branches and that it was not the proper business of the judiciary to deal with the pros and cons of testing or the political questions involved.

Another victory was achieved by the Division when the courts upheld the constitutionality of Public Law 88–108—the first federal statute requiring compulsory arbitration to resolve labor disputes other than those arising under collective bargaining agreements. Constitutionality was challenged by the Brotherhood of Locomotive Firemen and sustained by the courts in decisions that upheld the right of the President to intervene in the national interest to avert a threatened nationwide railroad strike.

Under the Trading With the Enemy Act in World War II, the United States seized enemy alien interests in a number of American corporations and businesses. Control of the seized property was vested in the Attorney General and administered by the Office of Alien Property, a separate division with an assistant attorney general in charge, that had been created out of a section of the Civil Division. One of the seizures produced one of the most vigorously contested cases in the history of the Justice Department. The stakes were high and the legal talent on both sides skilled and adroit.

The property was the General Aniline & Film Corporation, of which German interests, before the war, held 89 per cent of the stock. The government assumed that the shares belonged to I. G. Farben, a large German industrial complex. In 1948, however, a Swiss holding company known as Interhandel claimed ownership and sued to recover. As a Swiss corporation, Interhandel was not an alien enemy. Some 2,000 stockholders intervened, all claiming they were not enemies and entitled to recover.

The United States wanted to liquidate its alien property operations but could not sell General Aniline while ownership was in litigation. Some settlement with Interhandel was a prerequisite. During the administration of Attorney General Robert F. Kennedy, a complex agreement was worked out, whereby General Aniline shares were registered with the Securities and Exchange Commission and sold by competitive bidding to American nationals. The sale, on March 9, 1965, yielded $329,141,926.48, of which the United States received $208,281,419.27 and Interhandel $120,860,507.21. At the time of vesting, the General Aniline shares were worth less than $100 million. Their value had tripled under Justice Department management. The United States and Interhandel each made money on the deal.

Sale of General Aniline disposed of the last large property seized from World War II enemies. The Office of Alien Property was closed as a division and reverted to the status of a section in the Civil Division, and unless the United States should again become involved in a major war, it probably will disappear entirely.

VIII

Land and Natural Resources Division

The Land and Natural Resources Division of the Department of Justice is the lawyer for the largest land owner in the United States, namely, the United States Government. The federal government owns 768 million acres, or 34 per cent, of the entire nation, with its forests, plains, buildings, minerals and other natural resources, and navigable waterways.

The Department of Justice does not administer public lands and resources. That is the function, primarily, of the Department of the Interior, shared in certain areas with the Forest Service and Soil Conservation Service of the Department of Agriculture, the Department of Defense, NASA, the Department of Transportation, and, in the case of navigable waters, the U.S. Army Corps of Engineers. But if legal controversies develop, the Justice Department must act for the government, whether in the prosecution of a timber thief or the acquisition of land for the Manned Lunar Landing Project in Florida. As Ramsey Clark, at that time the assistant attorney general in charge of this Division, said in 1964, it "renders legal services to the other federal agencies at the courthouse. These agencies are its clients."

FUNCTIONS AND ORGANIZATION

The Division represents the interests of the United States in civil litigation involving the public domain. This litigation

137

includes enforcement of statutes concerning the use and disposal of public, reserved, and acquired lands; interpretation and cancellation of land grants, patents, leases, and contracts of sale; recovery of rents, royalties, and damages; trespass, evictions, and recovery of possession; removal of clouds on titles; foreclosure of mortgages executed in connection with the disposal of real property; determination of boundaries; establishing of mineral rights; conduct of condemnation proceedings for the acquisition of land or other property; defense of actions for damages resulting from acts of the United States, its officers, agents, or contractors in connection with real property, and in the prosecution and defense of actions pertaining to Indians and Indian property, real and personal.

In short, the Department of Justice, operating through the Lands and Resources Division, is the government's land agent—probably the busiest to be found anywhere in the world.

The officials of the Division are an assistant attorney general in charge, who is directly responsible to the Attorney General; a first assistant; and six chiefs heading the Land Acquisition, Appellate, Indian Claims, Appraisal, Administrative, and General Litigation sections. The attorney personnel fluctuates between 95 and 110. Small field offices are maintained in New York and Florida.

The Division was organized in 1910, reorganized in 1929, and was called the Land Division until 1965 when, because of its increasing involvement with matters relating to the development and conservation of natural resources, its title was changed to the Land and Natural Resources Division.

The laws under which the Division functions number more than 5,000—a vast, uncoordinated accumulation scattered through many titles of the U.S. Code and volumes of statutes. The laws reflect the development of national policy from the days when the colonists drove off the Indians to the present when federal laws pertain not only to the earth but to the waters thereof and the air above it. The Division now represents the United States in suits for abatement of water and air pollution and in navigation cases involving the handling and guidance of aircraft in the air.

U.S. LAND POLICY AND PROBLEMS

The area and resources of the United States were so vast when the nation was founded that development, rather than conservation, was government policy. Land was available to settlers on "give-away" terms; huge tracts were allotted to railroads to encourage construction of transcontinental systems; miners could stake claims and dig for gold or coal merely by paying a filing fee. The new nation was prodigal with its resources.

Early in the nineteenth century, the government and many citizens became concerned about the forests of the West. There were no laws that made cutting timber from public lands a crime, and saws and axes were denuding large areas of trees—especially red cedar and live oak, necessary to the building of ships. In 1817, Congress took a step toward conservation by authorizing the President and the Secretary of the Navy to set aside reserves of live oak and red cedar lands for future naval use. At the same time, cutting of those species of timber on reserved or other public lands was made a crime. But not until 1831 did Congress pass a law prohibiting the cutting of all kinds of timber from federal lands.

Enforcement of that law was sporadic. Such prosecutions as were undertaken were supervised by the solicitor of the Treasury until 1858, when the Land Office of the Interior Department took over the work. Violations were reported to district attorneys—not then subject to the authority of the Attorney General—and often no action was taken. In some areas, no effort was made to enforce the law.

Pioneers of the West pressed for legislation to permit settlers and others to purchase timber from government reserves. In 1878, a law allowing timber to be cut for building,
agricultural, mining, and other domestic purposes from land
not suitable for agriculture was enacted; the statute also provided that such timber lands might be purchased. But this
legislation failed to halt the rising tide of depredations.
Thieves did not buy timber or the land it grew on; they just
kept on stealing.

The Department of Justice undertook criminal prosecutions. Cases were referred to the Attorney General by the
Secretary of the Interior, and the district attorneys, who were
now under the Attorney General's control, were requested to
prosecute. By this time, big lumber companies, railroad corporations, and other commercial interests had begun strip-
ping the forests. When legal action to halt their plundering
was instituted, these interests fought back with powerful
legal resources.

A typical suit, instituted in April, 1886, accused the Sierra
Lumber Company of California of illegal harvesting of 16,-
000 trees, producing over 64 million feet of lumber valued at
$2,240,000. The government obtained a verdict in January,
1889, for $41,000, but an appeal was taken and litigation
continued until 1892, when the United States, in order to
avoid a new trial, accepted a compromise settlement of $15,-
000. The lumber company's success in avoiding a larger
judgment was due to its ability to prove inaccurate the original survey of the timber lands and to the government's difficulty in proving willful trespass.

The case of the Northern Pacific illustrates the trouble the
government had with the railroads over public lands. The
Northern Pacific was chartered by Act of Congress and given
grants of public lands ranging through two states and three
territories. The grants gave the railroad the odd-numbered
sections on each side of its line, the even-numbered sections

remaining public lands. The law permitted the railroad to cut timber from the odd sections. It provided also that the President of the United States would cause the land to be surveyed for forty miles on both sides of the entire line of the railroad—but that survey was not undertaken. The Montana Improvement Company, organized and controlled by the Northern Pacific, supplied the lumber for more than 900 miles of railroad, cutting trees indiscriminately from both the odd and even sections. When the government protested, the Company claimed that, until the land was surveyed, it could cut where it pleased. Civil and criminal suits were filed, but because of the difficulty in proving which timber had been cut legally for construction purposes and which had been cut illegally from public lands the suits were not brought to trial and eventually were dismissed.

(Other huge land grants made to the Union Pacific Railroad were the source of the Credit Mobilier affair that plagued the Administration of President Grant and Attorneys General of that era. Members of Congress and powerful financiers were linked to charges of fraud and corruption, which became an issue in the Presidential election campaign of 1872. Legal proceedings instituted by the Department of Justice concerned money, however, rather than land.)

Some forty years later, conservation of timber, coal, oil, water, and grazing lands led to a famous controversy and a national scandal. The first harrassed the Taft Administration, and the second disgraced the Administration of President Warren G. Harding.

THE BALLINGER-PINCHOT FEUD

President Grover Cleveland, acting by authority of an 1891 statute, had set aside millions of acres as forest reserve. President William McKinley followed Cleveland's policies of protecting the public domain. And conservation gained an ardent champion when Theodore Roosevelt succeeded to the Presidency.

In his first message to Congress, Roosevelt declared that forest reserves and water problems were the most vital concerns of the United States. He withdrew great tracts for the preservation of water resources, to protect sites for reservoirs, power plants, and game preserves, tracts within reclamation areas, and phosphate deposits. He also withdrew from entry some 68 million acres of coal lands in 7 states and about 8 million acres in the Territory of Alaska. In all this, he relied on the opinion of Gifford Pinchot, a professional forester and conservationist, that he had authority under existing laws to withdraw the lands from entry. Attorney General William H. Moody gave no opinion as to the legality of the President's actions.

When William Howard Taft became President, he named Richard A. Ballinger, a former commissioner of the General Land Office, as Secretary of the Interior. Ballinger's attitude toward conservation, although not antagonistic, was legalistic as opposed to the Roosevelt-Pinchot conviction of the righteousness of their acts and impatience with legal restraints. Ballinger questioned the legality of some of Roosevelt's withdrawals and restored some of the lands to entry.

When Clarence Cunningham, of Spokane, Washington, who had used names other than his own in making thirty-three entries on coal lands in Alaska, proposed to consolidate the holdings and transfer them to a Morgan-Guggenheim syndicate, a disagreement developed as to the interpretation of a 1908 statute permitting consolidation of small claims when "made in good faith." Without consulting the Attorney General, law officers of the Interior Department prepared an opinion that the statute should be liberally construed and technical objections as to good faith should not be allowed to frustrate Cunningham's plans.

Louis R. Glavis, Chief of the Field Division of the General

Land Office, investigated the Cunningham entries and disagreed with the opinion of the Interior Department's lawyers. He went to Attorney General George W. Wickersham,
who discussed the matter with Ballinger, and the documents
were submitted to the Attorney General. Wickersham ruled
that the Cunningham entries had not been made in good
faith as provided by the 1908 law, and the Land Office withdrew Glavis from the case. He took his troubles to Pinchot,
head of the Forest Service, who arranged for him to tell his
story to President Taft. On August 18, 1909, Glavis submitted to Taft a report charging that Ballinger and his subordinates were attempting to obtain for the Cunningham
interests patents on entries that were illegal. After consultation with Wickersham and other members of the Cabinet,
Taft sent Glavis a letter, drafted under the Attorney General's supervision, in which he asserted that the Glavis
charges were "only shreds of suspicion" and granted Ballinger the authority he had requested to discharge Glavis.

The President also wrote Pinchot that the discharge of
Glavis, to which Pinchot had objected, was in the interest of
"proper discipline" and urged Pinchot to use his efforts to
bring the controversy to a close. Pinchot replied with a blast
charging that the Interior Department's handling of coal
claims, Indian forests, water power, and reclamation had
been harmful to the public interest.

Congressional interest in the controversy was stirred by
the publication in *Collier's Weekly* of Glavis's side of the
story. The Senate asked Taft for the reports, statements, and
documents upon which he based his exoneration of Ballinger. Pinchot sent a letter to the Senate, to coincide with
receipt of the President's report, and, the next day, Taft
wrote Pinchot that his letter was a reflection upon the President and that it was now a matter of duty to direct Pinchot's
removal from office.

Conservationists were angered by Pinchot's dismissal.

Congress named a joint committee of both houses to investigate. After hearings, a majority of the committee, in a voluminous report, concluded that the evidence "failed to make out a case" and did not "exhibit Mr. Ballinger" as anything but a "competent and honorable gentleman, honestly and faithfully performing the duties of his high office with an eye single to the public interest." The minority said Ballinger had been "uncandid" and guilty of "duplicity" and should be asked to resign. Later, he did. Eventually, the Interior Department canceled the Cunningham entries, which had started the controversy.

TEAPOT DOME SCANDAL

In 1912, President Taft set aside two large areas of oil lands in California as reserves for naval purposes. In 1915, President Woodrow Wilson reserved another area in Wyoming. Wilson's first Attorney General, James C. McReynolds, opposed proposals to lease oil lands in the reserved areas to private interests. The Navy Department also expressed opposition, but Congress, in 1920, passed a bill authorizing the Interior Department to lease wells already drilled to claimants who had acted in good faith, and who would surrender claims to title and pay the government an amount not less than one-eighth of the oil and gas produced. Under the 1920 measure, leases on the Elk Hills and Teapot Dome reserves were granted, paving the way for a scandal that sent a Cabinet officer to prison. Albert B. Fall, a former U.S. Senator, who was Harding's Secretary of the Interior, and Edwin Denby, Secretary of the Navy, were the officials who had approved the leases. Fall was accused of accepting a $100,000 bribe from Edward L. Doheny, California oil man. He was convicted and served a prison term. Ironically, Doheny was acquitted of giving the bribe. No criminal charges were preferred against Denby, who continued in office after

Harding's death and resigned when Calvin Coolidge became President.

THE DEPARTMENT AS PROSECUTOR

The Department of Justice was on the periphery, as it were, of these conservation controversies. It was not concerned with policies, but had the responsibility of prosecuting those who plundered the nation's natural resources. The Attorney General gave opinions on legislative proposals and acts of the Chief Executive, and lawyers of the Department prosecuted Fall and Doheny, as well as other persons charged with illegal grazing on reserved lands, unlawful enclosure of lands, stealing timber, and setting fires in forests. In playing such a role, the Department was acting in the old tradition of the Office of Attorney General.

As the United States had vastly expanded its domain in the first half of the nineteenth century, acquiring millions of acres of land and adding billions to its national wealth, legal burdens had piled on the Office of Attorney General. The litigation that arose out of land cases involved persons, places, events, and policies that enliven whole chapters of American history.

Some fifty cases involving lands in the Louisiana Purchase reached the Supreme Court, and all required participation of the Attorney General in preparation and argument. Many of the claims were fraudulent. The Maison Rouge claim for thirty square leagues in upper Louisiana was based on forged certificates of survey; an Arkansas lawyer forged the name of a Spanish governor to 130 grants; claims of heirs to 400,000 acres in Mississippi were tainted with fraud. These and others were defeated in the courts.

The most famous Florida claim was filed by Fernando de la Maza Arredondo & Son, Havana merchants. They claimed a grant of 289,645 acres, embracing nearly the entire north-eastern coast of Florida, including the sites of the present cities of Jacksonville and Gainesville. They obtained the grant on a promise to establish a colony of 200 Spanish families to farm and raise cattle. A district court confirmed the grant, and the United States took the case to the Supreme Court, where General Richard Keith Call, later to be governor of Florida, Attorney General Taney, and former Attorney General Wirt represented the government. Daniel Webster and former Attorney General John M. Berrien were of counsel for the claimants. The government lawyers argued that the grant was made by an unauthorized official, that the lands were within Indian boundaries and not subject to grant, and that failure to establish the colony constituted nonfulfillment invalidating the grant. The Supreme Court rejected the government's arguments and confirmed the entire grant to the Arredondos and their assignees. Large areas already were in the hands of American speculators.

The Treaty of Guadalupe-Hidalgo gave the United States territory that included Arizona, New Mexico, California, Nevada, Utah, and Colorado west of the Rockies. Spanish and Mexican claimants filed 813 claims, covering 19,148 square miles of land. Their claims were opposed by American settlers, miners, and squatters, who poured into California after the discovery of gold—and by the U.S. Government, whose rights under the treaty were at stake. A board of land commissioners sent to California to adjudicate titles decided all of the 813 claims, finishing its duties in March, 1856, and the record in each decision was sent to the Attorney General, who was responsible for appeals to the courts.

Attorney General Caleb Cushing carried many of the California land cases to the Supreme Court. One of them involved a famous American soldier, General John C. Fremont, afterward a candidate for President of the United States. Fremont had purchased for $3,000, in 1847, a tract of land known as Las Mariposas that had been conveyed to

Juan B. Alvarado in 1844. The tract embraced ten square leagues, but its boundaries were vague. Hostile Indians had prevented Alvarado from colonizing it. Fremont was able to establish a cattle farm, but Indians continued to threaten the settlement. Cushing contended that Alvarado's grant was "a mere naked initiatory concession, upon paper" that had never been validated by survey. The Court, however, upheld Fremont's claim.

The grant to Alvarado was a "floating grant," permitting him to locate a tract of land anywhere within an area of upwards of 100 square leagues. Under the Alvarado title, Fremont claimed lands upon which gold mines had been developed. In a memorial to President Franklin Pierce, 120 settlers demanded the removal of the surveyor general of California, charging that he had surveyed the Fremont grant under the ruse of laying out township lines and had gerrymandered the tract so that the mines were within its boundaries. The Supreme Court confirmed the survey, and Fremont was able to include several mines in his "floating grant."

Altogether, Cushing had relatively small success in his appeals of California land cases, but his successor, Jeremiah Sullivan Black, was more successful.

A Frenchman named Jose Y. Limantour filed eight claims covering about 1,000 square miles of land. One included the city of San Francisco and another, islands in San Francisco Bay. Public property involved in these two claims was valued at $12 million and private property at $36 million. The Land Commission, in 1856, rejected six of Limantour's claims, but confirmed the two including San Francisco and the islands in the bay. Under investigation by Black, Limantour went to Mexico and returned with proofs purporting to support his claim. Black appointed Edwin M. Stanton, of Ohio, who was to be Lincoln's Secretary of War, a special counsel to handle the Limantour case. Stanton went to California and spent eighty-nine days on a survey of Mexican archives, scattered over the state in towns and pueblos from Sacramento to San Diego. He uncovered evidence of theft of portions of the archives, of false testimony by professional witnesses, counterfeit seals, and forged signatures. Several of Limantour's documents, it was disclosed, were on a style of paper that was not in existence at the time of the grants, and Limantour was revealed to possess eight blank titles signed by the Mexican governor. Faced with this evidence, Limantour's lawyers abandoned the case, and he fled the country.

Stanton's researches in California provided Black with evidence of fraud in other cases. He reported to President James Buchanan that the value of lands claimed under fraudulent grants was "probably not less" than $150 million. The bulk of Black's work during his tenure, which ended December 17, 1860, consisted of California land cases. In one of them he defeated the Sutter title to twenty-two leagues of land that had provoked riots among California settlers.

California land cases were before the courts for two decades, but by 1880 all but four of the 813 claims had been settled and suits for them were pending.

THE MASTER OF TITLES

In 1841, Congress made it the duty of the Attorney General to examine titles of land or sites that had been purchased or would thereafter be purchased by the United States for governmental purposes. Today, whether by condemnation or direct purchase, the federal government acquires land for a wide variety of purposes—a post office site in a prairie town, a shipyard in a coastal port, an airport for a metropolis, or a storage field for atomic missiles—and the Department of Justice represents the government in all the proceedings. The value of such accessions in recent years has averaged more than $100 million annually, and land acquisition involves nearly half the manpower of the Land and Natural Resources Division.

Acquisition requires appraisal. When the government plans a new building in Washington D.C., the Division first files a declaration of taking and then employs experts to evaluate the site upon which the building will be erected. The appraisals are used as a basis for negotiations with property owners, who almost always refuse to accept the government's first offers. Disputes are settled by compromise or by litigation; when claims for larger compensation are taken to the courts, the Justice Department is the lawyer for the government.

The Department's responsibility to protect government property is illustrated by the case of the sinking shipyard, titled *United States* v. *Anchor Oil Co. et al.* Producers pumping gas and oil from beneath the harbor of Long Beach, California, caused the subsidence of the $75 million United States Naval Shipyard at Terminal Island. In 1959, when the suit was filed, the shipyard had sunk from 2 to 22 feet below its original surface level.

The United States sued for damages. It sought also to compel the state of California, the city of Long Beach, and some 100 producers to cooperate in a repressurizing project. An agreement was finally reached, whereby the United States recovered $6 million in damages and the producers pumped vast quantities of water into the subsurface vacuum, halting the subsidence and saving the shipyard.

INDIAN CLAIMS

Protection of the rights and property of Indians and the defense of Indian tribal claims are major functions of the Land and Natural Resources Division. Many of the claims involve transactions more than 100 years old that require a prodigious amount of research by anthropologists, historians, surveyors, and lawyers, and great expenditures of time and money on investigations.

The Indian population of the United States numbers more than half a million, according to the 1960 census, and most American Indians live on reservations. Those reserves are not lands given the Indians, but areas they were allowed to keep when the United States obtained from them, by treaty and direct purchase, larger areas that were added to the public domain. The litigation of today arises because present-day Indians are not satisfied with the deals their forefathers made. Millions of acres of land and huge sums of money—in 1964 the government's liability in pending cases was estimated at $1 billion—are involved.

Timber, minerals, water for power, irrigation and reclamation purposes, fishing, grazing, and mining rights, treaty violations, and inadequate compensation for lands acquired by the United States are problems that the Indian Claims Section of the Land and Natural Resources Division must deal with. When Congress established the Indian Claims Commission, it gave the Commission jurisdiction over claims of Indian tribes arising before August 13, 1946. Claims after that date are under the jurisdiction of the Court of Claims. Decisions of the Commission or the Claims Court may be appealed to federal district and circuit courts and to the Supreme Court.

One of the difficult questions to solve relates to the value of land at the time the United States acquired it from the Indians. The government may have paid the tribe 87 cents an acre for arid lands in 1873. Half a century or more later, the tribe may claim the land was worth more at the time of acquisition. Old records must be searched, surveys made, new appraisals undertaken, and treaties studied. The Indian Claims Commission may decide that the value of the land at time of taking was $3.50 per acre and give the Indians judgment for the difference, or it may rule that the tribe got its money's worth when the deal was made. Either side may appeal, and the Justice Department may be involved for years in complex litigation.

Interpretation of treaty rights also presents difficulties. In the War of 1812, large numbers of the Creek nation sided with Great Britain. President Andrew Jackson thought that such disloyalty justified taking from the Creeks, as an indemnity, large acreages in Southern Georgia and Alabama, held by the Indians under treaty with the United States. When the Indians took their claim to the Indian Claims Commission, many years later, they said that the land should have been restored to them under the Treaty of Ghent, which ended the war. The Commission ruled, however, that the government's treaty with the Creeks in 1790 antedated the Treaty of Ghent, and President Jackson's seizure was justified.

Collectively, the Indian tribes have fared well in the matter of money judgments. Up to the end of 1965, they had been awarded more than $160 million. Where they have denied the right of the United States to take lands for reclamation, flood control, conservation, or power projects, they have been less successful. When the Seneca tribe, for instance, asserted that the government did not have the right to take lands in New York for a flood control dam on the Allegheny River, a project that would inundate Indian farms and homes, the Supreme Court held, in effect, that Indian Treaty rights could not bar projects that were in the public interest.

Since 1910, when it was first organized, the Land Division has handled thousands of cases arising out of the government's relations with Indians. In 1965, the Indian Claims Commission rendered decisions in 24 cases aggregating $56,-129,118.03, but it had 394 cases pending at the end of the year. During 1965, the Court of Claims handed down 5 opinions on appeal from the Claims Commission and had pending at the end of the year 5 cases in which it had original jurisdiction. Since the laws permit the Indians to keep on filing claims, for the Department of Justice the end of the trail is not in sight.

IX

The Internal Security Division

Internal security became an acute and controversial issue after both World War I and World War II. Fears that anarchistic elements would continue wartime activities led to drastic measures after World War I, and apprehension generated by the increase and zeal of Communists led to restrictive legislation after World War II. Strict laws were passed under which spies, saboteurs, and subversives of every rank and kind were prosecuted. Investigation and prosecution centered in the Department of Justice.

There were, of course, famous security cases in earlier days. One of the first was the Burr conspiracy, some aspects of which remain a mystery. It is still not clear whether Aaron Burr, a former vice-president of the United States, planned to wrest Louisiana from the Union, merely planned an unlawful expedition against Spanish Mexico, or intended to establish a colony in Louisiana. But Burr was tried for treason in assembling men for an attack on New Orleans, an act forbidden by the neutrality laws in effect at that time. Burr's array of counsel included Edmund Randolph, the first Attorney General. William Wirt was retained by the government to assist the district attorney in the prosecution and became the star lawyer of the trial. The Constitution says: "Treason against the United States shall consist only in levying war against them, or in adhering to their enemies, giving them aid and comfort." The government was unable to prove that Burr's actions or intentions came under this definition, and he was not convicted.

In Civil War days, charges of treason were bandied loosely about, and indictments were found in great numbers in some districts. Twenty-five indictments were returned during one term of a federal court in St. Louis. Most of the charges involved aid to the Confederate states. After the war, Jefferson Davis, president of the Confederacy, was indicted for treason and spent two years in prison and nineteen months on bail awaiting trial before President Andrew Johnson pardoned all who had participated in the Confederacy and the indictment was dismissed.

WORLD WAR I AND AFTER

Modern concepts of internal security, and what constitutes threats to it, first developed during World War I, generated by the activities of Kaiser Wilhelm's diplomats, spies, and saboteurs and by the lawless acts of native and alien anarchists. A bomb thrown during San Francisco's Preparedness Day Parade on July 22, 1916, killed ten persons and contributed to growing awareness that anarchists and revolutionaries were a menace to the government and its officials.

In April and May, 1919, bombs were sent, mostly through the mails, to prominent persons throughout the country. As mentioned in Chapter II, a man carrying a bomb ascended the front steps of the home of Attorney General A. Mitchell Palmer and was blown to bits when the missile exploded prematurely. No one else was injured, but the steps were wrecked and windows shattered in houses across the street. Palmer was increasingly urged to do something about the bombs and the threats, and the so-called Red or Palmer raids of 1919 were his response.

Federal officers swooped down on thousands of persons,

including writers, teachers, historians, even clergymen, and more than 5,000 persons were arrested. Those arrested were selected from a list of more than 60,000 names of persons allegedly identified with the radical movement or propaganda, which had been compiled by William J. Flynn, former head of the Secret Service. Palmer had installed Flynn as chief of a newly organized General Intelligence Division—a forerunner of the FBI.

The raids, and Palmer and Flynn, were roundly denounced in radical, and in some other, circles. Many bills to suppress peacetime sedition were introduced in Congress, but none passed. Since there were no applicable federal statutes, Americans arrested in the raids were turned over to state and local authorities for prosecution, and aliens to the Bureau of Immigration for deportation. Because of the shaky legal status, there were few prosecutions or deportations. Violence subsided, and so did national interest. The Presidential campaign of 1920 was concerned with what Harding called a "return to normalcy," and, when Harlan Fiske Stone was appointed Attorney General, he directed all investigators or agents of the Justice Department to confine their activities strictly to matters under existing federal law. Stone established the FBI, and federal laws still define its jurisdiction.

WORLD WAR II AND AFTER

The Communist Party, after World War II, came to be regarded as the foremost domestic threat to national security. The government's statutory weapons for dealing with the menace were the Smith Act of 1940, which provided punishment for conspiracy to teach and advocate overthrow of the government by force and violence and made membership in an organization that so advocated a crime; the Labor-Management Relations Act of 1947 (Taft-Hartley), which required that officers of labor unions desiring the services of the National Labor Relations Board execute non-Communist affidavits; and the Internal Security Act of 1950, which required all "Communist-action," "Communist-dominated," and "Communist-infiltrated" groups to register with the Attorney General. The Communist Control Act of 1954 and the Labor-Management Reporting and Disclosure Act of 1959 modified some of the provisions of those other laws, but did not alter their main objectives. Enforcement of those laws imposed heavy legal burdens upon the Justice Department's Internal Security Division.

INTERNAL SECURITY DIVISION CREATED

The Internal Security Division was established July 9, 1954, in an order issued by Attorney General Herbert Brownell, Jr., in compliance with a provision of the Communist Control Act. The order directed that the Division be headed by an assistant attorney general and "have charge of matters affecting the internal security of the United States." The Division took over all the functions of the Department relating to internal security other than those assigned to the FBI and the Immigration and Naturalization Service. Its first head was William F. Tompkins, who had been a U.S. attorney in New Jersey.

"Matters affecting the internal security of the United States" means more than just such subversive activities as treason, sabotage, espionage, sedition, or stealing government secrets. There are nearly 100 laws that the Division enforces, and under them persons may be prosecuted for interfering with homing pigeons belonging to the United States, importing paper lanterns from Communist China, enticing workmen from an arsenal, enticing desertion and harboring deserters, exporting arms, liquors, and narcotics to Pacific Islands, misuse of passports, and literally scores of other major and minor offenses.

The assistant attorney general is aided in the enforcement of laws under his jurisdiction by a first assistant; an executive assistant; a confidential assistant; chiefs in charge of Administrative, Appeals and Research, Registration, Criminal, and Civil sections; and a departmental security officer. Investigations are conducted by the FBI, and U.S. attorneys and their staffs in the judicial districts throughout the country present cases to grand juries, obtain indictments, and conduct trials in the district courts.

The Division was established and several of the laws it administers were passed during the period loosely described as the McCarthy Era. Senator Joseph McCarthy of Wisconsin was trumpeting charges that the Armed Services, the State Department, and other government departments and agencies were nests of traitors, Communist spies, and fellow-travelers. J. Edgar Hoover, Director of the FBI, was convinced—and still is—that the American Communist Party was dominated by Moscow and was a major threat to the security of the United States and its form of government. There were no "Palmer raids," but Hoover's investigators and Congressional committees unearthed enough evidence of disloyalty, subversion, and espionage to keep the newborn Division busy around the clock. (See Chapter XIII.)

So-Called Communist Cases

Even before the Internal Security Division was set up, the Justice Department dealt with so-called Communist cases that involved federal officials and employees and some nongovernment public figures. One of the latter was Charlie Chaplin, the film comedian. Chaplin had been accused of leftist beliefs and association with Communist organizations. When he went abroad, Chaplin, a British subject, held a re-entry permit, but Attorney General James P. McGranery ruled that if he sought re-entry a hearing would be held to determine if he was eligible. Under the immigration laws, aliens with Communist associations may be excluded from the United States. Rather than face a hearing, Chaplin surrendered his re-entry permit in 1953 and has resided abroad ever since.

Soviet agents were active in recruiting Americans to spy for them and one agent reached into the Justice Department itself to induce an employee to work for him. Judith Coplon, employed in the Department's Foreign Agents Registration Section, was arrested in New York on March 4, 1949, in the company of Valentine A. Gubitchev, a Soviet citizen employed at the United Nations. The FBI charged that Miss Coplon had in her purse, for delivery to Gubitchev, summaries of confidential reports to which she had access. She was tried for espionage, convicted, and sentenced to ten years in prison. She and Gubitchev were convicted of conspiracy to commit espionage and sentenced to fifteen years each. Gubitchev's sentence was suspended on condition that he leave the United States and never return. Miss Coplon won a reversal because some of the evidence against her was obtained by eavesdropping on conversations with her attorney. The government felt that court rulings with relation to evidence weakened its case and retrial. Recently, the government announced that it had dropped her case.

A famous case involving another government employee grew out of information given by Whittaker Chambers, a journalist and confessed Soviet agent. Chambers told a congressional committee that for several years his source of clandestine information was Alger Hiss, a State Department official. Hiss had been an adviser of President Roosevelt at the Yalta Conference and Secretary-General of the San Francisco conference at which the United Nations was organized.

Hiss denied he had given classified information to Chambers and swore that he had never seen Chambers during the period Chambers testified Hiss had divulged secrets to him, which he passed on to the Russians. Hiss was not arrested or tried for espionage, but a grand jury believed he had given false testimony and indicted him for perjury. He was convicted and sentenced to five years in prison.

The source of much of the information involving government employees with Soviet agents was Elizabeth T. Bentley, who had collaborated with the Communists during World War II. Miss Bentley gave a Senate judiciary subcommittee the names of a number of government employees, some in key positions, whom she said were members of or were aiding Soviet spy networks. Justice Department investigations and prosecutions that followed her disclosures sent several persons to prison for contempt in refusing to answer questions of investigative bodies or giving perjured testimony. None of the convictions was for espionage, as such.

Employee loyalty was of great concern to the government after World War II, and procedures were devised for ridding the federal service of those who were suspect and preventing employment of persons of doubtful devotion to the precepts and practices of the United States. Security apparatus was set up in government departments and agencies that functioned, in effect, as trial courts for those whose loyalty was questioned. In an effort to ensure impartiality in judgment, President Truman established, in 1947, a Loyalty Review Board to which employees discharged for loyalty reasons could appeal. In his State of the Union Message on February 4, 1953, President Eisenhower, declaring that it was the responsibility of the Executive Department to cleanse the federal payroll of the "disloyal and dangerous," disclosed that the loyalty program, which had been widely criticized, would be revised. An executive order, prepared in the Justice Department, abolished the Loyalty Review Board and made the heads of departments and agencies responsible for purging security risks and preventing infiltration by disloyal or dangerous applicants.

Membership in or affiliation or sympathetic association with totalitarian, Fascist, Communist, or subversive groups was cause for dismissal from government service or rejection of an application for employment. The Justice Department compiled a roster, known as the Attorney General's list, of organizations it classified in those categories and supplied it to all officials concerned with the hiring or firing of federal personnel. At one time, nearly 300 groups were on the list, ranging from the National Lawyers' Guild to the International Workers' Order, which the Department described as the chief fund raiser for the Communist Party.

The Internal Security Act of 1950, known as the McCarran Act, required Communist and Communist-front organizations to register with the Attorney General. That Act also established the Subversive Activities Control Board and charged it with determining whether an organization, when cited by the Attorney General, was subject to the requirements of the law. If the Board found that a group was in the prescribed category, it issued an order directing registration.

COMMUNIST PARTY CITED

On April 20, 1953, the SACB ordered the Communist Party of the United States to register as a Communist-action organization "nurtured by the Soviet Union," seeking to overthrow the government of the United States and establish a dictatorship of the proletariat. The order was the outcome of hearings that began in April, 1951, at the request of J. Howard McGrath, then the Attorney General, after the Communists had refused to register voluntarily in conformance with the McCarran Act.

The Communists fought the Justice Department every step of the way during the two years the hearings were in progress. After the order was issued, the Communist Party fought in the courts. And it did not register. The Supreme Court affirmed the SACB's order on June 5, 1961, eight years after it was issued. The Party was indicted on December 1, 1961, for failure to register, was convicted on December 17, 1962, and fined $120,000.

The Court of Appeals for the District of Columbia reversed that conviction on the ground that officers of the Party who should have signed the registration forms could avail themselves of the First Amendment's privilege against self-incrimination. The Supreme Court denied the government an appeal from that ruling. The Justice Department then obtained, on February 25, 1955, a second indictment alleging that a member of the Party was available and willing to sign the registration forms and the Party knew it. A jury in federal district court convicted the Party on twenty-three counts of the indictment, and Judge William B. Jones imposed a fine of $10,000 on each count—a total of $230,000. On March 3, 1967, the District of Columbia Court of Appeals reversed that judgment. The Justice Department did not take an appeal to the Supreme Court, and later dismissed the indictment. Thus, after fourteen years, the Party had won its fight to escape registration.

The McCarran Act also provided for registration of individual members of the Party, and the SACB issued registration orders. The Supreme Court invalidated those orders on the ground that the provision was unenforceable in view of the Fifth Amendment privilege against self-incrimination. Although the Supreme Court upheld the constitutionality of the McCarran Act, it consistently found defects in registration cases. The Justice Department's record of success in cases it has prosecuted under that Act is not imposing.

The Internal Security Division's responsibilities under other laws, however, keep its lawyers busy. In February, 1958, for instance, a federal grand jury in New York indicted Carlos Prios Socarras, a former president of Cuba, and eight others, charging them with conspiracy to organize military expeditions against the Republic of Cuba in violation of U.S. neutrality laws. In the same month, the Universal Leaf Tobacco Company, of Richmond, Va., was indicted for violations of the Trading With the Enemy Act.

Under the Labor-Management Relations Act, James E. West and others were indicted in January, 1958, for conspiracy to file false statements with the National Labor Relations Board. This was the first case in which labor union officials and functionaries were convicted for conspiracy to violate the false statements statute.

PASSPORT CASES

In June, 1958, the Supreme Court ruled against the government in a case involving the right of the Secretary of State to deny passports to persons who refused to answer questions as to Communist Party membership. The key decision was in the case of the artist, Rockwell Kent, to whom Secretary of State John Foster Dulles had refused to issue a passport. When the Supreme Court held that Congress had not delegated authority to the Secretary of State to withhold passports on those grounds, similar cases against Corliss Lamont, wealthy supporter of left-wing causes, the singer Paul Robeson, and Anna Louise Strong, an American journalist who had embraced Communism and now lives in China, were dismissed.

In the latter part of 1959, however, the Internal Security Division was successful in two cases involving the right of the Secretary of State to refuse to issue passports validated for travel to China. One involved William Worthy, a writer, whose passport had been revoked after he traveled to Communist China and Hungary despite specific restrictions on travel to those countries. Worthy asked renewal of his passport, but refused to promise not to go to the Chinese mainland. Renewal was denied. In the other case, a member of

Congress, Representative Charles Porter of Oregon. sued to compel the Secretary of State to validate his passport for travel to China. Each of these cases was taken to the Supreme Court, which affirmed the decisions of the Secretary.

Those rulings, however, applied only to specific cases of travel to a designated Communist country. In 1962, the Supreme Court, in a much broader decision, held that the right to travel was a constitutional right. The Court invalidated as unconstitutional the section of the Internal Security Act that made it unlawful for a member of a Communist-action organization to apply for a passport or use or attempt to use a passport. Under that section, the Secretary of State had revoked the passports of Elizabeth Gurley Flynn, then national chairman of the Communist Party, and Herbert Aptheker, then editor of *Political Affairs,* the Party's theoretical journal. The government's position was that the Internal Security Act's restrictions on the issuance and use of passports were a legitimate exercise of congressional authority to regulate the travel of Communists and revocation was justified when the Secretary of State determined that such travel was inimical and dangerous to the security of the United States. The Court, however, held that that section of the Act, as written, violated constitutional rights.

ATOMIC TRESPASSER PUNISHED

In 1958, the government was preparing an atomic test in the Pacific and restricted entrance to the area. Earle L. Reynolds sailed his forty-foot ketch into the Eniwetok Nuclear Testing Ground without authorization from the Atomic Energy Commission or the Department of Defense. When he refused to leave, he was arrested by the Coast Guard and taken to Hawaii, where he was convicted in a federal court and sentenced to two years in prison, with a proviso that after serving six months the balance of the sentence would be suspended, and he would be placed on probation for five years.

Protecting military posts and installations from security risks provided the Division with several cases. One that was regarded as important because of its possible application to civilian employees at posts abroad was decided in the governments favor in 1961. The superintendent of the Naval Gun Factory in Washington required Rachel Brawner, a cook in the cafeteria, to surrender her identification badge, thus revoking her security clearance. The Supreme Court upheld lower court judgments that the superintendent, in the exercise of his command responsibility, had authority to withdraw summarily the identification badge of an employee who failed to meet security requirements of the installation.

In an effort to prevent use of the mails for dissemination of propaganda, Congress passed a law authorizing the Postmaster General to withhold delivery of "Communist political propaganda" originating from a foreign country unless he received a request from the addressee to deliver the mail. In June, 1964, Corliss Lamont, doing business as "Basic Pamphlets," sued to test the constitutionality of the statute. On May 24, 1965, the Supreme Court held that the requirement that an addressee affirmatively state that he desired to receive the propaganda was an unconstitutional inhibition upon rights associated with freedom of speech.

At all times, the Internal Security Division has pending trials or appeals in cases arising out of asserted violations of the Neutrality Act, the Smith Act, the Taft-Hartley law, the Subversive Activities Control Act, the Foreign Agents Registration Act, and related statutes. Each year adds new cases to its work load. The Division bears the legal brunt of the government's battles to protect American citizens and institutions from the corruptive activities of enemies, foreign and domestic.

But spies are the enemies upon which the Division and the

FBI have declared unremitting warfare. Espionage cases attract more public interest than those in any other category. Some deal with sensitive international relations. Most arise out of the activities of agents of Soviet Russia.

THE CASE OF THE ROSENBERGS

The case of Julius and Ethel Rosenberg, the first persons to be executed under American laws for peacetime espionage, was a *cause célèbre*, bitterly fought in the courts and ended in a day of legal drama.

The Rosenbergs were indicted under the Espionage Act of 1917 as members of a spy ring that had passed atomic secrets to the Russians. They were tried and convicted before Judge Irving R. Kaufman in the U.S. District Court for the Southern District of New York. Judge Kaufman imposed the death sentence, permissible by the Act. Their execution was fixed for 11 P.M., June 19, 1953.

On the last day of its regular term, the Supreme Court refused to set aside Judge Kaufman's sentence. Attorneys for the Rosenbergs appealed to Associate Justice William O. Douglas for a recess stay of execution, and Justice Douglas granted the stay on June 16. Attorney General Brownell moved swiftly to ask Chief Justice Fred M. Vinson to convene a special session and set aside Justice Douglas's order. Justice Vinson reconvened the Court, on June 19, in one of the briefest and most dramatic sessions in its history.

Two legal points were at issue. One was the authority of Justice Douglas to grant the stay. That was disposed of by upholding the power of any justice to stay any proceeding when he believed his action warranted by circumstances. The second was whether the Espionage Act of 1917 was superceded by the Atomic Energy Act of 1946. The 1917 law permitted a judge to impose the death penalty; the 1946 statute provided that a death sentence be prescribed by a jury.

The Rosenberg's lawyers argued fervently that their clients had been improperly indicted under the 1917 act and that their conviction and sentence were illegal; the government contended with equal earnestness that the Atomic Energy Act did not nullify the Espionage Act as applied to the Rosenberg case. A solemn court listened to the arguments and retired to its conference room. The conference was brief and the justices returned to the bench. The Chief Justice announced that the Atomic Energy Act did not limit or repeal the provisions of the Espionage Act. The legal issues were settled; the sentences were upheld; the Rosenbergs must die.

Emanuel Bloch, chief attorney for the Rosenbergs, hastened from the courtroom to the White House, seeking to appeal to President Eisenhower for last-minute clemency. The President had previously denied a reprieve and did not receive Bloch. As the evening shadows lengthened across the White House lawn, Bloch departed, and just before sunset on June 19, the Rosenbergs died at Sing Sing in the electric chair.

Julius and Ethel Rosenberg were part of an atomic spy apparatus of which Klaus Fuchs, a German atomic scientist who became a British subject, was a key member. Fuchs worked on atomic projects in this country. After his return to England, information supplied British security officials by the FBI led to his arrest and conviction. Testimony at the trial pointed to associates in the United States. As a result, Harry Gold, David Greenglass (a brother of Mrs. Rosenberg), Morton Sobell, William Perl, and Alfred Dean were arrested, convicted, and given long prison sentences.

SOVIET DIPLOMATS AND AMERICAN SPIES

Almost all of the arrests for espionage involved in some way employees of the Soviet Embassy, the Soviet delegation to the United Nations, or other U.S.S.R. diplomatic agencies, who had induced Americans to supply them with secret information. In one case, the former head of the Russian Secret Police was named as a co-conspirator, although he was not assigned to an official post in the United States. In many cases, the Russians had diplomatic immunity and could not be tried, but were invariably declared *persona non grata* and ordered to leave the country. Their dupes bore the punishment. Among Americans imprisoned for spying for Russia were a New York psychiatrist, four former U.S. soldiers, a Navy man, an engineer whose work gave him access to "top secret" information relating to the communications system of the Strategic Air Command, and a former Second Secretary of the United States Embassy in Warsaw, Poland. There were many others as the Russians induced Americans of high and low estate to betray their country.

The prize case was that of Rudolph Ivanovitch Abel, a Russian who did not have diplomatic immunity. Abel was a colonel in the Soviet State Security System and a skillful operator, but he was trapped because he carelessly gave a newsboy a hollow nickel.

By whom the nickel's hollowness was detected is not of record, nor is it important. The fact that it was opened and found to contain what appeared to be a code message brought about Abel's downfall. The FBI spent almost four years trying to decode the cipher and find its source. Success came after Reino Hayhanem, a lieutenant colonel of the Soviet secret service, when he was ordered back to Moscow and feared reprisals for failures in his espionage assignments, asked for asylum. Using leads supplied by Hayhanem, the FBI followed trails that led to a studio in Brooklyn, near where the newsboy got the nickel. FBI agents described the studio as a "virtual museum of modern espionage equipment, such as short wave radios, cipher pads, cameras and film for producing microdots, a hollow shaving brush, cuff links, and other 'trick' containers." Abel was arrested as he entered the studio, tried in New York in October, 1957, convicted, and sentenced to thirty years in prison.

The Russian spy was serving that sentence in the Atlanta Penitentiary when, on February 10, 1962, he was exchanged for the American U-2 pilot Francis Gary Powers, who was in a Russian prison for spying on Russia from the sky.

X

The Immigration And Naturalization Service

Three centuries ago, British emigrants sailed to Jamestown and Plymouth, the Dutch settled New Amsterdam, a group of Swedes located at Fort Christina, Delaware, and Spaniards established colonies in Florida and the Southwest. They were the vanguard of a migration of peoples of all races, cultures, and creeds from all countries. They and their descendants made the United States a "nation of immigrants," with the most ethnically diverse population any country has known.

Each colony set up its own standards for the selection of immigrants. Policies varied. Persons unwelcome in one colony usually were acceptable to another. Immigration was uncontrolled and generally encouraged because of the need for labor as pioneers cleared the land and set up factories that were the forerunners of the era of industrialization. Colonial housewives welcomed immigrant maids, and masters of ships could always use a skillful sailor. The migrants, however, were by no means all menials; aristocrats and planters, merchants, teachers, physicians, lawyers, many preachers, and many who became the politicians of the period were among them.

There were doubts as to the wisdom of unrestricted immigration in colonial days and the early years of the Republic.

169

Benjamin Franklin noted the large number of Germans in Pennsylvania and wondered if interpreters might not be needed in the State Assembly. Thomas Jefferson, the ardent democrat, feared that too large an influx of aliens from monarchical governments might hamper the growth of democracy. George Washington took a cautious view of unrestricted immigration, and John Quincy Adams, Secretary of State in 1819, said that the government had never officially encouraged emigration from Europe and warned immigrants that they were not to expect favors. For almost a hundred years, national policy favored unrestricted immigration, however, and there were no federal laws governing the admission of aliens.

The first restrictive enactment was the Alien Act of 1798, adopted as part of the Alien and Sedition Laws, and it was very limited in its application, merely empowering the President to order the departure of any alien he deemed dangerous to the United States. Even this mild measure proved unpopular, and at the expiration of its two-year term it was not renewed.

TEN MILLION FROM EUROPE

Passage to America, for the immigrant in the early days, meant a hard trip in a crowded sailing ship that sometimes required three or four months to tack its way across the Atlantic. Supplies of food and water ran low, sanitary facilities were poor, cholera, typhus, smallpox, and other diseases took their toll, and angry seas increased danger and discomfort. When steamships entered the travel picture in the middle and late 1800's, they brought a new era in immigration. Accommodations were improved, and crossing time reduced to about two weeks. Agents of steamship lines solicited prospective emigrant passengers in Europe, land speculators and industrial interests urged emigrants to come, and immigrants already here provided money to bring relatives and friends to this country. Between 1820 and 1880, 10 million immigrants entered the United States. Most of them were from Northern and Western Europe.

The mounting flow alarmed many. American workmen feared the impact of cheap foreign labor upon rising wage scales. State and municipal governments became concerned over the cost of caring for immigrants who became public charges. Various states passed immigration laws, but the Supreme Court voided them as unconstitutional attempts to regulate foreign commerce. With their own restrictive laws nullified, some states became insistent that federal regulations be instituted.

The first fruit of that insistence was passage of the Act of March 3, 1875, which prohibited the admission of convicts and prostitutes. It was followed by passage of the first general immigration statute, which imposed a head tax of 50 cents upon immigrants and barred the admission of idiots, lunatics, and persons likely to become public charges.

CHINESE IMMIGRATION

Few Chinese immigrants came to the United States before 1850, but between 1850 and 1882 approximately 200,000 entered—mostly through West Coast ports. They provided a reservoir of cheap labor in mining and railroad construction camps, agriculture, domestic service and small business. Their competition aroused the hostility of white laborers, some of whom were immigrants themselves, and stirred animosities toward all Orientals—of which vestiges are still traceable in the attitudes of some West Coast citizens.

A treaty with China, adopted in 1880, permitted suspension of immigration of Chinese laborers, but did not allay pressure for more restrictive legislation. In 1882, Congress passed the Chinese Exclusion Act, which remained on the statute books until it was repealed on December 17, 1943. The exclusion act made entry of any Chinese illegal, but it did not stop ingenious Chinese from coming in. Smuggling across Canadian and Mexican borders and through seaports became a profitable business and plagued immigration authorities for more than half a century.

The first contract labor law, aimed at ending the practice of some employers of importing blocs of workmen, was passed in 1885, largely in response to pressure from representatives of the growing American labor movement to eliminate a depressant factor from the labor market. A supplemental law, enacted in 1888, authorized deportation of alien contract laborers within one year after entry.

FEDERAL CONTROL ESTABLISHED

Bartholdi's Statue of Liberty, bearing on its pedestal the inscription from Emma Lazarus's sonnet inviting the Old World to "give me your tired, your poor, your huddled masses," was dedicated on October 28, 1886. The United States still beckoned immigrants, despite a few minor exclusionary laws, but immigration was not subject to any organized federal control. Five years later, however, President Benjamin Harrison signed the Act of March 3, 1891, that established federal control over immigration and designated the first official to administer it. That was the seed from which sprouted the Immigration and Naturalization Service, today an important unit of the Department of Justice.

The 1891 measure provided for a superintendent of Immigration at a salary of $4,000 per year. He was not an official of the Justice Department, but was under the direction of the Secretary of the Treasury. The first superintendent was W. D. Owen. He was charged with supervising the inspection of arriving immigrants and with the housing and care of aliens detained at stations such as Castle Garden and, later,

Ellis Island. The law provided for medical inspection and added to excludable classes persons suffering from a "loathsome" or contagious disease, those previously convicted of a criminal offense involving moral turpitude, paupers, and polygamists. The statute also authorized deportation of immigrants who entered unlawfully. Decisions of inspecting officers were final, but adverse rulings could be appealed to the superintendent, whose decisions were subject to review by the Secretary of the Treasury. By the Act of March 3, 1893, Congress established boards of special inquiry and required shipping companies to supply passenger lists of vessel entering United States ports. Those lists provided the first material from which immigration statistics were compiled.

In 1895, Congress gave the agency and its head new titles. The Bureau of Immigration was created and the title of superintendent changed to commissioner general of Immigration. Commissioners of Immigration, to be appointed by the President for terms of four years, were established at several major ports of entry. The commissioner general was given an expanded staff. The Bureau remained a unit of the Treasury Department.

By 1900, administration of the Chinese exclusion law and the contract labor law were major problems of the Bureau of Immigration. Since both laws were primarily in the field of labor, Congress in 1903 transferred all the functions of the Bureau to the newly created Department of Commerce and Labor, in a general immigration law that added to excludable classes epileptics, professional beggars, and anarchists. The ban on anarchists was an aftermath of the murder of President William McKinley in 1902.

DEMANDS FOR MORE LEGISLATION

Restrictive laws and federal control did not slow the pace of immigration; rather, it increased phenomenally in the early years of the twentieth century. In 1905 alone, 1,026,000 immigrants were admitted to the United States. The addition of such hordes to the labor market increased demands for more restrictive legislation, and a commission was appointed in 1907 to study the problem.

The commission submitted a 42-volume report in 1911, but it was not until 1917 that legislation based upon it was enacted. A law passed on February 5, 1917, codified all previous exclusions and added two; a literacy requirement and an automatic exclusion of persons coming from a designated geographical zone, comprising most of Asia and the Pacific Islands. President Woodrow Wilson vetoed the Act because of the literacy provision, but Congress passed it over the veto. The Act defined the powers of immigration officers and gave discretionary authority to the Secretary of Labor to admit certain excluded groups for meritorious reasons. Aliens who entered in violation of the law, and those who committed certain serious offenses within the United States, were made deportable.

LIMITATIONS ON NUMBERS

Until after World War I, all restrictive laws related only to the quality or character of the immigrant. No limitations were placed upon the number of immigrants. The principle of numerical limitation was introduced by the Quota Act of 1921, a temporary measure, which permitted the entry annually of 3 per cent of the number of persons of each nationality in the United States in 1910. In 1924, Congress enacted a permanent quota law, which limited the number of immigrants to approximately 150,000 each year, basing the annual quota for each nationality group on the number of persons of their national origin in the United States in 1920. This national origins system of choosing among prospective immigrants remained in the law for more than forty years.

The 1924 Act, however, provided for the admission of certain nonquota immigrants, chiefly persons born in the Western Hemisphere countries of Canada, Mexico, Costa Rica, El Salvador, Guatemala, Honduras, Nicaragua, Panama, Cuba, the Dominican Republic, Haiti, Argentina, Bolivia, Brazil, Chile, Colombia, Ecuador, Paraguay, and Venezuela. Immigration visas were required for the first time under the 1924 Act.

The quota system was the product of concern lest an uncontrolled flood of immigration from war-ravaged countries of Europe descend upon the United States. Whether the fears were justified or not, the record shows that the system was effective in measurably reducing the movement of aliens into the country. Whereas some 350.000 were admitted in 1921, only 153,000 came in 1929—a manageable number under then existing economic conditions. From 1925 to 1929, nonquota immigrants averaged more than 125,000 a year. The principal source of Western Hemisphere immigration in those years was Canada, with a yearly average of more than 75,000.

A sharp decline in immigration took place during the Depression. Authorities strictly enforced the provision excluding persons likely to become public charges, and visas were issued only to applicants who had adequate financial resources. The Canadian average dropped to 13,000 yearly during the 1930's. In the years 1932–35, more people left the United States than came into the country to live.

With economic recovery, immigration resumed an upward trend. But World War II checked the climb. The total for 1939, the year the war in Europe began, was 82,998. It dropped to 70,756 in 1940, and during the entire period 1941–45 only 170,952 immigrants entered the United States, the low number being 23,725 in 1943—the smallest total since 1831. Immigration increased rapidly again after the war, and almost 4 million entered during 1946–62. More than 1 million were from the United Kingdom, Germany, and Italy, while almost 900,000 came from Canada and Mexico. Postwar immigration reached its peak in 1957, with 326,-867 entries.

"WAR BRIDES ACT"

Refugees and "war brides" contributed heavily to the migrant inflow after the war. In 1945, Congress passed the "War Brides" Act which waived some of the excluding provisions of the 1924 law and between July, 1946, and June 30, 1950, approximately 120 alien wives and husbands of United States Armed Forces personnel and their children entered the country. Most of the war brides came from Northern Ireland, Germany, Italy, Canada, Australia, and New Zealand. Some 50 per cent were from English-speaking peoples.

DISPLACED PERSONS

Between 1946 and 1962, more than 400,000 displaced persons were admitted under conditions specified by acts of Congress. Three-fourths of them were from Poland, Germany, Latvia, the Soviet Union, and Yugoslavia. In July, 1960, Congress passed a law, which is still in effect, authorizing the Attorney General to parole into the United States certain refugees who fled Communist countries and could not return for fear of persecution because of race, religion, or political beliefs. It was under this law that more than 125,-000 Cubans were admitted after the fall of the Batista regime and, by authorization of President John F. Kennedy, several thousand Chinese from Hong Kong who had escaped from Communist tyranny on the China mainland.

The experience gained in handling the early Cuban refugees, those from the Hungarian revolt in 1956, and the Hong Kong parolees in 1962, guided the immigration authorities in dealing with the thousands who fled from Castro's Cuba to sanctuary in Florida and elsewhere in the United States. From January 1, 1959, when Castro seized power, until the end of the 1965 fiscal year, some 227,000 Cubans were admitted in temporary status and 56,526 entered as immigrants.

How Citizens Are Made

Until a federal government was formed after the Revolutionary War, inhabitants of the American colonies were British subjects. With independence, they became citizens of the United States. Immigrants, however, were not citizens, and procedures had to be devised for their naturalization. The first Congress passed a naturalization law in 1790, entrusting the function to the courts and leaving it to the courts to prescribe their own rules. Each court made its own decision about whether a petitioner met the requirements as to residence, good character, education, and attachment to the principles of the Constitution. Each court designed its own naturalization certificate. Some were ornate with flags, eagles, scrolls, and other decorations; others so simple and cheap they could be copied easily in any print shop.

The Naturalization Act of 1906 established the first central federal agency to supervise naturalization of aliens and keep records. It created the Bureau of Immigration and Naturalization, to be headed by a commissioner general of Immigration and Naturalization, under the general supervision of the Secretary of Commerce and Labor. The courts retained power to grant or deny citizenship, but the Act formulated fundamental safeguards that are still in effect.

Under the 1906 Act, duplicates of every naturalization paper were filed with the central agency, uniform fees were fixed and clerks of court were required to account for fees, naturalization forms were prescribed, and each petitioner who arrived in the United States after June 29, 1906, was required to obtain and attach to his petition an official certificate of his lawful arrival. The applicant was required to sign his petition in his own handwriting and to speak the English language. Procedure was prescribed for cancellation of naturalization fraudulently or illegally procured.

Most naturalization laws were codified in the Nationality Act of 1940, and a later codification was made in the Immigration and Nationality Act, which became effective on December 24, 1952, and is now the basic statute. The 1952 Act removed all racial barriers to naturalization, established uniform procedures for naturalization of spouses of American citizens, changed the requirements for acquisition of citizenship by a child born to one alien and one citizen parent, modified the grounds for expatriation of citizens, and added new grounds for revocation of citizenship. "Illegal procurement" of naturalization as grounds for cancellation was removed by the 1952 Act, but was restored in 1961 by Public Law 87–301, which amended the 1952 statute by providing for the expatriation of persons convicted of offenses under sections of the U.S. Code relating to rebellion or insurrection, seditious conspiracy, or advocating overthrow of the government.

Instruction for Immigrants

Very soon after the 1906 Act established educational requirements for naturalization, officials recognized that citizenship education was an integral part of the naturalization process. If the "huddled masses" that came by millions were to be assimilated it was essential that they learn at least the rudiments of the language and the basic precepts of American constitutional democracy. Although the 1906 Act did not delineate the permissible nature or extent of federal activity relating to the education of the foreign-born, the first step toward federal sponsorship of courses in citizenship was taken in 1909.

The Bureau of Immigration and Naturalization proposed the establishment of classes in public schools to instruct immigrants in the use of the English language and concepts of citizenship rights and responsibilities. That was the beginning of a system of cooperation wherein federal naturalization officials provide the guidelines and materials and public schools the teachers to instruct aliens in the educational requirements and obligations their attainment of citizenship entails. No federal agency has ever been authorized to engage in the teaching function, but the cooperation of states and local communities has enabled millions of aliens to meet the requirements of the naturalization laws. In 1966, citizenship classes were held in forty states, serviced by extension divisions of state universities or state educational authorities. The *Federal Textbook On Citizenship,* published by the federal government and distributed free to all aliens desiring to become citizens, provided the principal study material.

THE MOVE TO THE JUSTICE DEPARTMENT

The 1906 measure created an anomalous situation, putting the administrative unit of the immigration service in Washington under the Department of Commerce and Labor, and the field force under the Department of Justice. The anomaly was removed in 1909 by transferring the field force to the Department of Commerce and Labor, leaving the Justice Department without functions in the immigration field.

Then, in 1913, immigration and naturalization were divorced. They became separate bureaus in the newly created Department of Labor, just separated from the old Department of Commerce and Labor. The bureaus operated separately for twenty years, until June 10, 1933, when they were reunited by Executive Order 6166 under the name of the Immigration and Naturalization Service, headed by a commissioner of Immigration and Naturalization. The Service remained in the Department of Labor.

Pursuant to the provisions of the Reorganization Act of April 3, 1939, a product of the Hoover Commission, President Franklin D. Roosevelt proposed to Congress the transfer of the Service from the Labor Department to the Department of Justice. The plan was approved, and the transfer became effective June 14, 1940. Since that date, the Service has functioned under the direction of the Attorney General. He is charged with the administration and enforcement of all laws relating to the immigration and naturalization of aliens, except insofar as such laws relate to the powers and functions of the President, the Secretary of State, and officers of the State Department. The Attorney General's rulings on questions of law, however, are controlling.

The Reorganization Act authorized the Attorney General to delegate authority and duties as he desires. Succeeding Attorneys General have promulgated regulations delegating much operating and administrative authority to the commissioner of Immigration and Naturalization. The commissioner is aided in the performance of his duties by an executive assistant, an associate commissioner for Management, an associate commissioner for Operations, and a general counsel. The Service has 4 regional offices, 32 district offices, and more than 300 field officers located throughout the United States, principally at ports of entry along land and sea borders. The Service has approximately 6,750 employees, of which more than 4,000 are classified as officers and the remainder as clerical. The officers include some 1,400 border patrolmen, 1,250 immigrant inspectors, 750 investigators, and 160 naturalization examiners.

REGISTRATION AND FINGERPRINTING

A wartime measure, enacted in 1940, was the Alien Registration Act, which required registration and fingerprinting of all aliens who were in the United States and all those who sought to enter thereafter. The merit of the law was the means it gave the immigration authorities to (1) count noses of the alien population, (2) check up on illegal entries, and (3) track down criminals and undesirables who gained admission despite exclusionist provisicns of the statutes. The Internal Security Act of 1950 required aliens in the United States to report their addresses annually to the Immigration and Naturalization Service. Under that Act, 2.5 million address reports were filed in 1951; in 1966, nearly 3.5 million reported. Failure to report an address subjects the alien to legal sanctions.

Checking aliens and inspecting them as they arrive at seaports or airports is relatively easy. Inspectors in many ports board ships and complete their examinations before the vessel docks. At airports, aliens are channeled into separate rooms, where immigration and public health officials check their visas and their health. Every alien seeking admission must first obtain a visa from a U.S. consulate abroad, which means that their eligibility for entry has been passed upon preliminary to arrival. Domestic officials may refuse admission despite the visas if their examination discloses exclusionary evidence not revealed to the consular official, or perhaps ignored by him. A consular visa is not a mandatory ticket of admission.

THE "WETBACKS"

The Service is responsible for patrolling more than 5,000 miles of Canadian and Mexican border, as well as the coastlines of the United States—a difficult task. Long stretches of border between ports of entry tempt unauthorized immigrants to cross with minimum fears cf detection. Once they are in the country, the problem of finding and deporting them becomes formidable. A primary cause of the problem was the postwar need for agricultural laborers in California, Texas, New Mexico, and Arizona. Thousands of Mexicans came each year to cultivate and harvest seasonal crops of fruit, vegetables, and other products. Most of them entered legally under laws authorizing temporary admission of farm labor, but hordes swam or waded the Rio Grande at shallow crossings or sneaked through gullies and ravines on moonless nights. In the vernacular of the border, they were known as "wetbacks." What caused immigration officers the most trouble was that they did not go back to Mexico. Even some of those legally admitted remained after their permits had expired.

In 1954, Border Patrol officers were apprehending some 3,000 illegal entrants a day, but hundreds were getting through. Commissioner Joseph M. Swing organized a task force to tighten controls and round up those in the country illegally. Known as "Operation Wetback," this special force apprehended more than 1 million aliens who were in the United States without sanction of law and sent them by truck, train, and airplane to the border, where they were turned over to Mexican authorities.

Congress later enacted the so-called Bracero Act which, by agreement with Mexico, permitted the entry of a specified number of temporary farm laborers. The measure was approved by the farmers of the Southwest and Pacific Coast but so strongly opposed by labor organizations, which asserted that aliens were depriving native labor of work and wages, that the agreement was not renewed when it expired in 1965. In that year, 29,693 Mexican aliens entered without inspection—and most of them came after the Bracero Act expired.

Commissioner Raymond F. Farrell reported that in 1965 a total of 110,371 deportable aliens were located, of which 55,349 were Mexicans, 8,063 Canadians, 1,808 Cubans, 5,925 Chinese, 4,699 Greeks, 1,982 from British West Indies and Honduras, and 8,700 from other Western Hemisphere countries. The remaining 23,845 came from all other countries.

More than 186 million persons, Commissioner Farrell reported, were inspected and admitted during the fiscal year 1965. That figure is indicative of travel volume, however, rather than immigration, because 96 per cent were multiple entries—persons who crossed the Canadian or Mexican borders many times or returned several times from trips abroad, and sailors who came into port on frequent voyages and were granted shore leave. Aliens accorded status as lawfully admitted permanent residents during the year totaled 296,697.

These statistics reveal that, despite restrictive laws and tightened controls, the United States is still a welcoming land of opportunity for those who come lawfully. But those who seek illegal entry are turned away.

THE BASIC LAW

The Immigration and Nationality Act, known as the McCarran-Walter Act, which became effective December 24, 1952, is the fundamental law administered by the Service. That measure was enacted after an investigation by the Judiciary Committee of the U.S. Senate of national immigration and naturalization policies and the enforcement and administration of the pertinent laws. The Act accomplished a complete revision and codification of previous laws, repealed many provisions of older statutes, and made major changes in the immigration system. It is a voluminous and complicated law, puzzling at times even to lawyers, and many of its provisions have required interpretation by the courts.

The law made major changes in the quota system. The total annual quotas remained the same, but the first 50 per cent of the quota from any quota area was allotted to highly skilled or educated persons whose immigration would be beneficial to the economic or cultural interests of the United States. The remaining 50 per cent was made available, on petition, to designated close relatives of U.S. citizens and lawfully admitted aliens. Alien husbands of U.S. citizens were accorded the same nonquota status enjoyed by wives of citizens. The Act provided rigid controls over alien crewmen, including requirements for issuance and revocation of temporary landing permits, and made violation of terms of admission grounds for summary removal of alien sailors.

The 1952 Act specified for the first time the administrative processes by which deportability of aliens are determined. Grounds for deportation in previous laws were codified, and the eligibility of deportable aliens for suspension of deportation was circumscribed by additional requirements and safeguards. Classes of aliens who might establish eligibility for suspension were enlarged and authority granted the Attorney General to withhold deportation to any country where the alien might be subject to physical persecution.

The law codified excludable categories and added narcotic drug addicts, persons convicted of two or more offenses whether or not involving moral turpitude, and certain classes of immoral persons.

REPEAL OF NATIONAL ORIGINS QUOTA

Various subsequent enactments revised, repealed or amended provisions of the McCarran-Walter Act, the latest being Public Law 89–236, which became effective December 1, 1965. The principal purpose of that legislation was repeal of the national origins quota and the substitution of a new system for the selection of immigrants. The end of the national origins method of selecting immigrants was set for June 30, 1968, but, in the meantime, new quotas were to be set up subject to a new preference system. Under the preference categories, numerical limitations were to be applied on a worldwide basis (exclusive of the Western Hemisphere), instead of the individual country quota basis.

A provision of the law, designed to rectify imbalances in the quota system, required that at the end of each year during the period from December 1, 1965, tc June 30, 1968, numbers assigned to each country that were not used be transferred to an immigration pool. Quota numbers in the pool would be made available to preference immigrants who otherwise could not obtain visas because the quota for their country was exhausted. The death of the pool arrangement was fixed for June 30, 1968, along with the national origins system.

Public Law 89–236 fixed an annual numerical ceiling of 170,000 immigrants and established preferential categories for first, unmarried sons and daughters of U.S. citizens; second, spouses and unmarried sons and caughters of permanent resident aliens; third, members of the professions, scientists, and artists; fourth, married sons and daughters of U.S. citizens; fifth, brothers and sisters of U.S. citizens; sixth, skilled or unskilled persons who are able to fill labor shortages in the United States; seventh, and the remaining 10,200 numbers under the over-all ceiling, refugees uprooted from their homes because of a natural calamity or who, because of persecution or fear of persecution on account of race, religion, or opinion, have fled from a Communist-dominated country or from a country within the general area of the Middle East. Unused portions of any preference may be allocated to other appropriate categories.

Another change made by Public Law 89–236 was the removal of epilepsy as ground for exclusion and the addition of sexual deviation. A semantic change was the deletion of "feeble-minded" and the substitution of "mentally retarded." Provision was made for waiver of mental retardation as grounds for exclusion if certain specified conditions are fulfilled. A person who has suffered an attack of insanity, formerly a mandatory ground for exclusion, may be admitted if the Public Health Service determines he has been free from mental illness long enough to demonstrate recovery.

A significant provision of 89–236 created a Select Commission on Western Hemisphere Immigration to study demographic, technological, and economic trends pertaining to Western Hemisphere nations and the operation of U.S. laws as they pertain to those countries.

THE "COURT OF APPEALS"

Independent of the Immigration and Naturalization Service but under the supervision of the Attorney General is the Board of Immigration Appeals. This is a five-man body, consisting of a chairman, who is designated by the Attorney General, and four members, each appointed by the President on the Attorney General's recommendation. The Board is responsible solely to the head of the Justice Department.

In a sense, the Board is the appellate court of the immigration and naturalization system. It has jurisdiction to review, on appeal, orders of special inquiry officers or orders entered by or under the direction of the commissioner of Immigration and Naturalization, in exclusion and deportation cases and related actions affecting the status of aliens and immigrants. It also has jurisdiction to consider and determine cases that are not appealed but are certified to it by the commissioner for final decision.

Decisions of the Board are certified to the Attorney General for review when he so directs, or when the chairman or a majority of the Board believes they should be referred to him, or when the commissioner requests that they be referred.

That procedure is followed only in cases presenting unusual or exceptionally important issues, or when national policies are involved.

XI

The Criminal Division

A strict reading of the Constitution of the United States, as ratified on June 25, 1788, would appear to limit the Congress to enactment of laws to define and punish only two categories of crime: (1) counterfeiting, and (2) piracies and felonies committed on the high seas. But the Constitution granted Congress many other powers and authorized it to "make all laws which shall be necessary and proper for carrying into execution" the powers granted to it. Under that authority, the federal legislature has enacted, piecemeal, a code of laws that prescribes offenses against the United States and punishment for them. Simple in the beginning, the code is now varied and complex.

The Department of Justice is the enforcer of that code, and its Criminal Division is responsible for the prosecution of those who violate it and for the enforcement of more than 600 criminal statutes that are not specifically within the jurisdiction of the Antitrust, Civil Rights, Internal Security, and Tax divisions. Certain civil matters, such as the immigration and naturalization laws, extradition proceedings, and seizure actions under the Food, Drug, and Cosmetics Act also are assigned to the Criminal Division.

The first criminal statute enacted by Congress on April 30, 1790, defined treason and made provision for its punishment. Likewise, it defined and prescribed the penalty for murder in a fort, arsenal, dockyard or any place under the jurisdiction of the United States. The penalty for each offense was death by hanging.

Section 31 of the first law also closed a loophole through which some offenders had been crawling. An old English statute, abolished in 1827, permitted certain persons charged with a felony to claim the benefit of clergy and be tried in ecclesiastical courts. The Americans wanted none of that, so Section 31 read: "That the benefit of clergy shall not be used or allowed upon conviction of any crime for which, by any statute of the United States the punishment is or shall be declared to be death."

The British system of criminal law had crossed the ocean with the colonists, but it represented the heavy hand of regal power, and, once the colonies threw off the British yoke, they adapted the system to the conditions and philosophies of the new republic. The process was gradual and, in the first decades of the nineteenth century, enforcement often desultory.

In 1850, Justice Joseph Story, an advocate of codification and enforcement, declared his belief that many members of Congress "imagine the laws were made to execute themselves." Laws were passed, but organized enforcement was lacking. Congress, said Justice Story, "seems to have forgotten that such a thing as organization is necessary."

The new Department of Justice, formed in 1870, began the slow process of reform, reorganization, and supervision of the officers of the courts—district attorneys, marshals, and clerks—and the development of methods and personnel for the detection of offenses against the laws. In 1883, Attorney General Benjamin H. Brewster recommended revision of the federal statutes with specific regard to reform of procedure and substance of the criminal law. Not until 1909, however, was a criminal code adopted, and the fragmentary criminal statutes did not become a part of the general code until the U.S. Code was adopted in 1928. That was the year, also, that a division was set up in the Justice Department for supervision of the administration of federal criminal law. It was the creation of the Attorney General, not of any statute.

Before then, the Attorney General himself had supervised administration of the criminal laws, with the assistance of a small staff.

PUNISHABLE OFFENSES UNDER FEDERAL LAW

In 1929, Arthur J. Dodge, a Department of Justice attorney, listed, in a report that was transmitted to Congress by the President, categories of criminal offenses punishable under federal law. They were:

Offenses against the existence of the government, such as treason, inciting to rebellion or insurrection, seditious conspiracy, criminal correspondence with a foreign government, and enlisting to serve against the United States.

Offenses against neutrality, including accepting commissions to serve against a friendly power; arming vessels against a friendly power; and organizing military expeditions against a friendly power.

Offenses against the elective franchise and civil rights of citizens by conspiracy to injure persons in the exercise of civil rights; search without search warrant; conspiring to prevent an officer from performing his duty, and unlawful presence of troops at the polls.

Offenses against the operation of the government; in this category are counterfeiting, possession of false papers, falsely representing to be an officer, agent, or employee of the United States, stealing personal property of the United States, threats against the President, desertion from the Army and Navy (there was no Air Force then), depredations on public lands or Indian lands, false impersonation in procuring naturalization, and false claims as to citizenship.

Offenses relating to official duties, extortion, unlawful use of public moneys, embezzlement, and the acceptance by members of Congress of "subscriptions" in matters affecting the United States.

Offenses against public justice, which includes perjury, destruction of public records, bribery of a judicial official, allowing prisoners to escape, and misprision of felony.

Offenses against the postal service. This category embraces illegal carriage of the mails, wearing carriers' uniforms without authority, injuring mail bags, stealing post office property, obstructing the mails, mailing libelous or obscene matter, counterfeiting money orders and postage stamps, and fraudulent use of official envelopes.

Offenses against foreign and domestic commerce, such as violent interference with foreign commerce, importing lottery tickets and transporting them in interstate commerce, importing and transporting obscene books, importing prizefight films, transporting stolen motor vehicles in interstate commerce, and larceny of goods in interstate or foreign commerce.

Offenses within the admiralty and territorial jurisdiction of the United States. These would include such crimes as murder, manslaughter, and felonious assault; loss of life by misconduct of officers of vessels; robbery, arson, etc.; larceny and receiving stolen goods; piracy, confederating with pirates, and piracy under color of foreign commissions or by aliens; inciting to revolt and mutiny on shipboard; and abandonment of marines in foreign ports.

Thirty years later, most of these laws remain on the statute books. Many others have been added to enable the Criminal Division to protect society against those who flout the law.

THE DIVISION'S FIRST ASSIGNMENTS

On December 30, 1933, Attorney General Homer Cummings' comprehensive reorganization of the Justice Department redistributed the functions assigned to the various divisions. Thirty-one specific functions were to be the responsibility of the Criminal Division, among which were enforcement of the national prohibition laws, kidnaping, and racketeering. To these might be added "any other assignments" the Attorney General chose to give the Division.

Federal prohibition of liquor and beer opened a lucrative field for the lawless and greatly widened the scope of the Criminal Division's operations and responsibilities. Violators operated in every corner of the nation, and rumrunners infested coastal waters. Organized bootlegging was big business, and it moved the country into an era of big crime.

Many dry law transgressions were violative of state, rather than federal, statutes, but the movement of illicit liquor in interstate or foreign commerce gave federal jurisdiction, especially in the cases of the rumrunners. The principal legal weapons of the Justice Department in federal enforcement during the decade of warfare against the illegal liquor traffic were the revenue and customs laws. Bootleggers who did not pay their income tax, or cheated on it, were sent to jail; the boats and cargo of the rum-running fleet were seized and confiscated; and the miscreants who brought in alcoholic beverages without paying customs duties, when they were caught, were vigorously prosecuted.

In terms of time and legal history, the prohibition laws were temporary. The Eighteenth Amendment, adopted in 1920, was repealed in 1933 by the Twenty-third. The official end of the American experiment in alcoholic aridity, however, did not abolish all of the law enforcement problems the Prohibition Era created, nor did it stop the manufacture and sale of liquor unprotected by excise stamps. Enforcement of alcoholic beverage regulations was one of the functions assigned the Criminal Division by Attorney General Cummings.

In 1959, for instance, the Criminal Division obtained the conviction of ten Pennsylvania and New Jersey men for operating, from April, 1957, to June, 1958, a still that produced 375,000 gallons of alcohol upon which no excise duty was paid—a tax fraud of $3,935,000. In 1964, a Nashville, Tennessee, police officer was convicted of operating a still; a South Carolina sheriff and his deputy were convicted of conspiracy to engage in the manufacture and sale of illicit liquor; and a Georgia state representative, a sheriff, and two others were found guilty of heading a large illegal liquor manufacturing and distributing organization that in 3 months produced 5,950 gallons of non-tax-paid whiskey, resulting in a tax fraud of $62,275.

When they could no longer make fortunes out of manufacturing and selling "needled" beer and diluted whiskey, the hard-core criminals of the Prohibition Era turned to other lucrative forms of wickedness, such as kidnaping for ransom, gambling, narcotics, extortion, prostitution, looting of labor union funds and treasuries, infiltrating and wrecking of legitimate businesses, the not-too-difficult corruption of prizefighting, and the bribing of professional and college athletes to "control" the scores of sports contests.

Awareness that criminal operations were being increasingly directed by syndicates led the Justice Department to the conclusion that its crime-fighting forces should be strengthened and its efforts intensified. Throughout several administrations, the policy of building up within the Criminal Division an organized unit of lawyers trained in the prosecution of criminals and the application of the pertinent statutes was followed. Eventually this unit developed into the Section of Organized Crime and Racketeering, established as such in 1958.

HOW THE DIVISION IS ORGANIZED

The Criminal Division is organized in five sections: Administrative Regulations, Fraud, General Crimes, Organized

Crime and Racketeering, and Appeals and Research.

The General Crimes Section supervises the enforcement of approximately 400 criminal statutes in four major categories: (1) integrity in government operations, (2) protection of the channels of interstate commerce, (3) protection of the postal system, and (4) general enforcement in special maritime and territorial jurisdictions of the United States.

The first category embraces investigation of bribery and attempts at bribery involving personnel of the Internal Revenue Service; Army and Navy personnel accepting money from Selective Service employees to falsify their medical histories; bribery, obstruction of justice, and conspiracy in attempting to sell Secret Service files or records; and embezzlement of Defense Department funds.

It was under the integrity in government operations function that James R. Hoffa, general president of the International Brotherhood of Teamsters, was convicted, with other defendants, of jury tampering in Hoffa's trial on other charges at Nashville, Tennessee. Hoffa's sentence of eight years in prison and a fine of $10,000 was upheld by the Supreme Court.

Protection of the channels of interstate commerce involves laws against theft from interstate shipments and destruction of property in interstate shipments, and the interstate transportation of stolen property, forged or stolen securities, and obscene material. Hijacking an airplane in flight would be an offense the General Crimes Section would prosecute. A case it did prosecute was the conspiracy in 1965 to blow up the Statue of Liberty, the Liberty Bell, and the Washington Monument.

Protection of the postal system includes enforcement of statutes proscribing robbery, theft from the mails, extortion, and the mailing of obscene material (the offense of which Ralph Ginzburg, publisher of *Eros,* was convicted in 1963).

A murder committed in a post office, a national park, on a

military post or an Indian reservation, aboard an American aircraft over international waters, or on an American ship plying the high seas, the Great Lakes, or parts of the St. Lawrence River constitutes a crime under the fourth category in the General Crime Section's jurisdiction.

In many and devious ways, frauds are perpetrated upon the United States. The Frauds Section supervises the laws involving banking violations other than robbery, and commercial frauds that involve the perpetration of swindles between private parties in which the mails, or interstate or foreign wire facilities, are used. A fraudulent bankruptcy comes within the Fraud Section's jurisdiction, as do illegal election practices and political activities.

The government is the largest single purchaser of goods and services in the world. Constant vigilance and scrutiny are required to preclude corruption in procurement operations and insure that fraud and corruption are detected and punished. Frauds involve contracts, large and small, from big-scale defense procurement to a false claim for moving a transferred service man's personal effects.

The category known as program frauds includes the procurement activities of such governmental organizations as the Agency for International Development, the Small Business Administration, the Department of Housing and Urban Development, Department of Commerce, Department of Agriculture, Department of Health, Education, and Welfare, and others that make, insure, and guarantee loans and engage in large-scale procurement of supplies and services.

Commercial frauds, in the Crimes Division category, are swindles, stock frauds, and bankruptcy frauds under the Securities and Exchange Act and the Bankruptcy Act. Banking violations involve misapplications and embezzlements proscribed by the Federal Reserve Act and the Federal Deposit and Insurance Corporation statutes, as well as federally insured savings and loan associations.

The mail fraud statute is the most useful weapon against those who exploit the small businessman, the consumer, or the general public. This wide category embraces schemes to obtain advance fees for financing small businesses; impractical "work-at-home" schemes predicated upon the purchase of overpriced sewing or knitting machines; sales of distributorship franchises; medical frauds, charity frauds, and fraudulent land subdivision sales.

That prosecution can reach into high places was evidenced by the conviction in 1959 of two members of Congress, Thomas F. Johnson of Maryland and Frank W. Boykin of Alabama, for conspiracy and conflict of interest in endeavoring to delay the prosecution for mail fraud of Kenneth Edlin, a savings and loan promoter.

In its capacity as legal protector of interstate commerce, the Criminal Division, in 1964, convicted Robert Bradford Murphy and his wife, Elizabeth Irene Murphy, of stealing 210 documents from the National Archives in Washington and transporting them to Detroit.

Smuggling is a serious offense against the customs laws, and the Criminal Division prosecutes smugglers who are caught. Illegal importation of narcotics is a profitable business for smugglers if they escape detection, and greedy criminals take great risks to smuggle diamonds in the hope of large profits. Many individuals have gone to jail and racketeering rings have been broken up because customs inspectors spotted travelers attempting to bring in contraband.

In October, 1963, customs inspectors seized 76 pounds of heroin, the largest seizure ever made at the Mexican border, at the international bridge at Laredo. Texas. Prosecuted by the Criminal Division, the courier received a 16-year prison sentence. Smuggling of 110 pounds of heroin worth between $14 million and $22 million into the United States from Italy brought about the extradition from Canada and the conviction in United States courts of 3 men who hid their contraband in quilted blankets and false trunk bottoms. A million-dollar smuggling syndicate was broken up in 1958 when a toy dog that arrived in the mails from a foreign country was found to contain $13,195 worth and a toy Indian club $22,380 worth of undeclared diamonds.

In cooperation with the Food and Drug Administration, the Justice Department has conducted a vigorous drive against dispensers of amphetamines, a habit-forming stimulant commonly known as "goof balls" or "bennies," and barbiturates, a depressant drug. "Goof balls" and "bennies" are sold to many truck drivers, who take them to keep awake on long night hauls over darkened highways. Dispensers are usually highway truck stops and pharmacists who sell the drugs without prescription. In the Justice Department's drive, large quantities of the forbidden drugs were seized and scores of dispensers prosecuted.

COPING WITH RACKETEERS

The Organized Crime and Racketeering Section has the responsibility of anticipating and being prepared to handle all potential criminal violations that reflect organized illegal activity of an interstate nature. It supervises and assists in the enforcement of the narcotics laws, the wagering tax laws, and antigambling statutes. It has on file more than 250,000 cards reflecting the movements and associations of several thousand known racketeers. It receives from and exchanges with twenty-six investigative agencies of the government information about the nefarious activities of gangsters. A major weapon in its arsenal is Section 1952 of Title 18 of the U.S. Code, which prohibits travel in interstate commerce to aid racketeering enterprises and the transportation of gambling information, machines, and paraphernalia in interstate commerce.

Two of the statutes the Section administers reach into the

field of labor racketeering. They are the Hobbs Act and the Labor Management Relations Act of 1947, which prohibit interference with interstate commerce by robbery and extortion, and "payoffs" between employers and representatives of employees, respectively. For example, a deal between an employer and a union official for a cash payoff to avert a threatened strike or obtain a favorable labor contract would be a federal offense. Embezzlement or larceny of union funds; deprivation of rights of a union member by force, violence, or threats; extortionate picketing; and the holding of office by a union official who has been convicted of certain crimes are criminal offenses under these laws. Violations of the Welfare and Pension Plans Disclosure Act occur when an individual embezzles money from, falsifies the records of, or receives money to influence his actions in relation to any employee welfare or benefit plan.

Since the Organized Crime Section was established, an imposing number of racketeers have been convicted. A famous case was that of the "crime convention" at Apalachin, New York, in 1957. A group of more than seventy managing directors of the underworld assembled at a remote mountain lodge, presumably to allot territories and fields of activity and plan strategy and organization. The lodge was stocked with fine food and good liquor, and shining limousines brought in crime lords from all sections of the country. They were dismayed when New York state troopers appeared and began asking questions as to what they were all doing there.

Seventy-three of those arrested were convicted, not of any overt acts, but of conspiracy to conceal the purpose of their meeting. An appellate court found this a rather tenuous charge and reversed the convictions, but as a result of the prosecutions there have been at least no more open gatherings at which gangsters met to plot against society.

In 1963, the Criminal Division began investigating the activities of the Cosa Nostra, a secret hierarchy of nationwide crime. Attorney General Robert F. Kennedy reported to President Johnson in January, 1964, that information provided by members and other sources helped develop criminal cases against a number of Cosa Nostra figures. He said that the help of defectors from Cosa Nostra ranks was of great value to law enforcement officials.

Among the notorious racketeers sent to jail by the Organized Crime Section have been an underworld boxing czar convicted of extortion by interstate transmission of threats of violence unless allotted a share of the earnings of a champion prize-fighter, a Midwest crime chieftain who got six years for filing false tax returns with the Internal Revenue Service, and a Los Angeles racketeer who got fifteen years for willful evasion of income taxes.

Indictments against 466 gangster figures were obtained in 1964 as the Criminal Division intensified its war on organized crime. In a speech on May 5, 1966, President Johnson called organized crime a "guerilla warfare against society" and asserted that "a society can be neither great nor just as long as organized crime exists." He made victory in the anticrime war an ultimate goal of the government. Former Attorney General Kennedy was not sure the goal could be attained. "The struggle against crime is as old as mankind and we cannot hope for either early or even ultimate triumph," he said. "What we can do is seek to control the racketeers and curtail their somber effect on American life."

The activities of the Criminal Division, as related in the foregoing pages, center upon the detection and prosecution of crimes against the United States. The vast majority of almost 3 million crimes committed each year—the murders, robberies, rapes, assaults—violate state and local laws over which the Justice Department has no jurisdiction. Realization that the rising national crime rate cannot be checked or controlled without federal and state cooperation led to the establishment of two special Department units.

NEW UNITS ESTABLISHED

A new agency of the Department established in 1964, is the Office of Criminal Justice. It is designed to provide a forum for discussion of difficult issues involved in the criminal law. Among the subjects it considers are the wide disparities between sentences imposed by judges in similar cases and reforms in bail and bonding procedures, how to reconcile law enforcement with the protection of individual rights, and how to preserve the right of an accused to advice of counsel without crippling the investigative function of police officials.

Another new unit is the Office of Law Enforcement Assistance, which operates under the Law Enforcement Assistance Act of 1965. That law authorizes the Attorney General to make grants to or contracts with local public or private nonprofit agencies in a program designed to strengthen local capabilities in the fields of law enforcement, criminal justice, corrections, and crime prevention and control. Its objectives are two-fold: 1) the improvement of law enforcement personnel through more effective training, professional education and selection procedures; 2) the improvement of capabilities and practices of law enforcement agencies through studies, testing, and demonstration of new and better ways of handling their work.

PARTNERSHIP AGAINST CRIME

On October 15, 1966, Ramsey Clark, then the acting Attorney General, told a Conference of State Planning Committees on Criminal Administration that

> as we move forward in a comprehensive attack on crime, foremost in our planning must be a firm commitment to maintain law enforcement as the primary responsibility of state and local government.

The role of the federal government in law enforcement is not central. Nor should it ever be. Nowhere among the powers delegated to the federal government is a provision for police protection. There is no more local phenomenon than ordinary crime in the streets. It is the very heart of the reserved powers, the police powers of the states.

Clark was expressing, in those words, a long-established policy of the federal government against the creation of a national police force.

President Johnson, however, emphasized the federal role in a war on crime that "takes scores of lives each year in gangland violence." In a White House statement on May 5, 1966, he said that the war must be fought "with every federal resource."

"There will be no instant victory," he said, "but today we serve notice on all syndicates of crime that victory will come. It will come through a new partnership between federal, state, and local governments."

Attorney General Homer Cummings once reminded the country that "there is no magic formula for the administration of criminal justice." The efforts of the Justice Department are increasingly concentrated, however, on evolving more efficient machinery for protecting the citizenry from the depredations of the lawless. The work of the Criminal Division will not be lessened by the achievement of that goal, but its hands will be strengthened.

XII

The Bureau of Prisons

No matter how sternly or benignly justice in its manifold forms has been administered, the problem of how to deal with criminals remains a major concern of organized society. No matter what laws are written, men will transgress them and incur the punishments prescribed.

In earlier times, punishment was usually severe. There were no prisons as we know them now, and sentences imposed upon those convicted were generally execution or banishment. There was little effort to make punishment fit the crime, and a man who stole a pig or slew a gamekeeper might be beheaded or shipped off to exile in some wild land. England sent exiled criminals to America until the colonists protested. Later, Australia became the place of exile for English convicts. The hardships men endured, either aboard convict ships or after being put ashore, were so shocking that Britons were aroused, and Parliament passed the General Prison Act of 1791, which was the beginning of the penitentiary system in England. The federal prison system in America did not develop until decades later.

AMERICA'S FIRST PRISONS

The first federal dungeon-keep in America may have been the burrows of an old mine near Simsbury, Connecticut, to which General George Washington consigned prisoners of the Revolutionary War. It remained Connecticut's prison until 1827. A chronicler wrote of it: "The horrid gloom of this dungeon can be realized only by those who pass along its solitary windings. The impenetrable vastness supporting the awful mass above, impending as if ready to crush one to atoms; the dripping water trickling like tears from its sides; the unearthly echoes responding to the voice, all conspire to strike the beholder with amazement and horror."

So-called work houses were established by several of the American colonies in pre-Revolutionary days. There those awaiting or serving sentences imposed by the courts were confined. These were by no means rest homes or reformatories, and inmates of some of them were subjected to appalling living conditions and mistreatment by brutal wardens. The first move toward reform was made in 1682 in Pennsylvania by William Penn, who established a penal code that was remarkable, considering the times, for its humanitarianism. It provided that each county of Pennsylvania "build a sufficient house for the restraint, correction, labor and punishment of all such persons as shall thereunto be committed by law." Penn's code was abolished after his death in 1718, and sanguinary treatment of prisoners was resumed in Pennsylvania, continuing until after the Revolutionary War. But Pennsylvania was to become, in a sense, the incubator of the American penitentiary system.

Benjamin Franklin and others formed, in 1790, the Philadelphia Society for Alleviating Miseries of Public Prisons. They obtained passage of a law that established the principle of solitary confinement of prisoners, strict discipline, and productive work. The Walnut Street jail in Philadelphia became the first penal institution in America in which dangerous criminals were segregated in solitary cells and lesser offenders housed in larger rooms and given indoor and outdoor work at reasonable wages and with reasonable hours of labor.

At Newgate, New York, in 1796, and at Lamberton, New Jersey, in 1798, prisons similar to the Walnut Street institution were established. By 1820, however, these institutions had become overcrowded and conditions so changed that segregation became impossible, and inadequate or incompetent personnel was unable to maintain industry or discipline. The Philadelphia Society worked out what was known as the Pennsylvania, or Separate, System under which all convicts were held in solitary confinement, day and night, and the monotony relieved only by a small amount of handicraft labor, Bible reading, and "moral instruction." Pennsylvania's Eastern Penitentiary was built in 1829 to house prisoners confined under those conditions and it is still used, with modifications, for the punishment of persons convicted in Pennsylvania courts.

Meantime, a new prison had been built at Auburn, New York, in 1816, which borrowed from the Walnut Street jail and Eastern Penitentiary systems. Inmates were housed in separate cells at night, but worked together in congregate workshops during the day in complete silence. This method, combining silence and profitable industry, became the pattern for other American penitentiaries, such as Sing Sing, New York; Wethersfield, Connecticut; Charlestown, Massachusetts and Baltimore, Maryland.

All of these were state institutions. There were no federal prisons. In 1776, the Continental Congress passed a law providing that state and county prisons might be used to incarcerate persons convicted of federal offenses, and each state, upon admission to the Union, passed laws authorizing acceptance of federal prisoners if suitable compensation for their subsistence was paid. Subsistence payments from the federal government became a coveted source of revenue to wardens and sheriffs. Contracts with the government required that jails be kept in good condition and prisoners supplied with "comfortable bedding and good, well-cooked food in sufficient quantity." But there were always some officials who cheated and enhanced their profits by ignoring their contractual obligations. As a result, deplorable conditions existed in a great many institutions designated to receive and care for federal prisoners.

NEED FOR FEDERAL PRISONS

The system of "farming out" convicts to serve their terms in state prisons was economical because, in that era, there were relatively few federal laws and consequently few offenders. To have built prisons solely to accommodate transgressors of federal statutes would have been costly. By 1890, however, both laws and prisoners had proliferated, the bills for keeping them in state jails were becoming quite a budget item, and public reaction to mistreatment of convicts in state prisons was becoming clamorous. Advocates of prison reform and government officials, who, for years, had been reminding Congress of the need for federal prisons, finally prevailed. In 1891, Congress authorized construction of three federal prisons but neglected to appropriate funds for purchase of sites or erection of buildings. Money for construction did not become available until several years later.

The first federal prison was built with convict labor. It was at Leavenworth, Kansas. The Army had a military prison, or barracks, at Fort Leavenworth, and, in 1895, it was transferred to the Department of Justice under a license from the War Department. The Army did not like the idea of civilian prisoners being incarcerated on a military post, however, so it suggested construction of a prison on an adjoining plot of land, which it deeded to the Justice Department. On this site, construction was begun, the laborers being marched each day from the military prison to where the walls of an institution that today houses more than 2,000 felons were slowly rising, and the new prison was opened in 1905.

The second prison was built at Atlanta, Georgia, with construction beginning in 1899. It remains a major institution in the federal prison system, and houses an average population of 2,210.

What were known as marshal's jails had been built in some of the territories. One was on McNeil Island, in Puget Sound, in what was then the Northwest Territory. When Washington was admitted to the Union, the territorial prison was offered to the new state, but the offer was declined. It then became the McNeil Island Penitentiary, the third among the three federal prisons authorized by Congress.

PENITENTIARIES, REFORMATORIES, AND JAILS

Those three were classified as penitentiaries. There is a difference between a penitentiary and a reformatory or a jail. A penitentiary is a place of strict discipline where hard-core offenders—the desperate, the dangerous, the intractable— are sent to serve sentences imposed by the courts. Reformatories are institutions in which prisoners deemed capable of rehabilitation, who are not regarded as serious disciplinary problems, are confined under less harsh conditions while participating in regenerative programs. A jail, in these times, is a place where offenders are kept while awaiting trial or serving short sentences—a place of detention rather than imprisonment.

After Leavenworth, Atlanta, and McNeil Island, three other penitentiaries were built. Lewisburg, Pennsylvania, was opened in 1932; Terre Haute, Indiana, in 1940; and Marion, Illinois, in 1963. The six today comprise the nation's penitentiary system, and are distinguished from centers in which regeneration, rather than punishment, is the primary objective.

The first reformatory in the United States was a state institution at Elmira, New York. It was designed to receive and rehabilitate first offenders between the ages of sixteen and thirty-two. Emphasis was placed on vocational training, and academic education and indeterminate sentences, contingent upon behavioral and educational progress, were imposed as incentives to reform. The Elmira experiment gave impetus to a developing movement for penological reform and pleas for adequate federal reformatories. It was not until 1925, however, that the reformers' pleas were heeded and construction begun of the first federal reformatory institution. Today there are four reformatories in the federal prison system. Until 1966, there were five, but the institution at Chillicothe, Ohio, first to be built, and opened in 1926, was closed for lack of inmates and leased to the state of Ohio.

The first prison for women opened at Alderton, West Virginia, in 1927. Prior to then, women prisoners had been kept in Leavenworth or boarded out in state institutions. At Leavenworth, the warden's mother served as matron, without pay, and the women were confined under conditions not differing greatly from those of the men. At Alderton, in the West Virginia hills, the women live in almost homelike surroundings, necessarily institutional in nature, but not forbidding. There are no men; warden and guards are all women. Discipline is strict but not oppressive.

The second of today's reformatories was opened at Petersburg, Virginia, in 1930; the third, at El Reno, Oklahoma, in 1933; the fourth, at Lompoc, California, in 1959. These reformatories are for male prisoners only.

Age limits at the reformatories, except at Alderton where there is no limit, are from seventeen to thirty-one. Alderton is for women convicted of felony or misdemeanors; El Reno for felons, and Petersburg and Lompcc for felons and misdemeanants.

Besides penitentiaries and reformatories, the federal government has eight correctional institutions—places where felons and misdemeanants serving short, or indeterminate, sentences are confined. It is the policy of the Justice Department not to commit to correctional institutions "hardened" offenders, dangerous criminals, or those who have escape records. There are no age limits.

The first of these correctional institutions was opened at La Tuna, Texas, in 1932, and the second at Milan, Michigan, in 1933. Another, at Tallahassee, Florida, opened in 1938, and three, at Danbury, Connecticut, Seagoville, Texas, and Texarkana, Texas, in 1940. Similar institutions were added at Terminal Island, Los Angeles, in 1955, and Sandstone, Minnesota, in 1959. All are for male prisoners, but Terminal Island has normal capacity facilities for 119 females.

YOUTH CENTERS

The housing and care of juvenile transgressors, an age-old problem, intensified in the twentieth century as juvenile delinquency increased. Public sentiment against confining youthful offenders in prisons, where they were taught ways of crime by habitual criminals, brought about the establishment by states and the federal government of institutions for juvenile offenders. The federal government now has four.

The oldest, strictly for juveniles under the age of seventeen, was opened in the District of Columbia in 1866 in troubled times after the Civil War, but long before gang rumbles disturbed the peace in major cities. It is still operating as the National Training School for Boys, and in normal times several hundred juvenile offenders committed by courts in various parts of the country are kept there. They are taught useful trades, afforded educational instruction, provided with recreational facilities, and an effort is made to inculcate in them a desire to become useful citizens instead of enemies of law and order.

Except for the National Training School, the other institutions for young offenders are of comparatively recent vintage. The Federal Youth Camp, at Tucson, Arizona, opened in 1933, and federal youth centers at Ashland, Kentucky, and Englewood, Colorado, in 1940. Age limits at Ashland and Englewood are sixteen to twenty-one, and at Tucson, sixteen to thirty-one.

OTHER PLACES OF DETENTION

A system of prison camps began in 1930 with the opening of one at Montgomery, Alabama. There are now three others: at Florence, Arizona, opened in 1952; at Safford, Arizona, in 1958; and at Eglin Air Force Base, Florida, in 1962. There is no age limit at any of these camps, and all are for felons and misdemeanants.

Two federal detention centers, in New York City and Florence, Arizona, are operated as places of temporary incarceration where persons under arrest are held while awaiting indictment or commitment to other institutions. The one in New York has existed since 1929; the Florence center since 1963.

A new departure in penology has been the establishment of what are known as "pre-release guidance centers." These are places where convicts, under the age of thirty, whose prison records justify the belief that they can become good citizens, are assigned, while awaiting expiration of their terms, to be familiarized with conditions they will face as they resume their places in society. They are not prisons, even in a technical sense, but what might be called convalescent homes for curables about to forsake the paths of crime and become law-abiding instead of lawless citizens. There are six of these centers, in Los Angeles, Chicago, Detroit, Kansas City, Missouri, New York, and Washington, D.C. All have been opened since 1961.

Another new step was taken when Congress passed the Prisoner Rehabilitation Act of 1965, establishing a work release program, under which selected inmates may hold employment or attend school near their institutions, returning to custody each night. Myrl E. Alexander, Director of the Bureau of Prisons, reported that 442 inmates were at work at the end of 1966 and that earnings of participants in the program through December 31, 1966, totaled $2,147,000. Alexander said that the program was "meeting its purpose of helping to bridge the gap between confinement and freedom, an enormous gap which too often has resulted in former inmates returning to crime."

Prisoners, like free men, become ill and sometimes insane. Minor illnesses and harmless feeble-mindedness can be dealt with in prison hospitals or infirmaries. But since ordinary prison facilities do not suffice when special treatment is required for serious or chronic ailments or mental disorders, the government established in 1933 the Medical Center for Federal Prisoners at Springfield, Missouri. Courts frequently send prisoners to Springfield for observation and tests to determine their physical or mental fitness to stand trial.

FROM ALCATRAZ TO SEAGOVILLE

In 1966, there were 36 penitentiaries, reformatories, correctional institutions, youth centers, prison camps, guidance centers, detention centers, and a medical center in the federal prison system. Total confinement in them was approximately 20,000.

The prison that became the symbol of harsh punishment was Alcatraz, an island bastille in San Francisco Bay. It was the "Devil's Island" of the American penal system and, during its lifetime, held within its forbidding confines, more vicious, intractable, irredeemable men than any contemporary institution. The purpose for which Alcatraz was acquired was to provide a place where such men could be kept apart from prisoners who were not a menace to discipline or prison safety. If punishment at times was harsh, or even cruel, it was no more so than the crimes for which the prisoners were paying the penalty.

Alcatraz, in 1933, was the War Department's disciplinary barracks. The Justice Department acquired it, adapted it to its needs, and staffed it with experienced guards and administrators trained to deal with situations bound to arise when desperate men flout discipline and resort to violence. Escape from Alcatraz was well-nigh impossible, and the few who did contrive to get outside the walls found themselves challenged by the swift tides of San Francisco Bay that even the strongest swimmers could not conquer. Changing types of prisoners and advanced penological theories and systems, however, made Alcatraz less necessary and less desirable in a humanitarian system of prison administration. In 1963, it was closed, and its inmates were transferred to other penal institutions.

The word "prison" conjures up an image of thick walls, mounted with towers manned by armed guards whose guns point constantly toward prisoners and who shoot at the first sign of trouble. Inside the walls, according to the image, are long rows of steel cells wherein men spend days and nights that become eternity. That concept can be applied to what are known as maximum-security prisons. It does not apply, however, to medium-security prisons, moderate-security prisons, and open- or minimum-custody institutions. Leavenworth and Atlanta are maximum-security prisons; Terre Haute and Lewisburg, medium-security; El Reno, moderate-security; and Seagoville, the outstanding example of the open-custody type.

Seagoville, a few miles away from Dallas, represents a

completely new kind of institution. There are no walls or frowning turrets, no armed guards, no cells, no iron bars or grilles, no lines of men marching in lockstep to work inside or outside the prison. The men live in small dormitories, almost like cottages at a tourist camp, or in furnished rooms in the main buildings. They have keys to their own quarters and may bring from their homes small conveniences to make life in confinement more comfortable. They may have razors, radios, and framed pictures of wives, children, or sweethearts. On visiting days, men may take their families to church and have dinner with them in the dining hall, where the *piéce de résistance* may be elk meat from surplus animals slaughtered on government game preserves. The buildings, surrounded by green lawns instead of bastions, resemble those of a college or a hospital or a public library. Inside, the foyers are adorned with pictures painted by "resident" artists.

There are, of course, guards and wardens, but they are more administrators than custodians. Seagoville has a form of self-government: forums are held at which inmates may state their grievances and offer suggestions as to better ways of doing things; complaints are investigated and, if found to be justified, efforts are made to correct conditions complained of. The whole idea is to create an atmosphere in which suspicion and hostility are replaced by respect and confidence. Seagoville is much more than just years away from Simsbury.

PRISON INDUSTRY

At all the prisons, whether maximum-security or open, inmates are required to work. Labor is a necessary adjunct to discipline; idleness breeds unrest, and unrest breeds trouble. Work done by inmates varies with the nature of the institution and the abilities of the prisoners. An effort is made to assign each man to the work he is most fitted to perform. A young offender who wants to learn a trade may work in a printing shop, a shoe shop, or a broom factory. Where farms are attached to correctional or medium-custody institutions, inmates raise pigs, milk cows, grow feed for livestock and vegetables and fruit for prison tables, or learn how to operate farm machinery. A high percentage of food consumed by the prison population is produced on scientifically managed farms attached to penal institutions. Skills and habits of industry acquired in confinement are an important part of the reformation that enables "graduates" to become productive workers and good citizens after they have paid their debt to society.

Prison wares, made in shops and factories, are sold only to the U.S. Government, but industries operated in penal institutions yield a profit. Federal Prison Industries, Inc., has annual sales that average more than $30 million and, since 1946, it has paid into the U.S. Treasury nearly $70 million in dividends.

Objections of private industry and craftsmen to competition from prison labor and commodities prevent prison industry from expanding into commercial markets. Congress prohibited Prison Industries from selling things it made to the public, and, consequently, all articles it produces are for consumption and use in government institutions or for sale to government agencies. Shoes that it makes are sold to the Navy; mail sacks manufactured at Atlanta are sold to the Post Office Department; brooms made at El Reno sweep floors in government hospitals and military barracks; calendars printed in prison shops hang on walls of government offices.

The primary purpose of Prison Industries, however, is not profit. It was established to accomplish three major purposes: to teach the prisoner sound work habits and specific skills; to build his self-respect by enabling him to earn wages, which he may contribute to the support of his dependents; and to help support the federal correction program, thereby lessening the burden on the taxpayer. Wages are paid to workers according to scales devised by prison authorities, commensurate with the skill of the worker and the nature of the work performed. Necessary equipment is purchased and operating expenses paid out of revenues.

Operational management and supervision is the function of officials in the prisons but the over-all direction, as in private industry, is provided by a Board of Directors, appointed by the President, and representing the Attorney General, the Secretary of Defense, agriculture, labor, retailers, consumers, and industry. Members of the Board meet twice a year and serve without pay.

BUREAU ORGANIZATION

The prison system that has been described in preceding pages is the largest organization of its kind in the world and the most advanced in its concepts of humanitarian administration. Its size is due to the growth of the country in population and the extension of federal criminal laws into areas once occupied solely by the states. That the United States has outstripped all other countries in balancing justice and humanitarianism, however, is largely due to one man.

Federal prisons were placed under control of the Attorney General in 1871. Until 1930, they were administered by an assistant attorney general in the Department of Justice. In that year, as a result of recommendations made by the United States Bureau of Efficiency, the United States Bureau of Prisons was established to direct, under the broad supervision of the Attorney General, the management of federal penal institutions.

James Van Benschoten Bennett was an investigator in the Bureau of Efficiency. He had investigated various government agencies—among them the federal prisons—with a view to recommending improved methods of operation. In 1929, he cooperated with a Congressional committee investigating federal prisons and drafted its report. Sanford Bates was named the first director of the new Bureau of Prisons, but it was logical that Bennett, at the age of thirty-four one of the best-informed men in the country on prison conditions and methods, should be appointed assistant director, and he was. Seven years later, when Bates retired, it was logical and inevitable that Bennett would be chosen as successor by Attorney General Homer Cummings. From 1937 until August, 1964, when retirement became mandatory at the age of seventy, Bennett ran the country's prison system.

A PHILOSOPHY OF PRISON MANAGEMENT

Bennett does not like the word "penology." He thinks it was coined in the early days by Francis Leiber, a theorist who believed that the seriousness of punishment could be proportioned to the seriousness of the offense, and developed a "science of penology" on that basis. "While this philosophy persists," Bennett once commented, "it seems naïve to believe that we can reduce to a science the unhappy task of punishing people."

It was Bennett's "unhappy task" to carry out the punishments prescribed by law and imposed by the courts, but he believed that the conflicting demands of social protection and reconstruction of the individual could be reconciled. More than any other man, he is responsible for the correctional institutions and what he calls "community prisons," such as Seagoville, that are a distinctive feature of the American prison system.

Bennett would not want to be called a reformer, but the fact remains that he did reform the prison system of the United States and, while so doing, became one of the best-known "penologists" in the world. His voice has been heard and his ideas propounded at international conferences for more than thirty years, and no laws affecting the management of prisons or the treatment of inmates have been passed by Congress in that period without benefit of his counsel.

He expressed his conviction that rehabilitation was the most important obligation of prison management when he said: "I'm not running a junk heap, but a repair shop."

XIII

The "G-Men"

On September 20, 1933, George "Machine Gun" Kelly was hiding out in a house in Memphis, Tennessee. Agents of the Federal Bureau of Investigation had been looking for him since July 22, 1933, the date when Charles F. Urschel, a wealthy Oklahoman, was kidnaped from his home in Oklahoma City. Kelly reputedly was an artist with a "Tommy" gun who could shoot the caps off bottles at fifty paces.

That September morning, the trail the FBI agents had followed for two months ended at the house in Memphis. The agents, reinforced by local officers, surrounded the house and called to Kelly, "We are federal officers. Come out with your hands up." They expected a machine gun blast from the gangster's gun, but instead the frightened desperado gasped, "Don't shoot, G-Men, don't shoot," and came out with his hands up.

Kelly received a life sentence for the $200,000 ransom kidnaping of Urschel and died of a heart attack in Leavenworth Penitentiary on July 17, 1954. But the name "G-Men," an abbreviation of "Government Men," became a classic appellation in the underworld and still clings to the FBI's employees.

The capture of Kelly was an incident in the era that brought the FBI its greatest fame—an era of kidnaping, bank robbery, murder, and other crimes of violence, when gangsters wore bullet-proof vests (and so did "G-Men") stole machine guns and other weapons, drove high-powered "get-away" automobiles, and hired professional killers to murder law enforcement officers and members of rival gangs.

Those were the years when Congress passed laws—the Federal Kidnaping statute, the Federal Extortion Act, the Federal Bank Robbery Act, the National Stolen Property Act, and others—to provide legal weapons the Justice Department needed to apprehend and prosecute the denizens of the underworld who, after the repeal of prohibition, turned to more lucrative, but also more dangerous, types of crime. It was during that period that FBI agents were authorized to carry guns and make arrests. Armed with legal and lethal weapons, the Justice Department waged war upon the lawless so successfully that, by the mid-1930's, the addresses of an increasing number of crime lords became Alcatraz, Atlanta, Leavenworth, and the cemetery.

No National Police Force

The FBI is not a national police force. It is the investigative unit of the Department of Justice, and its investigative authority is derived from laws passed by Congress or instructions of the President and the Attorney General of the United States. It investigates violations of federal statutes not in the jurisdiction of other agencies and collects evidence in cases in which the United States is or may become an interested party. The evidence it assembles is turned over without evaluation to the prosecuting officers of the Justice Department or to other agencies having statutory jurisdiction. It investigates violations of both civil and criminal laws and has more than 170 statutes in its jurisdiction.

There is no area of public administration that does not require some form of investigation. Many other government agencies employ investigators—notably the Secret Service—and another unit of the Department of Justice, the Immigration and Naturalization Service, has its own investigators. The FBI cooperates with but does not direct the activities of the investigating units of other agencies. In 1966, for instance, it disseminated more than 200,000 items of criminal intelligence to other law enforcement agencies, federal and state. Although not the command post for control of investigatory operations, it is the clearing house for information about crime wherever laws are violated within the United States.

The FBI, as it exists in the twentieth century, would have been inconceivable to the eighteenth century founders of the federal government, because they simply could not have foreseen the extensive jurisdiction over crime the government would one day assume. Moreover, the procedural change involved would have astonished them. For them, the grand jury system, inherited from England, was the medium for investigating violations of the law and reporting offenses to the courts. The grand jury then was a sort of secret town meeting to which righteous, or mayhap vindictive, citizens recounted the scandal and misdeeds of the community. Not only were there no law enforcement officers charged with investigative responsibilities, but the idea of federal snoopers prying into community affairs would have been repugnant.

Reliance upon grand juries was short-lived, however. When a system of federal district attorneys was created by the Judiciary Act of 1789, those officials became responsible for the detection of offenses against federal law and the collection of evidence to present to the courts. When the Department of Justice was established in 1870, the Attorney General instructed the district attorneys to "follow upon the heels of rumor, to investigate and to reach the truth of complaints." A later commentator said that they "thus filled the role of detective and village constable."

The United States marshals in each judicial district also

were expected to detect and apprehend violators of the law —especially in frontier areas, where the duty was also hazardous. Attorney General William H. H. Miller reported in 1890 that the number of marshals killed in Indian Territory while attempting to arrest notorious criminals averaged twenty per year. During eighteen years, fifty-seven deputy marshals, guards, and posse members were slain in the Western District of Arkansas alone. No federal law then imposed a penalty for killing a federal officer engaged in executing the laws, and local officials were not over-zealous in prosecuting crimes committed in their territories.

MONEY FOR DETECTION

Prior to 1870, more than one Attorney General had ruled that funds for the operation of United States courts could not be used to pay detectives. Enforcement problems arising out of Reconstruction days following the Civil War, however, convinced Congress that enforcement officers needed money to discover offenses against the laws, and, in 1871, $50,000 was appropriated to be expended by the Attorney General in the detection and prosecution of crimes against the United States.

The Department of Justice did not immediately set up its own detective force. Attorney General Amos T. Akerman asked the Secret Service to employ "capable and trusted persons" to operate in the South to unearth violations of the enforcement laws. In 1875, Attorney General George H. Williams appointed four "special detectives," one each for the New England States, the Middle Atlantic States, the Middle West, and the South. From time to time, the Department employed "agents" as designated by the district attorneys in special circumstances.

After 1878, the Justice Department employed a small force of examiners to investigate accounts of district attorneys, marshals, clerks of courts, and U.S. commissioners. The examiners worked under the direction of a general agent on the staff of the Attorney General. By 1905, their work load had become so heavy that additional personnel had to be added. Thirty-two operatives were borrowed from the Secret Service and appointed special agents under the supervision of the general agent. This act of borrowing was the origin of a new national investigative force.

A movement was also underway in the early years of the twentieth century to establish a federal bureau of criminal identification and information in the Department of Justice. Attorney General John W. Griggs and his successor, Philander C. Knox, were cool to the idea. They thought it would benefit the states more than the federal government, failing to see the interrelationship of federal and state law enforcement. In 1907, a new Attorney General, Charles J. Bonaparte, espoused the movement and persuaded Congress to appropriate funds for the collection, classification, and preservation of criminal records and their exchange with state officials.

Bonaparte (a grandson of Emperor Napoleon's brother) was passionately interested in good government and social reform. With the support of President Theodore Roosevelt, he began urging the establishment of a separate investigative force in the Justice Department to replace the borrowed Secret Service operatives. He told Congress that "a Department of Justice with no force of permanent police in any form under its control is assuredly not equipped for its work." Congress's reaction was to deprive the Justice Department of the Secret Service operatives borrowed from the Treasury.

President Roosevelt charged that the reason Congress did not want to provide the Department with a "police force" was fear that "the Congressmen themselves would be investigated by the Secret Service men." A senator and a representative had been convicted of land frauds in Oregon. Roosevelt suggested that if the executive branch was not to have power to prosecute criminals found in the legislative branch, Congress could put a clause in the law prohibiting investigation of members of the federal legislature.

Quite understandably, the legislators were irritated. They appointed committees to investigate the investigative agencies. Before anything concrete emerged, however, Roosevelt and Bonaparte had left office.

WICKERSHAM'S BUREAU OF INVESTIGATION

On March 16, 1909, twelve days after the inauguration of President William Howard Taft, Attorney General George W. Wickersham issued an executive order creating a new division, the Bureau of Investigation in the Justice Department.

Fields of investigation assigned by Wickersham to the Bureau included national banking laws, antitrust laws, laws relating to fraudulent bankruptcies, customs frauds, internal revenue frauds, post office frauds, immigration and naturalization cases, Chinese smuggling, impersonation of government officials with intent to defraud, thefts and murders on government reservations, offenses against government property, and offenses committed by federal court officials and employees. Nothing was said about investigating Congress.

Wickersham's Bureau had no statutory authority; it was created by an executive order. Its agents had no law enforcement powers. Not until 1934 were the investigative forces of the Justice Department authorized to carry arms, serve subpoenas, make seizures, serve warrants, and make arrests.

Wickersham believed that the Secret Service should be under the jurisdiction of the Justice Department instead of the Treasury, except for limited functions, such as counterfeiting, related specifically to Treasury matters. His view on the Secret Service did not prevail, but he worked out a *modus operandi* for cooperation with the Treasury and the investigative forces of other departments—the nucleus of a greatly expanded system that is still in force.

Some of the effulgence that was to bathe the latter-day FBI engulfed Wickersham's Bureau. It caught the public fancy and instilled a degree of public confidence, previously lacking, that crime would be punished and the rights of citizens preserved. A Boston newspaper expressed a popular concept when it called the director a "King Detective," who was as "direct as a stroke of lightning and as clear in his ideas as a mathematician" and who "reduced shadowing and other ancient arts of the detective to a minimum." That was extravagant praise and not entirely accurate, but it did reflect a widely held belief that more effective machinery in the hands of capable operators had been created to apprehend violators of the laws of the United States.

The Bureau of Investigation operated with varying success for several years until Harry M. Daugherty became head of the Justice Department in the Harding Administration. In 1921, Daugherty announced a "thorough reorganization" of the Bureau. The reorganization consisted of the appointment of William J. Burns, an elderly professional detective, who wore colored frock coats, as the Bureau's head. Burns recruited a staff of private detectives. Their principal activity was to obtain evidence Daugherty used in his post-World War I campaign to suppress Radicalism. Their tenure was described by a later Attorney General as a "sordid period."

Harlan Fiske Stone succeeded Daugherty in 1924. Stone knew the value of an efficient investigative force, and he set about readjusting the Bureau. He continued the policy of confining investigations exclusively to violations of the federal statutes, but he weeded out the unfit and replaced them with agents of legal education or a knowledge of accounting and required them to undergo rigid inspection and intensive training.

HOOVER BECOMES DIRECTOR

Stone picked a young lawyer on the staff of the Bureau to be its director. His name was John Edgar Hoover. Appointed in 1924, Hoover was still director in 1967. He had served under fifteen Attorneys General, only a few of whose names were long remembered and only six of whom were alive in 1967. His tenure extended over the terms in office of Presidents Coolidge, Hoover, Franklin D. Roosevelt, Truman, Eisenhower, Kennedy, and Johnson.

Hoover conditioned his acceptance upon assurance that there would be no politics in the Bureau; the organization would be a career service in which ability and character were to be the requirements for appointment, and performance and achievement the basis for promotion. Employees were to be subject solely to Hoover's orders and control; Hoover himself was responsible to the Attorney General. Stone and subsequent heads of the Justice Department accepted that basis of operation. As far as operations are concerned, Hoover today runs the FBI. In matters of policy, he conforms —not always happily—to those laid down by the Administration in office.

Hoover entered the Department of Justice in 1917. In 1919, he was appointed special assistant to the Attorney General, and from 1921 to 1924 he was assistant director of the Bureau of Investigation. He holds law degrees from George Washington University and honorary degrees from several other colleges and universities, and he has been admitted to practice before the United States Supreme Court. Born in Washington, D.C., January 1, 1895, he has lived there all his life.

In 1933, when Attorney General Homer S. Cummings put through his reorganization of the Department of Justice, he changed the name of the Bureau of Investigation to the Division of Investigation, but he retained Hoover as the head of it. In 1935, the Division became the Federal Bureau of Investigation, universally known as the FBI, still under Director J. Edgar Hoover.

THE FBI TODAY

Among the offenses within the FBI's investigatory jurisdiction are violations of the antiracketeering laws; the Atomic Energy Act; bank robbery and embezzlement; the Civil Rights Acts of 1960 and 1964; crimes on the high seas; espionage; the Internal Security Act of 1950; the antigambling laws; piracy of aircraft and other crimes aboard aircraft; sabotage, extortion; fraud against the government; theft of government property; labor-management laws; and unlawful flight to avoid prosecution, confinement, or giving testimony.

The headquarters staff is divided into 10 divisions, each headed by an assistant director. The Bureau has 57 field offices strategically located in 56 key cities in the United States and in San Juan, Puerto Rico. The personnel staff exceeds 15,000, of whom approximately 6,500 are special agents and some 8,500 are clerks. The annual appropriation exceeds $175 million—a vivid contrast with the $50,000 Congress gave the Attorney General in 1871 to detect and prosecute violators of federal laws.

Since mobility in pursuit of criminals or clues is essential to effective law enforcement, the FBI maintains a fleet of more than 3,500 automobiles. Hoover asked for 962 new ones in his fiscal 1967 budget, 50 of them to be assigned to investigators in the field of civil rights.

Training to Be an Agent

One of the first things Hoover did when he became director was to establish a training division to teach recruits how to be agents and sharpen the skills of veterans by refresher courses. New agents receive fourteen weeks of instruction and two-week retraining courses are held periodically for all. Courses taught range from study of the Constitution and federal rules of criminal procedure to investigative techniques and the collection, identification, and preservation of physical evidence.

The training school, known as the FBI National Academy, is located at Quantico, Virginia, near Washington. Academy buildings house classrooms, dormitories, dining halls, and a few shops where equipment, such as guns, is repaired and tested.

Since all agents must be prepared to defend themselves when their own and other lives may be in danger, they are given thorough training in the use of firearms and defensive tactics. They become skilled marksmen; some of the best pistol and rifle shots in the United States are FBI agents. Even though an agent is assigned to a desk job at headquarters or in a field office, he must maintain his skill with guns by periodic returns to the firing ranges. These ranges cover acres of ground at Quantico and comprise a rifle range, three pistol and machine gun ranges, electrical target ranges, and skeet ranges.

It is a tenet of the FBI that effective law enforcement requires efficient police officers at federal, state, and municipal levels. More than thirty years ago, the FBI National Academy, sometimes called "the West Point of law enforcement," was established to train selected members of nonfederal police forces in basic and special law enforcement methods. These officers are given an intensive twelve-week course designed to prepare them for positions as executives and instructors in police departments. The National Academy completed its thirty-first year in 1966, graduating 196 men. During those years, the school graduated 4,936 police officers.

The FBI's training division also provides instructors for police schools conducted by local law enforcement agencies in communities across the country. In 1966, there were 5,300 of these schools, attended by 163,000 officers.

A Data Bank on Criminals

Criminals, like most other persons, are creatures of habit, and a knowledge of their past activities often points an effective finger when a new crime is committed. Thus, the files of the FBI provide invaluable leads in investigations, not only for FBI agents but for nonfederal law enforcement officers as well. The central file at headquarters contains more than 50 million cards. A statistician once figured that, stacked one atop another, they would reach a height of about 6.5 miles. These cards are indexed so that the information they contain is readily accessible when a police officer anywhere asks for a criminal's record. In order to disseminate information rapidly, the FBI maintains a teletype network between headquarters and field offices, except those in Alaska, Hawaii, and Puerto Rico. This high-speed circuit operates 24 hours a day, 7 days a week, and handles an average of 10,000 messages a month.

In January, 1967, the FBI established the National Crime Information Center. Its core is a computerized information system whereby criminal information is sped to police in cities linked with the headquarters operation. If, for instance, a policeman in New York sees an automobile that arouses his suspicion, he notes the license number and radios the information to his dispatcher. Almost immediately, the information comes back to him that the car was stolen in Boston, and he is told to watch out for the driver, who may be armed. The facts are from the FBI's national data bank of criminal information, to which police everywhere report crimes as soon as they are committed. Electronically processed, the data is dispatched instantly wherever it is needed. Hoover said the information network signaled a new era in law enforcement that would result in greatly increased efficiency in apprehending those who break the law—whether a car thief or a murderer.

Millions of Fingerprints

The Identification Division of the Bureau contains the largest collection of fingerprints in the world. There are more than 177 million on file, and the number grows every day. The identification division was formed in 1924 from a nucleus of some 800,000 fingerprint cards maintained at that time in the Leavenworth prison. Twenty-five employees kept the records then. Today, it requires more than 2,000.

Fingerprints are not only invaluable in identifying criminals but also in identifying amnesia victims, missing persons, and victims of disasters. Fingerprint technicians are given special training and are adept in matching the whorls on their cards with the prints of a dangerous fugitive or the victim of an airplane crash. The files contain not only prints of known criminals but also those of aliens, prisoners of war, applicants for government employment, military personnel, and thousands of citizens who voluntarily submit their prints for personal identification reasons.

The Laboratory

The development of the FBI laboratory, one of its most important facilities, was slow. Hoover, a pioneer in scientific crime detection, began planning for a laboratory early in his tenure, but got scant encouragement from law enforcement agencies. He persisted, however, and in 1932 the FBI started a laboratory with one scientist and a meagre assortment of instruments.

From that small beginning, the laboratory has grown into a large complex of scientific instruments used by more than 250 employees, more than 100 of whom are special agents trained in a wide range of scientific fields. These scientists can determine, from a chip of paint, whose car it was that was involved in a hit-and-run death. They can analyze a smear on a suspect's clothing to tell whether it was left by animal or human blood. They can sometimes identify a murderer from the markings on a bullet. Laboratory examinations have trapped many criminals; they have also proved the innocence of many suspects.

Crime Records Division

The Crime Records Division is, among other things, the public relations office of the FBI. From this Division, reporters get the news when a noted bank robber is caught or a Soviet spy apprehended. Publications of the Bureau are edited in Crime Records, especially the *FBI Law Enforcement Bulletin,* issued monthly and distributed to police officers throughout the country. Booklets with such titles as *What You Can Do To Fight Communism* and *How Banks Can Help the FBI* are published from time to time to alert select groups to ways they can aid law enforcement. A great volume of information on crime and subversion pours into FBI headquarters daily from its field offices, local police agencies, and other sources. The Crime Records Division studies this material for information that may be useful to its own agents and police officers elsewhere and distributes pertinent data to appropriate agencies. Police Departments throughout the country supply the FBI with statistical information about criminal activities in their areas. This data is collated and analyzed by Crime Records and published, usually twice a year, as *Uniform Crime Reports,* giving in cold figures a picture of crime in the United States.

Main Business Divisions

Although the Training, Identification, Communications, Crime Records, and Laboratory divisions are essential to the Bureau's operations and contribute measurably to its effectiveness, they are subsidiary, in a sense, to the FBI's main business, which, today, is catching spies and criminals.

The three divisions in which those activities center are the General Investigative Division, the Special Investigative Division, and the Domestic Intelligence Division. The agents who staff those divisions are the ones who, in addition to their more routine work, shoot it out with gangsters, track down fugitives, and lurk in shadows ready to pounce upon an espionage operative keeping a rendezvous with a traitor who has stolen atomic secrets. If wire-tapping is done, they are in on it.

The success of the FBI in combating the "public enemies" of the 1930's firmly established the Bureau as the most effective foe of the lawless the country had known. The General Investigative Division was the unit whose men traced such notorious criminals as John Dillinger, gunned down on a Chicago street on July 22, 1934, when he tried to shoot it out with FBI agents; "Ma" and Fred Barker, leaders of the Barker-Karpis gang of kidnapers, robbers, and murderers, who answered demands to surrender with bursts from a Tommy gun and were killed in a four-hour battle; "Baby Face" Nelson, murderer of three FBI agents, who was slain in a gun battle on an Illinois highway while resisting arrest; and Alvin Karpis, who surrendered meekly to Director Hoover and a force of special agents as he emerged from an apartment building in New Orleans where he had been hiding out.

During World War II, the General Investigative Division was charged with investigating violations of the Selective Service Act and assisting the military in apprehending deserters. Under the Renegotiation Act, the FBI investigated and exposed fraud in many wartime contracts.

After the war, in the 1950's, criminals turned to bank robbing, gambling, and automobile theft as major sources of illicit revenue. On the evening of January 17, 1950, a group of armed men committed what was described as the "perfect crime." Wearing gloves, chauffeur caps, and Halloween masks, the men emerged from a building in Boston, Massachusetts, dragging bags containing $1,218,211.29 in cash and $1,557,183.83 in checks. This was the famous Brink's robbery. The FBI sought the perpetrators for six years. Finally, one Joseph James O'Keefe, on whose life three attempts had been made, turned against his associates and told the FBI the story. He named eleven criminals. Two were then in prison for other offenses, and one was dead. FBI agents apprehended the other eight.

Theft of automobiles became a major problem in the 1950's and continues to be. It ranks third behind burglary and larceny in the category of major crimes. The FBI's responsibility is the capture of thieves who drive stolen cars across state lines, and recovery of the vehicles. In its annual report for fiscal 1966, the Bureau reported recovery of 21,000 motor vehicles.

Gambling is one of the most remunerative activities of organized crime. Three laws signed by the President on September 13, 1961, gave the FBI jurisdiction to investigate interstate transmission of gambling information, interstate transportation of wagering paraphernalia, and interstate transportation or travel in aid of racketeering enterprises. These laws are among the most important legislative enactments ever passed to combat organized crime, and their enforcement has substantially curtailed gambling activities and racketeering. In fiscal 1966, ninety-eight persons—an all-time high—were convicted under these statutes.

When a crime in the FBI's jurisdiction has been investigated and the culprit identified, unless his whereabouts are known and he is quickly apprehended, he becomes a fugitive. Then the Special Investigative Division moves in, and a man hunt is on. Fugitives go to great lengths to avoid detection. Dillinger, for instance, underwent painful plastic surgery; some impersonate females; others dye their hair or whiskers; one shaved his pate to appear bald. FBI agents have pulled fugitives from holes in the ground, caves, secret compartments built into the walls of buildings and hideouts deep in dense woods. The agents plan arrests carefully to minimize the danger of violence but are not always successful. In the thirty years following the 1934 authorization to make arrests and carry guns, FBI agents killed forty fugitives and fourteen agents were slain by criminals.

One of the FBI's most effective procedures in catching fugitives is its "Ten Most Wanted" list. Ten of the most desperate criminals at large are always on the list; when one is caught another goes on. Their names are announced, and their pictures displayed in post offices, on police bulletin boards, and elsewhere. Newspapers and radio often are instrumental in enabling the FBI to "get its man." Since the program was inaugurated in 1950, nearly half of those caught were apprehended through information supplied by private citizens who had seen stories and pictures in the newspapers.

The Special Investigative Division directs efforts to locate escaped federal prisoners, deserters from the Armed Forces, and violators of major state laws who flee from state to state to avoid arrest.

THE FBI AND INTERNAL SECURITY

By a Presidential Directive issued on September 6, 1939, six days after Germany invaded Poland and World War II began, the FBI was charged with protecting the internal security of the United States. The scope of its authority included investigations of espionage, sabotage, subversive activities, and related matters. Director Hoover created a new division, first called the Security Division, but now known as the Domestic Intelligence Division. Counterintelligence activities of the Bureau center in this division, and agents attached to it are especially trained in techniques of catching spies.

Before the invasion of Poland, Nazi Germany operated a spy ring in the United States. Its "master spy" was Frederick Joubert Duquesne, who spied for Germany for forty years. The FBI spied on Duquesne for two years. It took photographs with a concealed camera showing him pulling blueprints of the new M-1 rifle, torpedo boats, and secret planes out of his sock to demonstrate to a paymaster newly arrived from Germany how clever he was in fooling the FBI. Over the weekend of June 28, 1941, Duquesne and thirty-two other German agents were arrested. Nineteen members of the ring pleaded guilty; the other fourteen were convicted by a jury. They were sentenced to prison terms aggregating 300 years and fines totaling $18,000.

As early as 1938, the FBI had been watching another German spy ring headed by Guenther Gustav Maria Rumrich. Rumrich, Johanna Hoffman, Otto Voss, and Erich Glaser were the first enemy spies arrested in the United States. Their apprehension so alarmed the Nazis that fourteen agents tied in with the German diplomatic service fled the country, and Nazi spies were removed from ships before they sailed from Germany.

The Rumrich and Duquesne rings were engaged in "peacetime espionage," confined mostly to obtaining secret information about the United States' military plans and strength. After Pearl Harbor, the saboteurs came. In June, 1942, two Nazi U-boats stole into American waters. One landed four saboteurs on Long Island; the other put four ashore on a beach near Jacksonville, Florida. They had $175,000 in U.S. bills and enough explosives to last for two years.

The saboteurs had orders to dynamite the Hell Gate bridge, destroy aluminum plants, place time bombs in railway station lockers, start fires in department stores, and spread terror in every place and way they could. But they were never able to carry out those orders. Within two weeks after they landed, all eight were in FBI custody. They were tried before a military commission and, on August 8, 1942, six were sentenced to death, one to life imprisonment, and one to thirty years. The FBI claims that not a single act of foreign-directed sabotage was committed in this country during wartime.

After World War II, when the Cold War struggle began, the FBI trailed agents of the Soviet Union and their American accomplices. Its investigations in 1950–51 led to the arrest and conviction for theft of atomic secrets of five members of the spy ring operated by Julius and Ethel Rosenberg. (See Chapter IX for the Department's Internal Security Division's role in the Rosenberg trial, and others of a similar nature.)

Cold War espionage activities on the part of the Soviet Union were largely directed by officials attached to the Russian Embassy in Washington or United Nations headquarters in New York, who have diplomatic immunity from arrest. From January 1, 1957, to January 1, 1967, twenty-eight Soviet officials stationed in the United States were declared *persona non grata* because of espionage activities and ordered to leave the country.

The diplomatic spies concentrated on persuading Americans to spy for them. From 1960 through 1966, twelve Americans were arrested for complicity in Soviet espionage activities. Among them was Nelson C. Drummond, sentenced to life imprisonment for delivering national defense information to Soviet agents; Robert Glenn Thompson, given a thirty-year sentence for obtaining and turning over to U.S.S.R. representatives information about missile sites; and Robert K. and Joy Ann Baltch, who gave a Russian agent information about rocket launching sites, atomic weapons in shipment, and other data relating to national defense.

Communism is an abomination to Director Hoover. He has utilized his responsibility for internal security to become what Senator James O. Eastland, Chairman of the Senate Judiciary Committee, called "this country's best-informed expert on Communism." He wrote two books, *Masters of Deceit* and *A Study of Communism,* in which he analyzed and exposed the aims and methods of the international Communist movement.

In order to know what the Communist Party of the United States is doing, Hoover's agents infiltrated the party. They attended conventions and meetings, shared the Party's secrets, and reported them to Hoover. The FBI knows virtually everyone in the United States who is a Communist and has dossiers on thousands of known sympathizers and "fellow travelers." That information has been the basis for prosecutions of Communist leaders and the Communist Party for alleged violations of the internal security laws.

THE FBI AND CIVIL RIGHTS

In recent years, an increasing investigative burden has been thrown upon the FBI by passage of the Civil Rights acts of 1960 and 1964. Director Hoover's appropriation request for fiscal 1967 included funds to add 165 full-time employees in the field to handle the growing volume of civil rights work. Resistance to or noncompliance with civil rights laws necessitates prompt and intensive investigation and requires a trained, tough, and mobile force as ready as firemen to respond to emergency calls.

A violation of civil rights consists of depriving a person of federally secured rights and privileges granted by the Constitution and laws of the United States. The 1960 and 1964 Acts forbid the obstruction of federal court orders, the interstate transportation of explosives with the knowledge or intent that they will be used to damage or destroy property, discrimination in public accommodations, facilities and education, and interference with the voting rights of citizens.

Enforcement of these laws involves both civil and criminal investigation. Most of the related crimes, such as murder, arson, dynamiting, police brutality, and so on are violations of state laws, but they come within the purview of the FBI because they are committed for the purpose of depriving persons of their constitutional rights. Thus, when a civil rights worker is shot and the President or the Attorney General orders the FBI in on the case, "FBI Investigates" often becomes a news headline.

Such cases usually are tried in state courts, and the evidence garnered by the FBI is made available to state prosecutors and juries. Reluctance of local courts and juries to punish home-town officials made it necessary in the 1960's for federal courts to assume jurisdiction increasingly, and, to gain the evidence needed by federal prosecutors, thousands of FBI agents were dispatched to Southern states, where they work with representatives of the Civil Rights Division in these cases. (See also Chapter IV.)

THE DIRECTOR AND POLICY

The FBI is not a policy-making body; Director Hoover never overlooks an opportunity to emphasize that its functions are purely investigatory. There can be no doubt, however, that in exercising its investigatory function the FBI gathers data that influences policy decisions of the executive branch and often legislation by Congress. The Attorney General may testify on proposed Civil Rights legislation, but his testimony will be largely based on information supplied him by the FBI.

His more than forty years as head of the FBI have embedded in Hoover's thinking definite ideas about methods of law enforcement. Law makers and administrators recognize that his experience qualifies him to advise on certain matters of policy. However reluctant he may be, the fact remains that he does give advice in public a. d in private on what he thinks should be done, legislatively and administratively. Sometimes this advice-giving involves him in controversy.

A 1967 instance involved him in a confrontation with Senator Robert F. Kennedy, former Attorney General. The issue was wire-tapping and veracity. Hoover believes that law enforcement officers should be allowed to use electronic devices to gather evidence of the activities of criminals. The FBI is forbidden, however, to use wire-taps except upon authorization of the Attorney General. Before Kennedy became Attorney General, a bill to legalize certain forms of wire-tapping was prepared in the Department of Justice and introduced in Congress. After he became Attorney General, Kennedy told Congress he wanted the legislation passed. When he shifted from law enforcement to law making, however, Senator Kennedy took a different position, and when the question was raised on whether he had authorized the FBI to listen in electronically in certain cases, he denied that he had given such authority. Hoover maintained that he had never used wire-taps without authorization from whatever Attorney General was in office and that Kennedy had sanctioned the electronic eavesdropping in question. The issue of veracity had not been clarified as this was written, nor had Congress enacted, or refused to enact, wire-tapping legislation. In the past, however, Hoover's attitudes have carried weight with Congress when legislation relating to law enforcement was under consideration.

In 1967, also, Hoover became involved in a matter of legislative and diplomatic policy. The Senate was considering ratification of a consular treaty with Russia. Hoover was quoted in Senate debate as having said that establishment of Soviet consulates in this country would make more difficult the FBI's task of ferreting out Russian spies. Opponents of the treaty cited Hoover's opinion as grounds for refusing to ratify the convention. Supporters of ratification denigrated the idea that a few consular establishments would bring in a horde of new spies. Hoover did not retract, but he modified his position by stating that the addition of consulates to the Soviet diplomatic establishment in the United States would create no problem the FBI could not handle. In this way, he avoided open opposition to a policy strongly advocated by President Johnson and the State Department.

The instances cited, and the FBI story as related in this chapter, demonstrate the significant role of the Bureau in the enforcement of laws. Because of its tremendous effect upon the lives of millions of citizens, and whether he considers himself a policy-maker or not, Director Hoover cannot disassociate himself completely from the policies behind the laws he, as head of the FBI, shares the responsibility of enforcing.

XIV

As Long as There Are Laws

The Justice Department is not, in the strictest definition, a policy-making agency—certainly not to the degree that the departments of State and Defense are. But, as a member of the President's Cabinet, and as the legal adviser of the President and his Cabinet, the Attorney General participates in the formulation of national and international policies. And in the field of politics, his position is bolstered by the fact that bestowal of an Attorney Generalship has been, and undoubtedly will be, a token of Presidential appreciation of political support.

Nor does the Department of Justice make laws in the sense that it enacts them. It does, however, draft and submit through the White House laws that Congress subsequently enacts. When the President sends to Congress a proposed bill relating to law enforcement, the measure almost certainly has been drafted in the Department. When it is considered by congressional committees, representatives of the Department explain its provisions and urge its enactment. A Civil Rights bill, for instance, is an effort by the executive branch to induce Congress to provide the legal machinery needed to carry out a national policy. To the extent that it prepares, submits, and steers through Congress legislation to enhance the effectiveness of law enforcement, the Department thus participates in the law-making process.

All laws are the product of their times and are made in response to public demands. Once a bill becomes law, it is the obligation of the Justice Department to enforce it equitably for the protection of the rights of society and the individual. In operating the machinery for enforcement of federal statutes, the Department further reflects and supports national policy.

The Department often concentrates its efforts in particular areas of enforcement. This is a matter of emphasis; it does not imply neglect of other areas. But the eyes of the law follow the spotlight of public interest, and if they focus upon events that attract widespread attention and arouse controversy, with resultant demands for federal action, the Justice Department inevitably will escalate its efforts to enforce pertinent laws.

That is why, in the sixth decade of the twentieth century, when organized crime and civil rights became matters of national concern, the Department expanded and strengthened its forces and demanded of Congress new laws and more money to operate effectively in those areas. The Department continued to enforce the antitrust laws, prosecute tax evaders, keep watch upon Communists, and break up narcotic rings, but its Criminal and its Civil Rights divisions were the most active and newsworthy. In both areas of responsibility, enforcement conformed to vigorously proclaimed Administration policies.

When national policies, social movements, criminal activities, or new legislation impose greater responsibilities upon the Justice Department, an increase in cost and personnel is inevitable. Civil rights guarantees have been in the Constitution since its adoption, and enforcement laws have been on the books since Civil War days, but when racial movements and large national support of the rights of Negro citizens produced new laws, it became necessary to set up, in 1957, a separate Civil Rights Division to enforce them. A larger staff and increased appropriations added pressures on departmental space and budgets.

Every new law that confers jurisdiction upon the Justice Department imposes added burdens upon its investigative arm, the Federal Bureau of Investigation. Consequently, when Director J. Edgar Hoover goes to Congress for his annual appropriation he asks more money to enable him to hire more men and install up-to-date equipment required by modern methods of crime detection and law enforcement. And he always gets it. The FBI's expansion pace in the past half century has been so rapid that it has outstripped the parent department. Congress has authorized construction of a separate building to house the Bureau and its ever-burgeoning personnel and activities. As long as Congress continues to make federal crimes out of offenses that once were in the exclusive jurisdiction of the states, the investigative responsibilities of the FBI will increase.

At present, federal penitentiaries and correctional institutions are crowded. The Bureau of Prisons is always faced with housing problems. Congress has been slow in the past to authorize new prisons, and, by the time a new one is ready, there are enough convicts awaiting transfer from existing institutions to fill it. The end of these conditions is not foreseeable, but humanitarian and reformative policies advocated and practiced by penal authorities are certain to require enlargement of the physical facilities of the prison system.

One area of activity in the Department of Justice appeared recently to be slackening somewhat, or at least to be reflecting a possible change in national attitudes. There is no doubt that the impetus for passage of the antitrust statutes came from a growing national fear in the nineteenth century that big business, by predatory methods or otherwise, would so dominate production and markets in basic industries that small business could not thrive and might even perish. In the mid-1960's, however, doubts were being expressed that the laws had accomplished their purpose or prevented concentration of economic power in the hands of oligopolistic industries.

The growth of government has kept pace with the growth of business, and some observers profess to see a decline in American antipathy to bigness and increasing acceptance within government of bigness as beneficial. Large business enterprises are necessary to successful operation of huge government projects in national defense, space exploration, nuclear research, atomic energy, the aircraft industry, and programs for the development of national resources. Whether as a matter of changed philosophy or economic necessity, a partnership has clearly developed between government and big business. Hostility to corporate size, once a cardinal tenet of antitrust doctrine, has receded.

But questions are being raised on whether revisions of existing statutes, or new laws, are needed to deal with the growing concentration of economic power, and, among some people, a belief is growing that antitrust enforcement must adapt to new concepts.

A study of measures enacted by Congress since passage of the first restrictive laws discloses changing national attitudes toward those who come from overseas seeking a new life in the United States. The invitation inscribed at the base of Bartholdi's statue is not as encompassing as it was almost a century ago, and the arms outstretched to enfold the immigrant are not so wide open. There are several reasons.

For one thing, fears of overpopulation govern policies more than did the need for labor on farms and in factories a hundred years ago. Fertile land that beckoned settlers has been settled, cities have grown to almost unmanageable proportions, and problems of congestion have multiplied almost everywhere in the country. Although the total labor force is greater than it ever was, the bulldozer, the steam shovel, and the dump truck do the work once done by pick and shovel, curtailing the need for manual labor supplied by the early immigrants. The preferences established by Public Law 89–236, which repealed the national origins quota of the McCarran-Walter Act, demonstrate that selective admission, in limited numbers, of unskilled workers has become immigration policy. In addition, some provisions of the McCarran-Walter Act still in force, and other statutes, are designed specifically to prevent the admission of immigrants who might become gangsters and racketeers or a menace to the government through subversive activities.

Currently, the Immigration Service administers laws that have erased racial bars and substituted entry preferences based on the immigrant's skills or the need to reunite families. But, although humanitarian considerations govern policy, as witnessed by elimination of the national origins quota system, and the admission of refugees from Communist tyranny and terror, they are weighed against domestic economic, scientific, and cultural interests, and international policies.

"In establishing preferences," President Johnson said in his 1964 State of the Union Message, "a nation that was built by immigrants of all lands can ask those who now seek admission 'what can you do for our country?' "

Since 1789, the Department of Justice has been the legal voice of the government, advising the President and his Cabinet on their constitutional and statutory powers, and expounding the government's position in litigation involving federal rights, states rights, and human rights. Over the years, as this book has shown, many other responsibilities, especially in the area of enforcement of the law, have been added.

Justice involves a balance between the rights of government and those of its citizens. Concepts of democratic justice change with the character and temper of the people, and the administration of justice attains complexity as the growth of populations creates new problems of political and social relationships. It has become the task of the Justice Department to adapt old laws to new conditions and enforce new laws in accord with their spirit and intent. This task requires flexibility, since inflexible justice can become injustice.

The only safe over-all prediction for the future of the Department of Justice is that it will grow as the country grows and continue to require more men and money to operate effectively in widened jurisdictions. What areas of enforcement it will emphasize will depend upon the pressures inherent in changing patterns of national life and thinking. Perhaps when the need for fighting organized crime and enforcing civil rights abates, the Department will turn to enforcement of laws of the space age. However, the certainty that so long as there are laws men will break them and society will demand punishment ensures continuity of that arm of the government whose motto remains *Qui pro domina justitia sequitur*.

Appendix I

An Act to Establish
The Department of Justice
(Forty-First Congress, Sess. II, 1870)

Be it enacted by the Senate and House of Representatives of the United States of America in Congress assembled, That there shall be, and is hereby established an executive department of the government of the United States, to be called the Department of Justice, of which the Attorney-General shall be the head. His duties, salary, and tenure of office shall remain as now fixed by law, except so far as they may be modified by this act.

SEC. 2. *And be it further enacted,* That there shall be in said Department an officer learned in the law, to assist the Attorney-General in the performance of his duties, to be called the solicitor-general, and who, in case of a vacancy in the office of Attorney-General, or in his absence or disability, shall have power to exercise all the duties of that office. There shall also be continued in said Department the two other officers, learned in the law, called the assistants of the Attorney-General, whose duty it shall be to assist the Attorney-General and solicitor-general in the performance of their duties, as now required by law.

SEC. 3. *And be it further enacted,* That from and after the time when this act takes effect, the solicitor of the treasury and his assistants, the solicitor of internal revenue, the solicitor and naval judge advocate general, who shall hereafter be known as the naval solicitor, and the clerks, messengers, and laborers employed in the office of the Attorney-General, and in the offices of the solicitor of the treasury, naval solicitor, and solicitor of internal revenue, and the law officer in the Department of State, now designated as the examiner of claims in said Department, shall be transferred from the Department with which they are now associated to the Department of Justice; and said officers shall exercise their functions under the supervision and control of the head of the Department of Justice.

SEC. 4. *And be it further enacted,* That questions of law submitted to the Attorney-General for his opinion, except questions involving a construction of the Constitution of the United States, may be by him referred to such of his subordinates as he may deem appropriate, and he may require the written opinion thereon of the officer to whom the same may be referred; and if the opinion given by such officer shall be approved by the Attorney-General, such approval so indorsed thereon shall give the opinion the same force and effect as belong to the opinions of the Attorney-General.

SEC. 5. *And be it further enacted,* That whenever the Attorney-General deems it necessary, he may require the solicitor-general to argue any case in which the government is interested before the court of claims; and as to cases coming by appeal from the court of claims to the Supreme Court of the United States, it shall be the duty of the Attorney-General and solicitor-general to conduct and argue them before that court as in other cases in which the United States is interested. And the Attorney-General may, whenever he deems it for the interest of the United States, conduct and argue any case in which the government is interested, in any court of the United States, or may require the solicitor-general or any officer of his Department to do so. And the solicitor-general, or any officer of the Department of Justice, may be sent by the Attorney-General to any State or district in the United States to attend to the interests of the United States in any suit pending in any of the courts of the United States, or in the courts of any State, or to attend to any other interest of the United States; for which service they shall receive, in addition to their salaries, their actual and necessary expenses, while so absent from the seat of government, the account thereof to be verified by affidavit.

SEC. 6. *And be it further enacted,* That whenever a question of law arises in the administration, either of the War or Navy

Department, the cognizance of which is not given by statute to some other officer from whom the head of either of these Departments may require advice, the same shall be sent to the Attorney-General, to be by him referred to the proper officer in his Department provided for in this act, or otherwise disposed of as he may deem proper; and each head of any Department of the government may require the opinion of the Attorney-General on all questions of law arising in the administration of their respective Departments.

SEC. 7. *And be it further enacted*, That the duties enjoined upon the auditor of the Post-Office Department by the fourteenth section of the act entitled "An act to change the organization of the Post-Office Department, and to provide more effectually for the settlement of the accounts thereof," passed July two, eighteen hundred and thirty-six, shall hereafter be performed by some officer of the Department of Justice, to be especially designated, under the direction of the Attorney-General, who shall also have the care of prosecutions for mail depredations and penal offenses against the postal laws.

SEC. 8. *And be it further enacted*, That the Attorney-General is hereby empowered to make all necessary rules and regulations for the government of said Department of Justice, and for the management and distribution of its business.

SEC. 9. *And be it further enacted*, That the several officers hereinbefore transferred from the other Departments to the Department of Justice shall hold their respective offices until their successors are duly qualified; and the solicitor-general, and whenever vacancies occur, the assistants of the Attorney-General, and all the solicitors and assistant solicitors mentioned in this act, shall be appointed by the President, by and with the advice and consent of the Senate. All the other officers, clerks, and employees in the said Department shall be appointed and be removable by the Attorney-General.

SEC. 10. *And be it further enacted*, That the following annual salaries shall be paid to the officers hereinbefore mentioned: To the solicitor-general, seven thousand five hundred dollars; to each of the assistants of the Attorney-General, five thousand dollars each; to the solicitor of the internal revenue, five thousand dollars; and to the other officers the salaries and fees now allowed by law; and the Attorney-General shall be allowed a stenographic clerk, with an annual salary of two thousand dollars, and he may appoint three additional clerks of the fourth class.

SEC. 11. *And be it further enacted,* That all moneys hereafter drawn out of the treasury upon the requisition of the Attorney-General, shall be disbursed by such one of the clerks herein provided for the Attorney-General as he may designate; and so much of the first section of the act making appropriations, passed March three, eighteen hundred and fifty-nine, as provides that moneys drawn out of the treasury upon the requisition of the Attorney-General shall be disbursed by such disbursing officer as the Secretary of the Treasury may designate, is hereby repealed.

SEC. 12. *And be it further enacted,* That it shall be the duty of the Attorney-General to make an annual report to Congress, in January each year, of the business of the said Department of Justice, and any other matters appertaining thereto that he may deem proper, including the statistics of crime under the laws of the United States, and, as far as practicable, under the laws of the several States.

SEC. 13. *And be it further enacted,* That the superintendent of the treasury building shall provide such suitable rooms in the treasury building as may be necessary to accommodate the officers and clerks of the said Department, or, to the extent that that may be found impracticable, to provide such rooms in some other building in the vicinity of said treasury building.

SEC. 14. *And be it further enacted,* That the Attorney-General may require any solicitor or officers of the Department of Justice to perform any duty required of said Department or any officer thereof; and the officers of the law department, under the direction of the Attorney-General, shall give all opinions and render all services requiring the skill of persons learned in the law, necessary to enable the President and heads of the executive Departments, and the heads of bureaus and other officers in such Departments to discharge their respective duties; and shall, for and on behalf of the United States, procure the proper evidence for, and conduct prosecute, or defend all suits and proceedings in the Supreme Court of the United States and in the court of claims, in which the United States, or any officer thereof, is a party or may be interested. And no fees shall be allowed or paid to any other attorney or counsel[l]or at law for any service herein required of the officers of the Department of Justice.

SEC. 15. *And be it further enacted*, That the supervisory powers now exercised by the Secretary of the Interior over the accounts of the district attorneys, marshals, clerks, and other officers of the courts of the United States, shall be exercised by the Attorney-General, who shall sign all requisitions for the advance or payment of moneys out of the treasury, on estimates or accounts, subject to the same control now exercised on like estimates or accounts by the first auditor or first comptroller of the treasury.

SEC. 16. *And be it further enacted*, That the Attorney-General shall have supervision of the conduct and proceedings of the various attorneys for the United States in the respective judicial districts, who shall make report to him of their proceedings, and also of all other attorneys and counsel[l]ors employed in any cases or business in which the United States may be concerned.

SEC. 17. *And be it further enacted*, That it shall not be lawful for the Secretary of either of the executive Departments to employ attorneys or counsel at the expense of the United States; but such Departments, when in need of counsel or advice, shall call upon the Department of Justice, the officers of which shall attend to the same; and no counsel or attorney fees shall hereafter be allowed to any person or persons, besides the respective district attorneys and assistant district attorneys, for services in such capacity to the United States, or any branch or department of the government thereof, unless hereafter authorized by law, and then only on the certificate of the Attorney-General that such services were actually rendered, and that the same could not be performed by the Attorney-General, or solicitor-general, or the officers of the department of justice, or by the district attorneys. And every attorney and counsel[l]or who shall be specially retained, under the authority of the Department of Justice, to assist in the trial of any case in which the government is interested, shall receive a commission from the head of said Department, as a special assistant to the Attorney-General, or to some one of the district attorneys, as the nature of the appointment may require, and shall take the oath required by law to be taken by the district attorneys, and shall be subject to all the liabilities imposed upon such officers by law.

SEC. 18. *And be it further enacted,* That the Attorney-General shall from time to time cause to be edited and printed an edition of one thousand copies, at the government printing office, of such of the opinions of the law officers herein authorized to be given as he may deem valuable for preservation, in volumes which shall be as to the size, quality of paper, printing, and binding, of uniform style and appearance, as nearly as practicable, with the eighth volume of said opinions, published by Robert Farnham, in the year eighteen hundred and sixty-eight, which volumes shall contain proper head-notes, a complete and full index, and such footnotes as the Attorney-General may approve. Such volumes shall be distributed in such manner as the Attorney-General may from time to time prescribe.

SEC. 19. *And be it further enacted,* That this act shall take effect and be in force from and after the first day of July, eighteen hundred and seventy.

APPROVED, June 22, 1870.

Appendix II

Attorneys General of
The United States
1789-1967

	State	President
Edmund Randolph Sept. 26, 1789–Jan. 2, 1794	Virginia	Washington
William Bradford Jan. 27, 1794–Aug. 23, 1795	Pennsylvania	Washington
Charles Lee Dec. 10, 1795–Feb. 18, 1801	Virginia	Washington and John Adams
Levi Lincoln Mar. 5, 1801–Mar. 3, 1805	Massachusetts	Jefferson
John Breckenridge Aug. 7, 1805–Dec. 14, 1806	Kentucky	Jefferson
Caesar A. Rodney Jan. 20, 1807–Dec. 11, 1811	Delaware	Jefferson and Madison
William Pinckney Dec. 11, 1811–Feb. 10, 1814	Maryland	Madison
Richard Rush Feb. 10, 1814–Nov. 13, 1817	Pennsylvania	Madison

William Wirt Nov. 13, 1817–Mar. 3, 1829	Virginia	Monroe and John Quincy Adams
John M. Berrien Mar. 9, 1829–July 20, 1831	Georgia	Jackson
Roger B. Taney July 20, 1831–Sept. 4, 1833	Maryland	Jackson
Benjamin F. Butler Nov. 15, 1833–Sept. 1, 1838	New York	Jackson and Van Buren
Felix Grundy July 5, 1838–Dec. 1, 1839	Tennessee	Van Buren
Henry D. Gilpin Jan. 11, 1840–Mar. 4, 1841	Pennsylvania	Van Buren
John J. Crittenden Mar. 5, 1841–Sept. 13, 1841	Kentucky	Harrison and Tyler
Hugh S. Legare Sept. 13, 1841–June 20, 1843	South Carolina	Tyler
John Nelson July 1, 1843–Mar. 3, 1845	Virginia	Tyler
John Y. Mason Mar. 6, 1845–Sept. 9, 1846	Virginia	Polk
Nathan Clifford Oct. 17, 1846–Mar. 17, 1848	Maine	Polk
Isaac Toucey June 21, 1848–Mar. 3, 1849	Connecticut	Polk
Reverdy Johnson Mar. 8, 1849–July 20, 1850	Maryland	Taylor
John J. Crittenden July 22, 1850–Mar. 3, 1853 (second term)	Kentucky	Fillmore

	State	President
Caleb Cushing Mar. 7, 1853–Mar. 3, 1857	Massachusetts	Pierce
Jeremiah S. Black Mar. 6, 1857–Dec. 17, 1860	Pennsylvania	Buchanan
Edwin M. Stanton Dec. 20, 1860–Mar. 3, 1861	Ohio	Buchanan
Edward Bates Mar. 5, 1861–Nov. 24, 1864	Missouri	Lincoln
James Speed Dec. 2, 1864–July 17, 1866	Kentucky	Lincoln and Johnson
Henry Stanbery July 23, 1866–Mar. 12, 1868	Ohio	Johnson
William M. Evarts July 15, 1868–Mar. 3, 1869	New York	Johnson
Ebenezer R. Hoar Mar. 5, 1869–June 23, 1870	Massachusetts	Grant
Amos T. Akerman June 23, 1870–Jan. 10, 1872	Georgia	Grant
George H. Williams Dec. 14, 1871–May 15, 1875	Oregon	Grant
Edwards Pierrepont Apr. 26, 1875–May 22, 1876	New York	Grant
Alphonso Taft May 22, 1876–Mar. 11, 1877	Ohio	Grant
Charles Devens Mar. 12, 1877–Mar. 6, 1881	Massachusetts	Hayes
Wayne MacVeagh Mar. 5, 1881–Oct. 24, 1881	Pennsylvania	Garfield
Benjamin H. Brewster Dec. 19, 1881–Mar. 5, 1885	Pennsylvania	Arthur

	State	*President*
Augustus H. Garland Mar. 6, 1885–Mar. 5, 1889	Arkansas	Cleveland
William H. H. Miller Mar. 5, 1889–Mar. 6, 1893	Indiana	Harrison
Richard Olney Mar. 6, 1893–June 7, 1895	Massachusetts	Cleveland
Judson Harmon June 8, 1895–Mar. 5, 1897	Ohio	Cleveland
Joseph McKenna Mar. 5, 1897–Jan. 25, 1898	California	McKinley
John W. Griggs June 25, 1898–Mar. 29, 1901	New Jersey	McKinley
Philander C. Knox Apr. 5, 1901–June 30, 1904	Pennsylvania	McKinley
William H. Moody July 1, 1904–Dec. 17, 1906	Massachusetts	Roosevelt
Charles J. Bonaparte Dec. 17, 1906–Mar. 4, 1909	Maryland	Roosevelt
George W. Wickersham Mar. 5, 1909–Mar. 5, 1913	New York	Taft
James C. McReynolds Mar. 5, 1913–Aug. 29, 1914	Tennessee	Wilson
Thomas W. Gregory Aug. 29, 1914–Mar. 4, 1919	Texas	Wilson
A. Mitchell Palmer Mar. 5, 1919–Mar. 5, 1921	Pennsylvania	Wilson
Harry M. Daugherty Mar. 4, 1921–Mar. 28, 1924	Ohio	Harding
Harlan Fiske Stone Apr. 7, 1924–Mar. 2, 1925	New York	Coolidge

	State	*President*
John C. Sargent Mar. 17, 1925–Mar. 5, 1929	Vermont	Coolidge
William D. Mitchell Mar. 5, 1929–Mar. 3, 1933	Minnesota	Hoover
Homer S. Cummings Mar. 4, 1933–Jan. 2, 1939	Connecticut	Roosevelt
Frank Murphy Jan. 2, 1939–Jan. 18, 1940	Michigan	Roosevelt
Robert H. Jackson Jan. 18, 1940–July 10, 1941	New York	Roosevelt
Francis Biddle Sept. 5, 1941–June 30, 1945	Pennsylvania	Roosevelt
Tom C. Clark June 15, 1945–Aug. 24, 1949	Texas	Truman
J. Howard McGrath Aug. 24, 1949–Apr. 7, 1952	Rhode Island	Truman
James P. McGranery May 27, 1952–Jan. 20, 1953	Pennsylvania	Truman
Herbert Brownell, Jr. Jan. 21, 1953–Nov. 8, 1957	New York	Eisenhower
William P. Rogers Nov. 8, 1957–Jan. 20, 1961	Maryland	Eisenhower
Robert F. Kennedy Jan. 21, 1961–Sept. 3, 1964	Massachusetts	Kennedy
Nicholas de B. Katzenbach Sept. 4, 1964–Oct. 2, 1966	Illinois	Johnson
Ramsey Clark Mar. 3, 1967–	Texas	Johnson

Appendix III

Jobs in Justice

The Department of Justice employs more than 30,000 men and women and almost always has openings in its many divisions, bureaus, and offices. Young lawyers especially are always in demand.

In order to assure annual replenishment of the legal staff, Attorney General Herbert Brownell, Jr., instituted in 1953 the Attorney General's Employment Program for Honor Law Graduates. Each year since then the program has brought into the Department fifty to sixty honor graduates of leading law schools.

These recruits are chosen from the upper 20 per cent of their class. They usually apply upon the advice of the dean of their school. Each year, an Assistant Attorney General visits the law school and interviews the applicants.

Consideration is given to the student's undergraduate record, courses, and grades in law school, law review work, extracurricular activities such as moot court competition, legal aid, student bar association, etc., personal attributes, and general potential as an attorney. Much information regarding these qualifications is obtained from faculty members.

Selections are made by January 1 of each year, based upon the report of the Department official who conducted the interviews. Those selected report for duty at the end of the school year.

The students may express their preferences for assignment. Some may seek to join the staff of the Civil Rights Division; others Antitrust; still others choose the Criminal Division. Preferences are given priority in assignment consistent with the manpower needs. Where preferential assignment is not possible, the student is placed in the Division judged to be most suitable to his training and capabilities.

The entrance salary is $7,696 annually (Civil Service Grade GS-9). After a year of satisfactory service, the appointee is eligible for promotion to GS-11, carrying an annual salary of $9,221. Thereafter, appointees are considered along with other attorneys in the regular promotion program of the Department. Usually, after 2½ to 3 years with the Department the salary rises to $10,927. Although no lawyers are under Civil Service, they are graded for salary purposes by the Civil Service scale.

Fringe benefits include a retirement plan, based upon length of service; group life insurance at low cost, based upon annual salary, and group medical and hospitalization plans. Part of the cost of insurance and medical plans is paid by the government.

The Honor Law Graduate Program is designed to provide an opportunity for outstanding law school graduates to work with the Department in its role of providing legal counsel for the United States. The Department expects many of the appointees to make a career in the government's legal service. Because the value of the young lawyer is enhanced by experience, the Department prefers students who will remain at least four or five years.

Not all attorneys in the Department are honor graduate recruits. Many are lawyers who have turned to a government career after experience in private practice.

Clerical employes—secretaries, stenographers, clerks, messengers, etc.—are under Civil Service and are recruited from those who have passed the classified service examinations.

FBI OPPORTUNITIES

The FBI, which employs fully as many people as the Department itself, has its own system of recruiting. Its top jobs are in law and accountancy.

Special Agents must possess the following qualifications:

Be male citizens of the United States;

Be graduates of accredited law schools and have completed at least 2 years of resident, undergraduate college work;

Be at least 5 feet 7 inches tall without shoes;

Have uncorrected vision of not less than 20/40 (Snellen) in one eye and at least 20/50 in the weaker eye without glasses, and at least 20/20 in each eye corrected. No applicant will be considered who is color blind;

Be able to hear ordinary conversation from at least 15 feet with each ear;

Be able to perform strenuous physical exertion and have no defects that would interfere with their use of firearms or with their participation in raids, dangerous assignments, or defensive tactics;

Be willing to serve in any part of the United States or Puerto Rico; and

Have reached their 23rd but not their 41st birthday.

All applicants must have a valid license to drive an automobile.

The above requirements apply to all Special Agents, whether lawyers or accountants. Accountants, however, are required to be graduates from a resident 4-year college with a major in accounting with at least 3 years of practical accounting or auditing experience. The entrance salary for special agents is GS-10, or $8,421.

In addition, the FBI employs translators, who usually are required to have a knowledge of 3 or more languages. Their salaries depend upon the number of languages spoken and general experience.

FBI jobs are also open to photographers with at least 3 years commercial experience; radio maintenance technicians; laboratory technicians such as chemists, physicists, metallurgists, document examiners, cryptanalysts, and fingerprint technicians.

These positions, as those of clerks, typists, stenographers, etc., are under Civil Service, and entrance salaries are in various grades from GC-2 ($3,925) to GS-10 ($8,421).

All FBI agents are covered by the provisions of the Civil Service Retirement System, which permits retirement after age 50 with a minimum of 20 years' service in hazardous work involving primarily investigation, apprehension, or detention of persons suspected or convicted of federal criminal offenses.

Life insurance and medical insurance programs are available to FBI employes as to other Justice Department personnel.

OTHER DIVISION OPENINGS

The Immigration and Naturalization Service, the Bureau of Prisons, and other units of the Department of Justice have job opportunities that require specialized skills and training. They do not operate extensive recruitment programs similar to the main Department and the FBI. Except for clerical Civil Service positions, employment in these agencies usually is obtained by direct application to the agency an applicant wants to work for.

Bibliography

Considering the importance of the Department of Justice and its long history, remarkably few books or informative articles about it have been published. The author had the privilege of access to documents not for commercial distribution, or on file in the Department only for internal use, such as certain biographical materials, organizational manuals, and the like.

Much of the material listed below can be found in the Library of Congress as well as the library of the Justice Department, which, although not open to the public, may make some of its resources available to students at the discretion of the librarian. Included among this material are the Law Reviews and the many volumes of the opinions of the Attorneys General over the years.

The author acknowledges his particular indebtedness to the following:

CLARK, TOM C. "The Office of the Attorney General," *The Tennessee Law Review*, XIX (1946), 150–59.

CUMMINGS, HOMER S., and MCFARLAND, CARL. *Federal Justice, Chapters in the History of Justice and the Federal Executive*. New York: Macmillan Co., 1937.

CUSHING, CALEB. "Office and Duties of the Attorney General," *The American Law Register* (Philadelphia), V (December, 1856), 65–94.

DODGE, ARTHUR. *The Origin and Development of the Office of Attorney General* (70th Cong., 2d sess.; H.R. Doc. 510). Washington, D.C.: U.S. Government Printing Office, 1929.

EASBY-SMITH, JAMES S. *The Department of Justice: Its History and Functions*. Washington, D.C.: W. H. Lowdermilk and Co., 1904. Out of print. The only known copy is on file in the Justice Department Office of Information

FAIRLIE, JOHN A. "The United States Department of Justice," *The Michigan Law Review*, III (1905), 352–59.

KENNEDY, ROBERT F. *The United States Department of Justice: A Brief Account of Its Organization and Activities*. A Department document prepared in 1961 and subsequently revised.

LANGELUTTIG, ALBERT. *The Department of Justice of the United States*. Baltimore, Md.: The Johns Hopkins Press, 1927. Out of print. There is a copy in the National Archives.

NEALON, RITA W. "The Opinion Function of the Federal Government," *New York University Law Review*, XXV (1950), 825–43.

Official Opinions of the Attorneys General of the United States Advising the Presidents and Heads of Departments in Relation to Official Duties. Washington, D.C.: U.S. Government Printing Office, 1963. Prepared in 1963 as a Departmental Series.

ROBB, ARTHUR. *Biographical Sketches of the Attorneys General*. A Department document not for public distribution, compiled from the records of the Department and other sources.

Index

Abel, Rudolph Ivanovich, 45, 167–68
Adams, John, 17, 112, 250
Adams, John Quincy, 170, 251
Adams, Sherman, 118
Addyston Pipe and Steel Co. v. United States, 98–99
Administrative Division, 62
Admiralty and Civil Division, 124
Admiralty and Shipping Section (of Civil Division), 125–26
Agriculture, Department of, 129
Akerman, Amos Tappan, 37–38, 73, 219, 252
Alcatraz, 209–10
Alexander, Myrl E., 209
Alien Act of 1798, 170
Alien and Sedition Laws, 170
Alien Property, Office of, 135–36
Alien Registration Act, 180–81
Aliens, 180 ff.; *see also* Immigration
Alvarado, Juan B., 147
American Bar Association, 48
Antitrust Division, 44, 45, 63, 87–109
Antitrust Laws, National Committee to Study the, 87
Antitrust policies, 39–41, 45, 87 ff., 109, 240–41
Appellate Section (of Civil Division), 126–27, 129
Aptheker, Herbert, 163
Archives, National, 34
Arredondo, Fernando de la Maza, 145–46
Arthur, Chester Alan, 252
Assistant attorneys general, 61–63, 68, 71, 124
Atomic Energy Act of 1946, 134, 165–66, 224

Attorney General: appointment of, 3, 11, 29; civil rights enforcement by, 43, 45, 46, 63, 70–86; in Civil War, 122–23; colonial, 5–6, 8; Congress and, 6, 8 ff.; and district attorneys, 65–68; duties of, 6, 7–8, 12, 13, 20–21, 24, 31 ff., 42 ff., 47–53, 65, 121, 124, 145, 148; establishment of office, 5–7, 29–30, 244 ff.; land title examination, 148; marshals and, 65–68; and national policy, 51–53, 238; *Official Opinions of the Attorney General*, 21, 24; and pardons and parole, 50–51, 56; protocol, 29–30; salary, 9–10, 36; seal of, 30–32; and selection of judges, 47–50; Teapot Dome scandal, 144–45; *see also* Attorneys General
Attorneys, federal, 50, 57, 64, 157
Attorneys General: appointed to Supreme Court, 27–28; from 1789–1870, 15–27; list of, from 1789–1967, 250–54

Ballinger, Richard A., 142–44
Ballinger-Pinchot feud, 141–44
Baltch, Robert K. and Joy Ann, 234
Barker, "Ma" and Fred, 229
Barnett, Ross, 80
Barratry, 125–26
Bates, Edward, 25–26, 123, 252
Bates, Sanford, 214
Bay of Pigs, 53
Beck, Dave, 119
"Beef Trust" case, 40, 101
Bell, Alexander Graham, 94
Bennett, James Van Benschoten, 213–15

261